Forest and Shade Trees of Iowa

SECOND EDITION

IOWA'S FORESTS ARE AS DIVERSE AS THE TOPOGRAPHY THEY CLOTHE. From north to south, from east to west, and from ridgetop to bottomland they reflect changes in climate, soils, and land use. These changes are both recent and as old as the forces of nature that created Iowa's landscape. Each forest community, through its composition of species, tells of a particular history as well as present interactions with native animal residents and with people. If we take the time to observe, to listen, and to wonder, the forest and shade trees of Iowa tell fascinating stories about our state and about ourselves.

IN THE NORTHEASTERN CORNER OF THE STATE, balsam fir and white pine (above) and paper birch and aspen (right) indicate Iowa's proximity to the Northern Forest Region. These northern species and others speak of an ancient time when northern forests spread across all of Iowa.

AT THE TIME OF EUROPEAN SETTLE-
MENT, prairies covered 85 percent of Iowa's
landscape. Although flatland prairies have
been converted almost entirely to rich farmland, native prairie grassland is still harbored
by untillable, steep slopes in northeastern
Iowa (above left, with paper birch, common
juniper, and eastern red cedar) and in the
Loess Hills region of western Iowa (left and
above right, with bur oak, cottonwood, and
eastern red cedar).

MOST OF IOWA'S FORESTS are characteristic of the Eastern Deciduous Forest Region. In these forests, oaks of various species are the most important element both ecologically and economically, especially in well-drained upland sites.

Forest and Shade Trees of Iowa

SECOND EDITION

PETER J. VAN DER LINDEN
THE MORTON ARBORETUM, LISLE, ILLINOIS

DONALD R. FARRAR
DEPARTMENT OF BOTANY
IOWA STATE UNIVERSITY, AMES, IOWA

IOWA STATE UNIVERSITY PRESS • AMES

WHERE THE PRAIRIE and Eastern Deciduous Forest Regions met, the bur oak and the prairie grasses shared space. Early accounts of Iowa's native vegetation describe open, parklike stands of bur and white oak occurring commonly across much of Iowa.

Peter J. van der Linden is a curator at the Morton Arboretum in Lisle, Illinois. He served as director of the Iowa Arboretum from 1981 to 1987.

Donald R. Farrar is a professor in the Department of Botany at Iowa State University, Ames.

∞ Printed on acid-free paper in the United States of America

First edition, 1984
Second edition, 1993

Library of Congress Cataloging-in-Publication Data
Van der Linden, Peter J.
    Forest and shade trees of Iowa / Peter J. van der Linden, Donald R. Farrar. — 2nd ed.
        p.   cm.
    Includes bibliographical references (pp. 133–35) and index.
    ISBN 0-8138-0734-4
    1. Trees — Iowa — Identification. 2. Shade trees — Iowa — Identification. I. Farrar, Donald R. II. title.
QK160.V36   1993
582.1609777 — dc20   93-19285

The U.S. government has the right to reproduce, publish, or otherwise use this work for governmental purposes.

CONTENTS

WORTHLESS TREES? Not to wildlife who see them as room and board. Eastern red cedar, sumac, wild grape, poison ivy, and many other species in a fence row produce a smorgasboard of wildlife food. Gnarled and hollow trees provide necessary nest and den sites for dozens of Iowa's birds and mammals.

PREFACE

AN OLD HOLLOW WHITE OAK may be home to a variety of animals including, as in this one, a hive of honey bees.

THIS BOOK IS A GUIDE to the identification, distribution, natural history, and uses of Iowa trees. It includes all native woody plants known to reach tree size in Iowa and those introduced species important in landscaping and conservation. For this book, a tree is defined as a woody plant at least 12 feet tall with a single erect stem that is 3 inches or more in diameter at breast height. Several large native shrubs are described and briefly discussed in a separate section near the end of the discussion of individual trees (Chapter 4).

The book is written for persons having little or no formal training in botany but includes precise botanical descriptions for the professional. Technical terminology has been kept to the minimum necessary to maintain standards of accuracy and conciseness in the descriptions. The author-date citation used refers readers to the bibliography that follows the text. All terms used are defined in Chapter 3.

Measurements are given in English units. Measurements reflect the range of variation among typical individuals and should not be regarded as absolute limits to the size of plant parts for a species. Note that the checkerboard ruler in the photographs of bark is 12 inches long.

Keys to trees in both summer and winter conditions are included. They should prove especially useful to students of Iowa flora, to professional botanists and foresters, and to other persons interested in the identification of trees. The authors would appreciate suggestions for improvement from users of the keys.

Most photographs of tree leaves, twigs, and fruits and many of the photographs of tree bark are the work of John Wee. Other photographs were contributed by John E. van der Linden, W. H. Bragonier, and the authors. The line drawings in the keys and Chapter 3 were prepared by Carol Peck.

Sources of information are not cited within the text to save space, avoid repetition, and make the book more readable. However, all references used are included in a bibliography at the end of the book. Sources used repeatedly include the manuals of Fernald (1950), Gleason and Cronquist (1963), Preston (1976), Rehder (1940), Rosendahl (1955), Sargent (1922), and Trelease (1931) for taxonomic characteristic; the dissertations of Carter (1960), Cooperrider (1958), Davidson (1957), Eilers (1964), Fay (1953), Hartley (1962), Monson (1959), and Van Bruggen (1958) for distributions of native trees; the books of Bard (1978), Peattie (1966), Settergren and McDermott (1964), Smith (1952), and the USDA Forest Service (1976) for natural history of native trees and the properties and uses of their woods; and the publications of Carter (1975), Dirr (1975), Erdmann (1966), and Wyman (1965) for culture of trees.

To guide readers who are unsure which trees to plant, the authors have commented on the growth of various species and their relative merits for different uses. In some cases these opinions will differ from those of other persons who are knowledgeable about trees and who have more experience in a local area. It is best to remember that trees are biological organisms, and it is not always possible to predict their "behavior." Individual trees may grow better or worse than is typical for their species.

The authors would like to thank the Forestry Section of the Iowa Conservation Commission for its generous financial support during the research and writing of this book. We are also grateful to the following persons for their assistance: John E. van der Linden, Lois H. Tiffany, Richard B. Hall, Roger Q. Landers, Donald R. Lewis, Abraham H. Epstein, Cecil R. Stewart, Jean C. Bodensteiner, and Paul H. Wray.

PREFACE TO THE SECOND EDITION

SHRUBS PROVIDE WILDLIFE COVER as well as browse. Members of the birch family such as these alders are especially important because of their nutritious catkin buds held above winter snow cover.

FOLLOWING THE PUBLICATION of *Forest and Shade Trees of Iowa,* it became apparent that a second edition would be needed. Reviewers made several helpful suggestions for improvement, as did students using the keys. Research provided new information about the status of Iowa's forests, the distribution of some native species, and the growth and culture of trees. Revisions in the rules of botanical nomenclature required some changes in the way tree names are spelled.

Portions of the manuscript have been expanded or rewritten, including sections of Chapters 1, 2, 4, and 6. Additional horticultural information has been provided throughout, corrections have been made, and the text has been updated and clarified where needed. I hope these changes will make the book more useful to its readers.

I am indebted to the Morton Arboretum for support in the preparation of this edition and for the many opportunities it has provided me to expand my knowledge of midwestern trees and their culture. Kris Bachtell, Tom Green, and George Thomson reviewed portions of the new material for this edition, and I thank them for their assistance. Of course, the responsibility for any errors or omissions are mine.

Peter J. van der Linden

Forest and Shade Trees of Iowa

SECOND EDITION

IDLED FARMLAND THROUGHOUT MOST OF IOWA reverts to forests through early succession of light-loving trees and shrubs—eastern red cedar and elm (top), sumac and cottonwood (middle), hawthorne, elm, and cottonwood (bottom).

TREE COMMUNITIES of mature forests vary with the topography of the landscape. Oaks and hickories (top left) dominate dry upland sites, whereas sycamore, cottonwood, elm, ash, and walnut characterize bottomlands (top right foreground).

MOIST SLOPES support maple and basswood, and in northeast Iowa, white pine. Eastern red cedars (foreground) cling to thin soils on cliff tops.

IN OLD UPLAND FORESTS of northeastern Iowa, sugar maples establish under the canopy of 100-ft. tall red and white oaks.

1: IOWA'S FORESTS

MOST PEOPLE consider Iowa to be a prairie state, but forests also have been an important feature of the landscape for thousands of years. Nearly 6 percent of the state is forested today, down from am estimated 12 to 20 percent at the time of settlement. The forests that remain are one of our most important natural resources, providing timber, wildlife habitat, watershed protection, recreation, and natural beauty.

HISTORY OF IOWA'S FORESTS

The history of Iowa's forests can be summed up in a single word—change. Just as today's forests are much different from those at the time of settlement, Iowa's forests of a century ago bear little resemblance to those that grew here immediately following glaciation. By studying pollen extracted from ancient bogs, notes made by the original surveyors, accounts written by early travelers, and changes in Iowa's soils, we have learned much about these forests of long ago.

Ten thousand years ago, after the last glacier left the state, Iowa had a much cooler, moister climate than it does now. Then the landscape probably supported a spruce-fir forest similar to that of modern-day Canada. When the climate later became warmer and drier, the conifers migrated northward and were replaced by oaks, maples, and other deciduous trees. As the trend toward a warmer, drier climate continued, the deciduous trees largely gave way to heat- and drought-resistant prairie plants.

This warm, dry period peaked about four thousand years ago and was followed by a climate again more favorable to the growth of deciduous trees. Nevertheless, the prairie plants remained the dominant vegetation until the arrival of white settlers. The persistence of prairie in a forest climate is usually attributed to fire, set naturally by lightning and deliberately by native Americans.

Prairie plants were adapted to these fires, but the seedlings of most trees were not. During wet years young trees became established in the prairie, but dry weather always returned, accompanied by fire. If not killed outright during a burn, the trees died back to the ground and resprouted from the roots, continuing to grow until the next fire occurred. After repeated cycles of burning and regrowth, the tree roots formed tough, knotted clumps in the prairie soil. These "grubs," as the settlers called them, were very difficult to remove when the land was cleared for farming.

Most of Iowa's presettlement forests were confined to stream valleys, being especially prevalent in eastern and south central Iowa. Strips of forest also occurred around the larger natural lakes in the north central part of the state. Many of these presettlement forests were more open than our woodlands today, with widely spaced oaks and other trees. Where fires regularly burned into these woods, the understory was prairie grasses and wildflowers.

Despite recurrent fires and drought, forests were slowly invading the prairie in some parts of Iowa when the settlers arrived. The advance of the forest was led by the bur oak, which was naturally resistant to drought and fire. Settlement accelerated this process by bringing an end to the fires, allowing trees to rapidly resprout from long-suppressed "grubs" in the soil. In some places the acreage of natural woodland actually increased despite the amount of land being cleared by settlers.

Groves of trees were also planted by the settlers, creating "forests" in place where only prairie had existed before. Many settlers took great pride in their woodlots and orchards, competing with one another for the largest plantation or the greatest variety of species.

At the same time these new forests were being planted, Iowa's native forests were being cut to provide lumber, fencing material, railroad ties, fuelwood, and other products and to clear land for farming.

These two phenomena—the growth of new forests and the depletion of others—have continued to the present day. In a few places, such as in the rugged loess hills along Iowa's western border, forest continues to advance on what remains of the prairie, creating a management problem for those seeking to preserve our native grasslands. In most parts of Iowa, however, there probably has been a net loss of woodland since settlement.

A 1990 survey by the United States Forest Service indicates that Iowa's forests may be on the increase. Preliminary figures showed an acreage of about 2 million in 1990, compared to about 1.5 million in 1974. According to State Forester William Farris, much of the increase can probably be attributed to a decline in livestock numbers, which has resulted in woodlands replacing pasture. Tree planting programs also have played an important role.

These changes are welcome news indeed for all those who enjoy Iowa's woodlands and appreciate the many benefits they provide.

CONSERVATION OF IOWA'S FORESTS

Although the total acreage of Iowa's forests may have increased in recent years, some of our woodlands are not in good condition. Grazing, fire, insects, and diseases pose an ongoing threat to the health of our forests.

Grazing by livestock is of particular concern. Although the use of woodland for this purpose may provide short-term economic benefits, livestock cause many unfavorable changes in the woodland environment. The soil becomes compacted and loses fertility, runoff and erosion increase, the canopy trees lose vigor and decline, and the young trees needed to regenerate the forest are destroyed. The forest eventually dies, and with it die many other benefits it once provided.

Forest conservation need not conflict with use of the forest for economic purposes. For example, when the economic returns of sawlog and fuelwood production are compared to those generated by converting a forest to pasture, the forestry alternatives can be superior (Countryman and Kelley, 1981). These benefits are provided without destroying the forest resource and without diminishing its suitability for wildlife or its value for recreation.

To encourage the conservation of Iowa's woodlands, the General Assembly has adopted the Iowa Forest Reservation Laws (Code of Iowa, Chapters 161 and 441). Under the provision of these laws, farm groves and natural forests may be exempted from taxation if they have a minimum size of two continuous acres and a minimum number of 200 trees per acre, no buildings are present, and livestock is excluded. Applications should be made to the county assessor's office.

Information and assistance in the management of woodlands for timber, wildlife, soil conservation, and recreation can be obtained through the Iowa Department of Natural Resources, the Soil Conservation Service, and the Cooperative Extension Service of Iowa State University.

DISTRIBUTION OF NATIVE TREES

The number of native tree species is distributed unevenly across the state. Diversity is greatest in eastern Iowa and gradually declines toward the west as one species after another disappears at the edge of its geographical range. For instance, five species of hickory, ten species of oak, and three species of ash grow naturally in the forests of southeastern Iowa but only one of each occurs in the woodlands of the northwest. The difference is presumably due to the colder, drier, windier climate in western and northern Iowa, which is less favorable for the growth of trees than the relatively mild climate in the east and south. Only a few hardy species grow satisfactorily in the northwestern part of the state.

FOREST COMMUNITIES

Individual species of trees may occur in a variety of environments, but each has a particular environment or habitat in which it is most commonly found. Topography and soils are especially influential in determining where a species will grow, because they strongly affect moisture, temperature, exposure, and the availability of essential nutrients.

A species usually is most common where the environmental conditions are optimum for its growth and development but may also do well elsewhere. Cottonwoods and willows are usually confined to wet, low-lying areas near streams because their seeds require a moist, bare mineral soil in which to germinate, but they will grow well when transplanted to fertile upland soils. Other species, such as

black and blackjack oaks, are usually limited to dry, sandy soils because they are unable to compete with other trees on better sites.

Not surprisingly, species having similar environmental requirements often grow together. For example, cottonwood and silver maple regularly grow together along streams, while oaks and hickories nearly always dominate dry upland sites. When two or more species occur together again and again over a large geographic area, they are referred to collectively as a *community, association,* or *forest type.*

Forest communities, like human communities, change over time. Fast-growing, short-lived, shade-intolerant trees and shrubs will be the first to colonize a site; they will eventually give way to long-lived, slow-growing species that can reproduce and grow in the shade of the woodland floor. These species will persist as the dominant members of the community until fire, logging, or some other disturbance starts the cycle anew.

Communities also change over distances because the geographical distributions of their constituent species do not exactly coincide. A species usually becomes increasingly less common as it approaches the edge of its range and is replaced by others that are better adapted to the climate there. Iowa is an excellent place to observe this phenomenon because so many species reach the limits of their ranges at some point between the relatively moist eastern and dry western boundaries of the state.

Forest communities, then, change over both time and space, making the task of naming and classifying them enormously complicated. Yet several basic types can be recognized. They are delimited by topography for the most part, although individual stands may occur in atypical topographical positions if the soil or available moisture is particularly well suited to their development (or unfavorable to the growth of the species that would normally occur).

Most of the natural forest stands in Iowa can be placed in one of the five following communities:

1. The *oak-hickory* community occurs on dry uplands and on south- and west-facing slopes. Its *canopy* (uppermost layer of foliage) is usually dominated by one or more of the following trees: white oak, bur oak, black oak, Hill's oak (northern pin oak), chinkapin oak, and shagbark hickory. Other common canopy trees include white ash, black cherry, quaking and bigtooth aspens, red oak, and basswood and, in southeastern Iowa, post oak, blackjack oak, shingle oak, and mockernut hickory. The *understory* (lower layer of foliage) is usually dominated by ironwood or chokecherry, though saplings of larger trees such as white ash, hackberry, elms, and hickories may also be abundant. Shrubby, thicket-forming species such as prickly ash, hazelnut, and dogwoods are often common in clearings or in stands with open canopies.

2. The *oak-maple-basswood* community occurs in moist but well-drained uplands, especially on north- and east-facing slopes and terraces in the larger stream valleys. Its canopy is usually dominated by some combination of red oak, hard maple, and basswood, with the maples decreasing and the other two species increasing from east to west. Hard maple drops out entirely in western Iowa and

red oak in the extreme northwest. Other large trees frequently encountered in this community are white oak, shagbark and bitternut hickories, black walnut, butternut, white and black ashes, and formerly the American elm. The understory and shrub layers are often sparse, with ironwood and hard maple saplings the usual dominants. Hornbeam, bladdernut, serviceberries, dogwoods, witch hazel, Ohio buckeye, and the saplings of ashes and hickories are also common locally.

3. The *bottomland hardwoods* community occurs on primary floodplains and low-lying terraces in the larger stream valleys. Its canopy dominants are typically one or more of the following species: silver maple; green ash; hackberry; black walnut; cottonwood; and, in certain parts of eastern Iowa, the river birch. American elm was once a conspicuous feature of this community but large trees of this species are now scarce because of the Dutch elm disease. Many other species of large trees are also characteristic of this community though they seldom take up more than a minor part of the canopy: sycamore, honey locust, Kentucky coffee tree, black and peachleaf willows, bitternut and shellbark hickories, pecan, pin oak, shingle oak, swamp white oak, butternut, rock elm, and black ash. The understory is commonly dense with woody vines and saplings of the canopy species, but where the canopy is fairly open the understory is often replaced by tall herbaceous plants such as jewelweed and nettles.

4. The *riparian* community forms a narrow belt on lakeshores, stream banks, mud flats, and sandbars. It is usually dominated by one or more of the following: cottonwood; silver maple; boxelder; river birch; and sandbar, rigid, black, and peachleaf willows. Several other species from the adjacent bottomland hardwoods community may also occur to a greater or lesser extent.

5. The *northern conifer-hardwoods* community occurs on steep, moist, usually north-facing slopes in extreme northeastern Iowa. This community is centered in the Great Lakes states and many of its most characteristic species drop out in Minnesota or Wisconsin. The trees and shrubs that do range into Iowa are more often found as minor constituents of the oak-maple-basswood or oak-hickory communities than as a discrete community. They include white pine, balsam fir, Canada yew, paper and yellow birches, mountain maple, quaking and bigtooth aspens, black ash, speckled alder, highbush cranberry, red elderberry, and red-osier dogwood.

AUTUMN COLOR

The turning of the leaves in autumn is an annual event that draws thousands of spectators—especially in the rugged northeastern corner of the state where the climate, abundance of forest, and diversity of tree species combine to create a display unmatched elsewhere in the state. The timing of this spectacle differs from one part of Iowa to another and varies from year to year within the same locality, but usually the color is best during the first or second week of October. At this time the bright yellows, oranges, and reds of the hard maples and other early coloring species are at their peaks, while the deep reds and purples of the oaks are just beginning.

The coloring and subsequent falling of the leaves in autumn result from a series of chemical changes that occur in the leaf tissues during late summer and early autumn. These changes are initiated by the steady increase in the length of the nights, although the exact timing, intensity, and duration of the display depends on the weather. The best color occurs when conditions are clear, dry, and cool but not freezing. Contrary to popular opinion, frosts actually detract from the show because they kill the leaf cells responsible for the bright colors and cause the leaves to fall early. Driving rainstorms and strong winds shorten the display by causing the leaves to drop prematurely.

The colors of leaves come from four groups of pigments: chlorophylls, carotenes, anthocyanins, and tannins. Some of these are present in the leaves throughout the summer, while others appear only in autumn.

Chlorophylls, the principal photosynthetic pigments of plants, give the green color to leaves. They continuously break down during the summer months but are normally replaced as fast as they are lost. In early autumn, chlorophyll production slows and the green color fades.

Carotenes and their close relatives, the *xanthophylls,* are responsible for the yellows and oranges of maples, elms, ashes, hickories, aspens, locusts, and other familiar trees. These pigments occur in the leaves throughout the growing season but are masked by the chlorophylls until autumn. These pigments also give carrots, butter, egg yolks, corn, squash, and marigolds their characteristic colors.

Anthocyanins produce the reds and purples of hard maples, oaks, sumacs, dogwoods, white ash, and Virginia creeper. They are manufactured from soluble sugars in the cell sap during autumn. Anthocyanins also occur in beets, cranberries, and purple grapes.

Tannins give oak leaves their brown color. Like carotenes, they are present throughout the growing season but are revealed only when other pigments have faded. They are found also in tea, acorns, and tree bark.

MYCORRHIZAE

Of the many relationships that have been discovered in our natural woodlands, few are more intriguing or important than one that occurs underground, entirely hidden from view. This relationship begins when the slender, threadlike structures of certain soil fungi enter the roots of forest trees and other plants, often causing them to swell noticeably. Instead of harming the plants, as one might expect, the fungus forms an intimate and mutually beneficial (symbiotic) relationship with the roots. This association is called a mycorrhiza.

The principal benefit of mycorrhizal associations for trees seems to be the increased absorption of nitrogen, phosphorus, potassium, and other soil nutrients through the roots. Recent research suggests that mycorrhizal fungi may also benefit trees by protecting the roots from parasitic soil fungi. The association is so important that tree seeds planted in soils lacking the appropriate mycorrhizal fungus may not grow into normal, healthy seedlings.

Like other soil fungi, mycorrhizal fungi produce above-ground fruiting structures. Many of our common woodland mushrooms, including some edible species, are the fruiting structures of these fungi.

A NATURAL DISTURBANCE IN BOTTOMLANDS, meandering streams topple mature trees while at the same time depositing new soil for establishment of tree seedlings. (*Photo by Gary Hightshoe*)

NATIVE STREAMSIDE TREES include cottonwood, willow, and silver maple (top); river birch (above); and sandbar willow (right).

2: SELECTING AND TRANSPLANTING TREES

THIS CHAPTER offers suggestions on tree planting in Iowa, based on the experience of the authors and others who have worked with trees in the state. These suggestions may be added to or somewhat altered by individuals with experience in a local area.

Local nursery personnel are knowledgeable of species that have been grown successfully in an area and can provide professional assistance in selection and planting. Their advice and any written instructions that accompany a purchased tree should be followed carefully in the planting and subsequent care of the tree.

TYPES OF PLANTING STOCK

Nurseries offer several kinds of planting stock. *Bare root* trees have little or no soil attached to the roots. *Container-grown* trees have been grown in a pot or similar container, while *containerized* trees have been dug from the nursery and placed in a container. *Ball-and-burlap* trees have the root system in a round ball enclosed by burlap.

WHEN TO TRANSPLANT

Trees are best transplanted when they are dormant (not actively growing). Most deciduous trees can be planted in either spring or fall, although some kinds—such as oaks, willows, and birches—should be planted in spring. Pines, spruces, and firs are best planted from mid-August through September, but they can be planted in spring if necessary. Most other needle-leaved evergreens can be planted in either spring or early fall.

HOW TO TRANSPLANT

To begin, dig a planting hole that is the same depth as the root-ball of the tree and two to three times its diameter. If the tree is container grown or containerized, remove it carefully from its pot or container. Peat pots and other biodegradable containers may be left around the ball if soft and friable.

Place the tree in the center of the hole, taking care that the top of the ball is flush with the surface of the ground. If the tree is container grown, cut or pull out any roots that are encircling the edge of the ball. If planting a ball-and-burlap tree, cut the twine or rope wrapped around the root-ball, and remove the burlap from the up-

per half of the ball. Next, fill the hole with good, firmly settled soil. Water the tree thoroughly and mulch it as described below.

Staking is probably unnecessary if the tree is small, but a large tree may need additional support. If in doubt, consult the nursery. When tying a tree to a stake, use nylon hosiery, sturdy twine, or cloth; avoid wire unless you cover it with a piece of rubber hose where it contacts the tree.

The nursery can advise as to whether any initial pruning is required. Trees dug from a wild area should have some of their branches removed to help compensate for the roots lost in transplanting.

MAINTENANCE

Trees need ongoing maintenance if they are to remain healthy and attractive. *Watering, mulching, pruning,* and *protection from mechanical injury* are especially important.

Watering is the most critical practice in maintenance of trees. Both too much and too little water can be harmful. After a tree is transplanted, it can take as long as 3 months for newly grown roots to absorb appreciable moisture from soil outside the root-ball. In the meantime, the root-ball can dry out very quickly, even though the surrounding soil is very moist. During times of intense summer heat and drought, even established trees may require additional moisture. To determine if watering is needed, probe the soil around the roots with a metal rod or similar object. Water thoroughly whenever the soil feels dry.

Mulching conserves moisture and moderates temperature in the soil. It also helps control the growth of turf grasses and weeds, which compete with the tree for water and nutrients. Mulch should be applied three to four inches deep to the entire area shaded by the tree's crown, except for a small circle immediately around the trunk. The best mulch is compost topped by aged wood chips, but any coarse-textured, partially composed organic material can be used. Rock mulches are less beneficial and in some cases may be harmful; for example, white, lime-containing rocks placed around pin oaks or red maples may increase problems of nutrient deficiencies in these species.

Pruning serves to maintain a healthy, natural shape to the tree and prevent growth defects. Unless you wish the trees to be multiple-stemmed, maintain a single main trunk (leader) by pruning back competing stems. Select branches that will someday form the main limbs of the tree, and remove other branches that crowd, rub, or cross them.

The widest crotches are usually the strongest and least likely to split, so remove young branches that form narrow angles with the trunk.

Pruning can be done almost anytime, although late winter is ideal for most broadleaf species. Maples, birches, and some other species may "bleed" sap if pruned then, but this does not harm the tree. In areas where oak wilt occurs, avoid pruning oaks in May and June. Most conifers do not need regular pruning.

When removing a branch, cut it as close to the trunk as possible without severing the *branch bark ridge,* a raised, collarlike area that serves as a natural barrier against infection. In most cases it is not necessary to apply pruning paint to the wound, but painting is appropriate if one is forced to prune at a time of year when a disease such as oak wilt or Dutch elm disease may be transmitted to the tree.

Protection from mechanical injury is also important. Avoid hitting trees with lawnmowers and do not disturb the soil around their roots. To prevent sunscald and injury by rabbits and mice during winter, cover the trunks of young broadleaf trees with tree wrap in late fall. Remove the wrap in early spring, when the tree begins to grow for the year.

Healthy, vigorously growing trees do not require regular fertilization. However, if a tree shows signs of a nutrient deficiency, such as yellowish (chlorotic) foliage, fertilization may be necessary or helpful. Before a fertilization program is started, it is wise to test the soil to determine if any nutrient is deficient. Contact the Cooperative Extension Service for information and assistance.

For additional information on tree maintenance, including illustrations on how to prune, consult Shigo's "Homeowner's Guide for Beautiful, Safe, and Healthy Trees" and other publications cited in the bibliography of this book.

DISEASES AND INSECTS

Diseases and insects often injure cultivated trees. As is so often true, an ounce of prevention may be worth a pound of cure. Where a particular disease or pest is known to be troublesome, susceptible tree species should not be planted. (For example, avoid white-barked birches where the bronze birch borer is a problem.) Disease and insect problems are most common on trees stressed by drought, injury, transplant shock, or old age, so it is important to maintain trees in good condition by using proper planting and cultural techniques. (See discussion above.)

When an established, otherwise healthy tree is attacked by a disease or insect, it may be necessary to apply a suitable pesticide. Before using any pesticide, be sure to correctly diagnose the problem and determine whether the situation is serious enough to warrant control. Apply all pesticides carefully, according to label instructions, and only for registered uses. Specific pesticides are not recommended in this book because changing government regulations and the introduction of new products quickly make such recommendations obsolete. For more information, consult your local Cooperative Extension office.

SELECTING TREES

Although many species of trees thrive in Iowa if planted in good soil and given proper care, not all are equally suited for the various purposes for which they may be planted. Unfortunately, there is no such thing as the ideal tree. A species should be chosen only after thoughtful consideration of its environmental requirements; winter hardiness; purpose in the landscape; ultimate size and shape; and susceptibility to diseases, insects, and other problems.

Trees recommended for planting in Iowa are listed in Tables 2.1 and 2.2. These recommendations are guides for

Table 2.1.   Conifers recommended for planting in Iowa

	Land-scaping	Ever-green	Autumn color	Wild-life	Reforest-ation	Wind-break	Dry soil	Wet soil	East only
Large (50 to 100 feet)									
Baldcypress	x							x	
Douglas-fir	x	x		x		x			
Fir, white (concolor)	x	x		x		x			
Hemlock, eastern	x	x		x					x
Larch, European	x		x		x	x			
Pine, ponderosa	x	x		x	x	x	x		
Pine, red	x	x		x	x	x			x
Pine, Scots	x	x		x	x	x	x		
Pine, white	x	x		x	x	x			x
Spruce, blue	x	x		x					
Spruce, Norway	x	x		x		x			
Spruces, white & Black Hills	x	x		x		x			
Medium (20 to 40, occasionally 50 feet)									
Arborvitae (white cedar)	x	x		x		x		x	x
Pine, jack		x		x	x	x	x		
Pine, limber	x	x		x					
Redcedar, eastern	x	x		x	x	x	x		
Small (under 20 feet)									
Junipers	x	x		x					
Pine, mugo	x	x		x					
Yew, Japanese	x	x		x					

Table 2.2. Broadleaf trees recommended for planting in Iowa

	Land-scaping	Autumn color	Flowers	Wild-life	Reforest-ation	Wind-break	Dry soil	Wet soil	East only	South only
Large (50 to 100 feet)										
Ash, green	x	x			x	x	x	x		
Ash, white	x	x			x					
Basswood (American linden)	x				x					
Cottonwood, eastern					x	x		x		
Ginkgo	x	x								
Hackberry	x			x	x	x	x	x		
Hickory, shagbark	x			x	x		x			
Kentucky coffee tree	x									
Maple, hard (sugar, black)	x	x		x	x					
Maple, silver				x	x	x		x		
Oak, bur	x			x	x		x			
Oak, red	x	x		x	x					
Oak, swamp white	x			x				x	x	
Oak, white	x	x		x	x		x			
Sycamore	x							x		x
Walnut, black				x	x					
Medium to Moderately Large (30 to 50 feet)										
Birch, river	x							x		
Buckeye, Ohio	x	x								
Cherry, black	x	x	x	x	x					
Linden, littleleaf	x									
Maple, red	x	x	x	x				x	x	
Maple, Norway	x	x		x						
Mulberry, white				x		x	x	x		
Oak, shingle	x	x		x		x	x	x		x
Osage orange				x		x	x	x		x
Pear, callery	x	x	x							
Small (under 30 feet)										
Chokecherry		x	x	x			x			
Crab apple, flowering	x	x	x	x						
Dogwood, alternate-leaf	x	x	x	x					x	
Hawthorn	x	x	x	x		x				
Hornbeam, American	x	x							x	
Ironwood (hop hornbeam)	x						x			
Lilac, Japanese tree	x		x			x				
Magnolias, saucer & star	x		x							x
Maple, Amur	x	x		x		x	x			
Plum, American	x		x	x		x	x			
Redbud	x		x							x
Serviceberry	x	x	x	x						
Sumacs, staghorn & smooth	x	x		x			x			
Willow, native pussy	x		x					x		
Willow, sandbar				x				x		
Witch-hazel	x	x	x						x	

persons seeking advice on which tree to plant; they are not intended to be complete lists of trees available for specific purposes in Iowa. Trees recommended for a particular use or especially noted for a certain characteristic are indicated with "x." Uses and characteristics included in the tables are discussed below.

Landscaping. Included in this category are plantings for shade and beautification. When selecting a tree for an urban or residential area, consider its ultimate size and shape.

Large, broad-crowned trees such as oaks, ashes, and pines should be planted at least 20 feet from buildings, utility wires, or existing trees. If this requirement cannot be met, consider a smaller species. One or two large trees are enough for the average front lawn.

Autumn color. Species differ markedly in the color of their autumn leaves, and surprising variation can occur between trees of the same species. The best color is provided by such native trees as white oak, hard maple, white and green ashes, aspens, and sumacs. Many trees introduced from Europe, Asia, or other parts of North America color poorly or unreliably in Iowa. Autumn color is discussed in more detail in Chapter 1.

Evergreens. Evergreens are trees whose foliage is green at all times of the year. They have long been valued for planting in Iowa because they provide year-round color, shelter from the wind, and cover for wildlife.

The foliage of evergreens sometimes turns brown during winter and early spring. This is usually caused by rapid temperature fluctuations or by warm, dry winds that desic-

cate the foliage. (Roots cannot quickly replenish lost moisture at this time of year because plant tissues are dormant
and the soil is frozen.) If no new growth appears by late
spring, affected foliage is dead and should be removed by
pruning. Mulching the tree and watering it in autumn may
help prevent this injury.

Winter injury should not be confused with the natural
discoloration and loss of older needles that may occur in
the autumn or spring. This process affects only the foliage
farthest back on the twig, whereas winter injury also affects the youngest leaves at the twig apex.

Flowers. All species of broadleaf trees except the ginkgo
produce flowers sometime during the growing season, generally in the spring. The most colorful blossoms are found
on the smallest trees, although some large species such as
catalpa and horsechestnut also provide attractive displays.
Most of our large shade and forest trees have tiny, inconspicuous flowers that few people notice.

Wildlife. Trees benefit wildlife by providing cover and
nesting sites, by producing edible foliage and fruits, and
by attracting insects that are eaten by birds. All trees are
probably used by wildlife to some extent, but some species
are much more valuable than others. Species especially
valuable for cover have evergreen foliage, dense thorny
crowns, or a tendency to form thickets; examples include
the pines and other conifers, hawthorns, osage orange,
and wild plum. Species especially valuable for food include oaks, pines, cherries, dogwoods, maples, sumacs,
hackberry, and redcedar for their fruits and seeds; and
maples and aspens for their buds, flowers, twigs, and foliage.

Reforestation. Both conifers and broadleaf trees are desirable for reforestation in Iowa. Geography, topography,
and soils should be considered when selecting species, because trees that thrive in one part of the state may grow
poorly in another and many species will not tolerate exces-
sively dry or wet soils.

Windbreaks. Conifers are preferred for windbreaks because their dense, evergreen foliage provides more protection from winter winds than do the leafless branches of
broadleaf trees. However, most conifers require a well-
drained soil and broadleaf trees are usually substituted for
them on wet sites. Some species of small broadleaf trees
are also useful for borders along the edges of windbreaks.

Information on the establishment and maintenance of
windbreaks is found in the extension bulletin by Wray
(1976a).

Dry soils. Some trees, such as jack pine and redcedar, are
able to grow on dry, well-drained, sandy soils that will not

support the growth of other species. However, even the
most adaptable trees will usually grow more slowly on
such sites than they will on a site where the soil is moist
and fertile.

Wet soils. Tree roots require air as well as water, so most
species grow best where the soil is moist but well drained.
Nevertheless, some species are notable for their tolerance
of soils that are frequently saturated or even flooded, provided that water does not stand for more than a few weeks
at a time. Other species can survive but will grow much
less vigorously in wet places. Most trees that are adapted
to poorly drained soils grow naturally in river bottoms.

East only. Some species that thrive in the eastern one-
half to two-thirds of Iowa are unreliable in western Iowa.
If planting these species in the west, use locally proven
nursery stock and select a sheltered site with moist, fertile,
and neutral-to-acid soil.

South only. Many trees are not reliably hardy in northern Iowa. However, individuals from locally proven
sources may do very well if planted in a sheltered area with
good soil.

PROBLEM TREES

The species listed below have one or more objectionable features that should be considered before planting
them as street and yard trees. These features include short
life (*l*); limited hardness (*h*); a tendency to be messy because of dropped fruit or limbs (*m*); weediness due to vig-
orous reproduction (*w*); and susceptibility to storm damage (*s*), diseases (*d*), insect pests (*i*), or physiological
problems (*p*).

Large willows (*m, s, l*)	White mulberry (*m, w*)
White poplar (*m, w, s*)	Sweetgum (*h*)
Black walnut (*m*)	Mountain-ash (*l, d, i*)
Butternut (*d, m, l*)	Honey locust (*d, i*)
Paper birch (*i, l*)	Black locust (*i*)
European white birch (*i, l*)	Tree-of-heaven (*m, w, s*)
Pin oak (*p*)	Silver maple (*s*)
Siberian ("Chinese") elm	Boxelder (*w, s, l*)
(*m, w, s, d, i*)	Flowering dogwood (*h*)
Russian-olive (*l, d*)	Austrian pine (*d, i*)

Although these features may limit use of these trees in
urban or residential settings, they may not be objectionable in rural areas. In fact, some of the trees listed are
excellent for reforestation (see Table 2.1). Others, such as
white mulberry and boxelder, are useful to wildlife and
tolerate difficult environments where few other trees will
grow.

BEAUTY IS UNFORTUNATELY TRANSIENT in species prone to disease (American elm, above) or with naturally short life spans (Lombardy poplar, right).

3: IDENTIFYING TREES

IDENTIFYING A TREE is a two-step process. The ultimate goal is to determine which *species* or particular kind it is, but first it is necessary to assign it to a *genus* (plural *genera*) or group of closely related species. Most tree genera are natural, clearly defined groups that are easy to recognize; familiar examples include the oaks, maples, willows, and pines. Species are distinguished by less obvious characteristics than genera, so their identification is often more difficult. Identification of species is especially frustrating within such large and diverse genera as oaks, willows, crab apples, and hawthorns, whose constituent species are notorious for their similarity to one another and frequent hybridization (crossing between species). Although most species of trees can be learned by the amateur botanist with a little practice, identification within some of the more difficult genera may require the aid of an expert.

Several approaches can be followed. One is to simply page through an illustrated book, comparing a leaf or fruit of the tree in question with the drawings or photos in the book. This approach is quite satisfactory when dealing with a common species and using a well-illustrated book covering a limited geographical area. If the species is uncommon and not illustrated in the book or the book covers a large geographical area and hence many species, the "paging through" approach may be impractical. It is also of little value when attempting to identify a tree in winter, because differences between the twigs of species are not so easily illustrated.

A better approach is to track down the unknown tree in a special identification device known as a key, which is a series of sequentially numbered pairs of descriptions that allows one to determine the identity of the tree through a process of elimination. Keys often appear formidable to people who have not used them; but they are easy to use if followed carefully, one step at a time. Read the first description pair, or *couplet,* and decide which of the two choices best describes the tree in question. This decision points the way to another couplet, and the process is repeated until the tree is identified. It is wise to check all identifications against illustrations and botanical descriptions of the species to ensure that a mistake has not been made along the way.

If all else fails, a specimen of the tree can be sent to an expert for identification. Most colleges and universities employ one or more persons skilled in plant identification who are glad to help the amateur botanist, providing good specimens are sent. A twig with several representative leaves from the tree should be placed between two sheets of newspaper, taking care that the leaves lie flat (not folded). Place a heavy book on the newspaper and allow the specimen to dry thoroughly. When dry, it should be inserted between two stiff sheets of cardboard in a large envelope and mailed. The collector's name and address should be included, as well as the dimensions and specific location of the tree. Fruits or flowers should also be sent when present.

NAMES OF TREES

Trees are known by *common* names and *botanical* names. Most people prefer to use common names, since they are easy to spell, pronounce, and remember. Botanical names, which are taken from Latin, Greek, or Latinized words of other languages, seem unnecessarily complicated; but they have an important advantage in being standardized by international convention and thus more precise. An excellent example is provided by two small trees in the birch family that grow together in woodlands across much of Iowa. One is called either ironwood or hop hornbeam; the other is variously known as ironwood, hornbeam, blue beech, and musclewood. Despite this confusion of common names, no doubt exists when using the botanical name; there is only one for each—*Ostrya virginiana* for the first and *Carpinus caroliniana* for the second.

Another advantage of botanical names is that they are based on natural relationships. The common names green ash, mountain-ash, and prickly-ash all contain the word *ash,* but they have little resemblance to one another and each species belongs to a different botanical family. Only the first is a true ash. Likewise, Russian-olive is not an olive, Douglas-fir is not a fir, and Kentucky coffee tree is not related to the coffee of commerce. Conversely, poplars, aspens, and cottonwoods belong to the same genus and have similar characteristics but the common names indicate no relationship.

Each botanical name consists of two parts, the *generic name* and the *specific epithet.* The generic name appears first and is always capitalized. It designates the genus to which the tree belongs. The specific epithet follows and is never capitalized, even when taken from a proper name. It refers to the particular species. Both the generic name and the specific epithet are italicized or underlined in print. The generic name may be used alone but the specific epithet is meaningless by itself and must always be preceded by the generic name or its initial.

In formal writing, the specific epithet may be followed by the abbreviated surname of the botanist who originally described the species. This part of the botanical name is capitalized but never underlined or italicized. If further study reveals that a species belongs to a different genus than the one to which it was originally assigned, the abbreviated name of the botanist who first named the species is placed in parentheses before the abbreviated name of the botanist who made the change. The "L." following so many botanical names stands for Carl Linnaeus, a Swedish scientist who designed the modern system of biological nomenclature and published the first description of a large number of species.

Many species have been subdivided into *varieties*. The varietal name, when indicated, follows the specific epithet but precedes the botanist's name. It is underlined or italicized in print but not capitalized. The unitalicized abbreviation "var." sometimes precedes it to indicate that it is a varietal name.

Within a species or variety, it is sometimes desirable to distinguish and name plants for horticultural purposes. The term *cultivar* is used for a group of plants that share some useful nursery-selected feature or features. For example, *Fraxinus pennsylvanica* 'Marshall's Seedless' is a cultivar of the green ash, selected because it produces no seeds and has attractive, dark green leaves. Cultivar names are always capitalized and enclosed in single quotes.

Many but not all cultivars are *clones*. This means that they originated from a single parent tree and are propagated vegetatively to insure that each tree is an exact genetic replica of the original.

CHARACTERISTICS USED IN IDENTIFYING TREES

Many plant parts or *organs* of trees are used in identification. Leaves, twigs, flowers, and fruits are the most definitive organs, but bark and silhouette are helpful when other parts are out of reach or the tree is seen from a distance. The characteristics of the various organs that are especially useful in identification are defined and discussed below.

Leaves. Leaves are the most conspicuous feature of trees and one of the best means of identification when present. Figure 3.1 illustrates leaf characteristics. The leaves of most species are remarkably consistent from one individual to the next, but in some species considerable variation

FIG. 3.1. LEAF CHARACTERISTICS

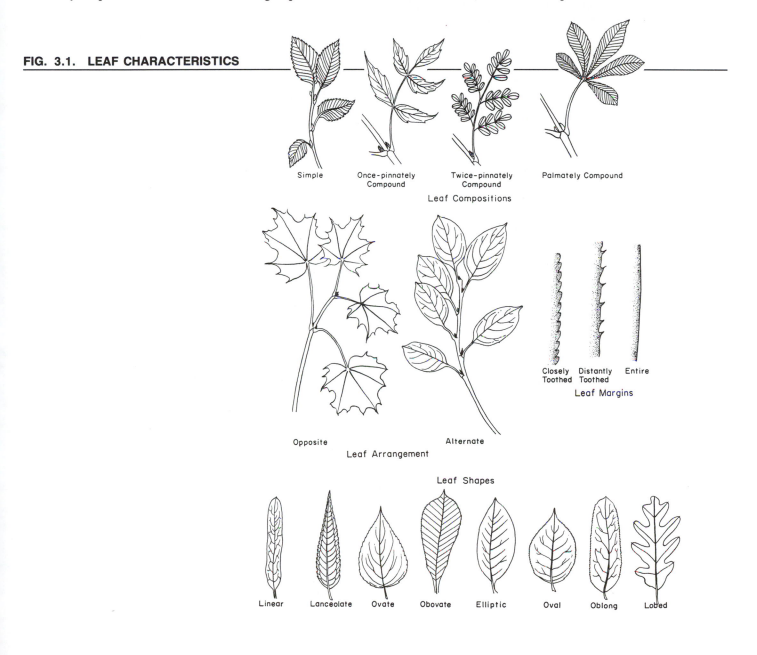

Simple   Once-pinnately Compound   Twice-pinnately Compound   Palmately Compound

Leaf Compositions

Closely Toothed   Distantly Toothed   Entire

Leaf Margins

Opposite   Alternate

Leaf Arrangement

Leaf Shapes

Linear   Lanceolate   Ovate   Obovate   Elliptic   Oval   Oblong   Lobed

occurs between individuals or even within an individual. The oaks are a notorious example, and species within this genus frequently cannot be identified without referring to buds and fruits in addition to leaves.

Leaf characteristics especially useful in identification are composition, arrangement, shape, margin, and surfaces.

Leaves should be collected from healthy, vigorously growing twigs when possible. Leaves from *root sprouts* (suckers) should be avoided because they are often unusually large and atypically shaped.

LEAF COMPOSITION. A leaf consists of two parts: (1) a broad, green, flattened portion called the *blade* and (2) a narrow stalk or *petiole.* The leaves of most trees, including such familiar types as oaks, maples, elms, and willows, have a single blade. Such leaves are said to be *simple.* Other species have leaves composed of many separate blades or *leaflets* and are said to be *compound.* If the leaflets are arranged along two sides of a central axis, like the barbs of a feather, the leaves are *once-pinnately compound.* Familiar examples include ashes, walnuts, and sumacs. In a few other species, notably the honey locust and Kentucky coffee tree, the leaf axis is branched with the leaflets arranged in two rows along each of the branches; these leaves are *twice-pinnately compound.* Two Iowa trees, the Ohio buckeye and its close relative the horse-chestnut, have leaflets arranged around a single point, like the fingers of a hand, instead of being attached to an axis. These are *palmately compound leaves.*

The composition of a leaf should be the first characteristic noted when identifying a tree. Do not mistake a leaflet of a compound leaf for a simple leaf or vice versa—a mistake easily made in spring when the new twigs are green and succulent. Remember that a bud occurs in the angle formed by the twig and each of its petioles, whereas buds are never present in the angle formed by a leaflet-stalk and the axis of a compound leaf.

ARRANGEMENT. A node is a slightly swollen, leaf-bearing portion of a twig. The leaves of most trees are *alternate*—only one leaf appears at each node. Maples and ashes have two leaves at each node, one on either side of the twig; this arrangement is called *opposite.* One Iowa tree, the catalpa, has three leaves at most nodes, an arrangement called *whorled.* When determining the arrangement of leaves, look along the main portion of the twig and avoid twig tips and spur shoots—the alternate leaves of oaks, birches, crab apples, and several other common trees are so close together at the tips of twigs or spur shoots that they may give the false impression of being opposite or whorled.

SHAPE. Leaf shape is usually consistent within a species. Leaves with very large indentations are said to be *lobed.* The projecting portions of the blades of these leaves are known as *lobes* and the spaces between the lobes are called *sinuses.*

MARGINS. The *margins,* or edges, of the leaves of most tree species consist of tiny alternating points called *teeth.* If the teeth are close together, the margin is *closely*

toothed; if the teeth are widely spaced, the margin is *distantly toothed.* An unbroken leaf margin is *entire.*

The difference between teeth and lobes is arbitrary and based only on size. A few species of oaks have projections of intermediate size that can justifiably be called either teeth or lobes, depending upon one's definition of these terms. However, in most cases there is little doubt as to whether the leaf itself or merely its margins are indented.

SURFACES. The upper surfaces of some leaves are noticeably *glossy* (shiny) while the leaves of other species are quite *dull.* A leaf surface may also be more or less covered with tiny hairlike projections, in which case it is said to be *pubescent* or *hairy.* A leaf with no hairs on its surfaces is *glabrous.* Some leaves are glabrous except for tufts of hairs beneath in the angles of the larger veins. The pin oak is a good example of this.

Winter twigs. Some people do not attempt to identify trees during winter, thinking the task is hopeless without leaves. Fortunately, the winter twigs of most trees are as distinctive as their leaves, so no one need give up identification when the branches are leafless. Even when leaves are present, one must often depend on twig characteristics, especially buds, to accurately identify species. Figure 3.2 shows twig characteristics.

The term *twig* as used here refers only to the current year's growth of the stem. Twig characteristics especially useful in identification are the arrangement, shape, and size of leaf scars; the number and arrangement of bundle scars; the color, number, and arrangement of bud scales; the presence or absence of terminal buds and stipule scars; the color and composition of the pith; and the occurrence of various special modifications. A magnifying glass is useful in examining these distinctive structures.

LEAF SCARS. When the leaf of a deciduous tree falls in autumn, its petiole leaves a mark on the twig called a *leaf scar.* Leaf scars of most species are small and somewhat semicircular in shape, but in some trees they are shield shaped or heart shaped and quite large. Each leaf scar encloses one or more small dots called *bundle scars* that mark the spots where the *vascular bundles* or veins of the leaf entered the twig.

Since leaf scars mark the positions of the leaves, they are likewise arranged in one of three ways: *alternate,* if solitary at the nodes; *opposite,* if in pairs at the nodes; and *whorled,* if in threes. One can also deduce the composition of a leaf in many species by examining its leaf scars. Compound leaves usually have large leaf scars with many bundle scars while simple leaves typically have small leaf scars with only 1 to 3 bundle scars. Several notable exceptions to this generality include mulberries, oaks, and the honey locust.

BUDS. A bud consists of a twig and leaves in the initial stages of development, prior to elongation. The buds of most trees are formed fairly early in the growing season but remain dormant until the following spring, since their principal function is to permit the vegetative parts of the tree to survive the winter. The buds of some species pro-

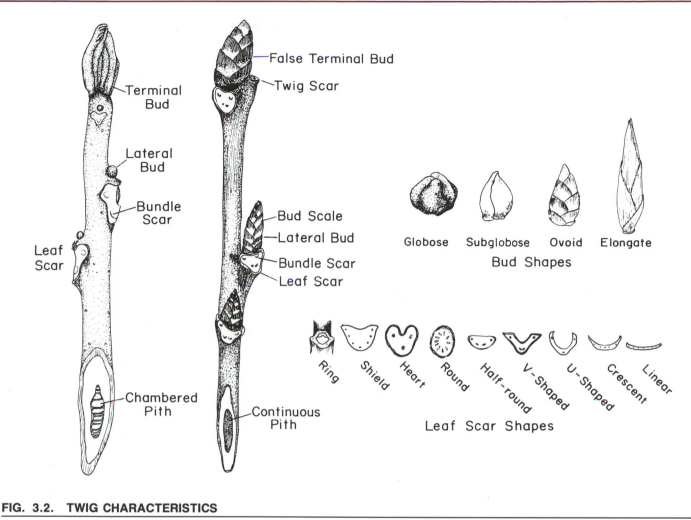

FIG. 3.2. TWIG CHARACTERISTICS

duce both leaves and flowers, in which case they are called *mixed buds;* but in other species the leaves and flowers come from different buds. *Flower buds* are usually larger and sometimes markedly different in shape than *leaf buds* of the same species. The buds of some trees are embedded in the twigs or the leaf scars and are apparently absent; these buds are *hidden buds.*

The buds of most species are covered with one or more thin, chaffy structures called *scales* that prevent the delicate tissues within from drying out during winter. The buds of poison ivy and a few small, uncommon trees lack scales and are said to be *naked.* Naked buds are often protected by a dense covering of long hairs.

In walnuts, cottonwoods, and maples, a single up-right bud called the *terminal bud* forms at the tip of each twig by midsummer. This bud, which limits elongation for the remainder of the growing season, is usually much larger than the *lateral buds* growing farther down the twig in the axil of each leaf.

Elms, willows, and sycamores do not produce true terminal buds, although their tender twig tips usually die back to a lateral bud sometime during the growing season, leaving it in a terminal position. This bud, which is called a *false terminal bud,* can usually be recognized as a lateral

bud by its size, shape, and frequently slanting aspect. The most definitive way to distinguish it from a true terminal bud is to look for the presence of either a stub or *twig scar* at its base. Twig scars often resemble leaf scars in size and shape but never enclose bundle scars.

STIPULE SCARS. Stipules are small leaflike appendages occurring in pairs on the petioles or twigs of many trees. Those attached to the twig leave two small horizontal lines where they fall, one on either side of the leaf scar. Sometimes one of these will be much more prominent than the other. Stipule scars of sycamores, magnolias, and tulip trees form a line that completely encircles the twig at each node.

PITH. If a twig is cut in *cross section* (in a plane perpendicular to its length), three concentric rings of tissues can be seen. These, in order from the outside to the center, are the bark, wood, and pith. All aid in identification, but the *pith* or core of the twig is especially useful. In some species, such as the Kentucky coffee tree and smooth sumac, it is brightly colored and occupies a disproportionately large portion of the twig; in other species it is very small and practically indistinguishable from the wood. Its outline likewise varies from round to conspicuously angled or even star shaped.

A cut made lengthwise through the center of a twig exposes the pith in a *longitudinal section*. The pith of most species then appears as *continuous* pith, an unbroken strand of tissue. In the magnolias and a few other less common trees, the pith consists of small pieces of solid tissue separated by thin cross walls; this type is known as *diaphragmed* pith. A third type, *chambered* pith, is composed of thin cross walls separating empty space. Chambered pith occurs in walnuts and intermittently in hackberry.

SPECIAL MODIFICATIONS. The twigs of some species bear specialized structures that aid in identification. The most useful of these are thorns, spines, spur shoots, and catkins.

A *thorn* is a modified twig with a sharp point and a smooth, often glossy surface. True thorns, such as those of the honey locust and hawthorns, do not have buds or leaf scars except at their bases. A few species, notably the wild plum and wild crab apple, often have short, sharply pointed twigs resembling true thorns, but these have buds and leaf scars like ordinary twigs.

Spines are stipules that have become sharply pointed and somewhat woody. They occur in pairs, one on either side of each leaf scar. The black locust is the only Iowa tree with spines, although several shrubby species also have them.

A *spur shoot* is a short, stubby twig that grows only a fraction of an inch each year. Its outer surface is covered with closely packed leaf scars and there is a terminal bud at its tip. Spur shoots occur sporadically in a large number of species but are especially common in crab apples, birches, and the ginkgo.

The *catkin* is a special type of flower cluster found in many trees. The catkins of most species remain hidden within the buds until spring, but in the birches and ironwood the immature staminate catkins become visible on the twig tips in summer and remain there throughout winter. They resemble tiny sausages covered with minute overlapping scales.

Flowers. All species of broadleaf trees except the ginkgo bear flowers sometime during the growing season, though the blossoms of many trees are so tiny and inconspicuous they are seldom noticed. Tree flowers are usually distinctive when present but their usefulness as a means of identification is limited by their short life. One reason willows, serviceberries, and hawthorns are so difficult to identify is that flowers are needed to differentiate among the species, and they are present for only a week or two in spring! Fortunately, most species of trees can be readily distinguished by more persistent features such as leaves, buds, and fruits.

Flower characteristics useful in identification are type of inflorescence (Fig. 3.3), number of stamens, placement of various flower parts with respect to the ovary, and presence or absence of petals. When petals are present, note their number, shape, and color and determine if they are joined or separate.

Tree flowers are not described in detail in the species descriptions here unless floral characteristics are necessary to distinguish species that closely resemble one another in other features. Further information on the flower structure of tree species can be found in Rogers (1935) or in a standard botanical work such as Fernald (1950).

FLOWER PARTS. Most of our common garden flowers (such as the petunia, tulip, and snapdragon) have four whorls or groups of parts. These, in order of arrangement from the outside of the blossom to the center, are sepals, petals, stamens, and carpels. All four are present in the blossoms of most small ornamental trees, but one or more are usually missing in the flowers of large shade and forest trees.

Sepals and *petals* are small, leaflike structures at the

FIG. 3.3. TYPES OF INFLORESCENCES

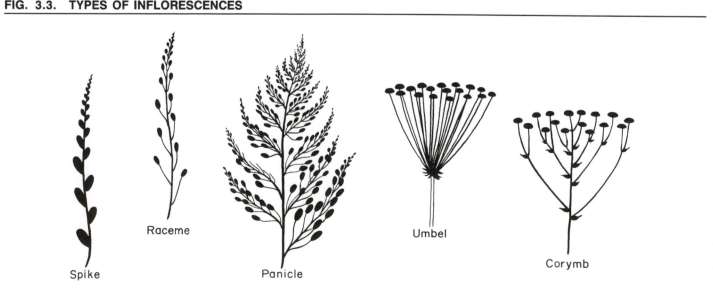

Spike Raceme Panicle Umbel Corymb

base of the flower. Sepals are usually green and the petals white, pink, or some other bright color, but in some species sepals and petals are the same color. The sepals are collectively known as the *calyx* and the petals as the *corolla*. A flower without petals is said to be *apetalous*.

Stamens are the male part of the flower and *carpels* the female part. Each stamen is composed of a slender stalk or *filament* and a pollen-bearing sac called the *anther*. The carpels in each flower form one or more flask-shaped structures called *pistils*. The pistil of most species is composed of a bulbous basal portion called the *ovary*, a slender neck or *style*, and a swollen tip or *stigma*. If the stamens, pistils, and sepals of the flower appear to arise from the summit of the ovary, the ovary is an *inferior ovary*; if they arise from the base of the ovary or are attached to the rim of a cuplike structure that surrounds (but is free from) the ovary, it is a *superior ovary*. The numbers of carpels can usually be inferred by counting the pistils or, if only one is present, by counting the compartments of the ovary or the lobes of the stigma.

A flower containing both stamens and pistils is said to be *perfect*; one bearing either stamens or pistils but not both is called *imperfect*. Thus each imperfect flower is either male or female. If the imperfect flowers are found on separate trees, the species is *dioecious*; if they occur on the same tree, it is *monoecious*. A species with both perfect and imperfect flowers is *polygamous*.

ARRANGEMENT OF FLOWERS. A cluster of flowers is called an inflorescence. Several common types of inflorescences are defined below.

The *spike* and *raceme* are unbranched in florescences. They each consist of a single unbranched stem to which several flowers are directly attached. However, the flowers of a spike are sessile (unstalked) on the stem, while those of the raceme are distinctly stalked. The *catkin* is a special type of spike found in willows, poplars, oaks, birches, walnuts, and hickories. It consists of numerous tiny, imperfect, apetalous flowers grouped closely together, forming a long, slender, often drooping inflorescence resembling a cat's tail. Catkins are produced in spring, often before the leaves.

The *umbel, corymb, cyme,* and *panicle* are branched inflorescences. The flower stalks of an umbel are attached to a single point and more or less equal in length, much like the ribs of an umbrella. An umbel may be flat topped or round topped. A corymb resembles the umbel in shape but has flower stalks of different lengths attached at varying levels along a central stem. The outermost flowers in corymbs bloom first, but in the cyme (which is often little different from a corymb in appearance) the innermost flowers are the first to expand. A panicle is an open, often highly branched inflorescence.

Fruits. To the botanist a fruit is any seed-bearing structure derived from the ovary of a flower. This definition includes a number of dry, one-seeded foods such as corn, walnuts, pecans, sunflower "seeds," and cereal grains as well as squash, tomatoes, green beans, and a number of other "vegetables." Even such inedible things as milkweed pods, sticktights, and cattail "seeds" are properly considered to be fruits.

Fruits are perhaps the most useful of all the plant parts used in tree identification, and in some of the larger genera they are virtually indispensable in distinguishing species. The fruits of willows, cottonwood, and a few other trees are as short lived as their flowers—they are available for a week or two at most—but most tree species have fruits that persist for several weeks or even months. Nuts are especially valuable in identification, since they can usually be found on the ground beneath the tree throughout the winter.

Characteristics of fruit used in identification are type, shape, size, and color. The two principal types of fruits are dry fruits and fleshy fruits.

Dry fruits are subdivided into two categories. *Dehiscent* fruits are podlike, splitting open along definite seams. Each may contain one to many seeds, depending on species. *Indehiscent* fruits do not split open and are usually one seeded. Some indehiscent fruits have husks or other accessory structures derived from a part of the flower other than the ovary.

Follicles, legumes, and capsules are three common kinds of dehiscent fruits. The *follicle,* which is derived from a superior ovary containing only one carpel, has a single chamber and splits open along one seam (the milkweed pod is a familiar example). The *legume* has a pair of seams, although it may split open along only one, and one internal chamber (pods of pea, soybean, and honey locust are examples). The *capsule,* which is derived from an ovary having two to several carpels, commonly has two or more seams and at least two internal chambers (catalpa, cottonwood, and lilac have capsules).

Common indehiscent fruits are the achene, samara, and nut. The *achene* is a tiny, one-seeded fruit present in many species of weeds but relatively uncommon among trees. Many achenes have long, cottony hairs or prickly hooks to aid in dispersal. *Samaras* are similar to achenes but have dry membranous wings that allow them to catch the wind (maples, ashes, and elms have samaras). *Nuts* are relatively large, one-seeded fruits with hard shells. Most nuts (including those of such familiar trees as oaks, hickories, and chestnuts) are at least partially enclosed by a husk, cup, or similar structure. The tiny nutlike fruits of birches, ironwood, and hornbeam are called *nutlets* (little nuts).

Fleshy fruits include the drupe, berry, and pome. A *drupe* or "stone fruit" has a single seed with a thick bony covering. This pit or stone is in turn surrounded by a juicy or mealy flesh (familiar examples are the olive, cherry, peach, and plum). *Berry,* though often used as a general term for small, juicy fruits, is technically defined as a fruit that is entirely fleshy with two or more seeds distributed throughout its pulp (tomatoes, grapes, and persimmons are examples; bananas, cranberries, melons, cucumbers, strawberries, raspberries, and citrus fruits also fit this description but are more properly placed in special categories because of their different development and structure). *Pomes* may also resemble berries but differ in their seeds being confined to the center of the fruit with a thin, cartilaginous wall separating them from the outer pulp (apples and pears are pomes). Pomes are derived from an inferior ovary, so the remnants of the calyx can often be seen at the end of the fruit opposite the stem.

Bark. The differences between the trunk barks of trees are less obvious than differences in leaves, twigs, and fruits; but with practice one can learn to identify most species by bark alone. A knowledge of the barks of our native trees is indispensable when attempting to identify species in the woods, where foliage and twigs are often out of reach. The barks of most trees can be described as being smooth, scaly, platy, warty, furrowed, or shaggy.

Smooth bark is tight fitting and unbroken. Most species have smooth bark when young but only a few trees retain it as they mature. Beech, hornbeam, and serviceberry are examples.

Scaly bark is broken into small, thin, loosely attached pieces with upturned edges. Black cherry is the best example.

Platy bark is broken into small, roughly rectangular pieces that are usually appressed to the trunk and more or less arranged in rows. White oak, silver maple, and ironwood have this type.

Warty bark is unique to the hackberry. It consists of small warty outgrowths on a smooth background.

Furrowed bark is by far the most common. It is composed of ridges alternating with valleys (or furrows), much like a three-dimensional map of a mountain range. Species can be distinguished by the color of the bark, depth and width of the furrows, thickness and length of the ridges, and regularity of the pattern. Black walnut, green and white ash, sugar maple, cottonwood, and many oaks have furrowed bark.

Shaggy bark occurs in the shagbark and shellbark hickories. It consists of elongate, irregularly shaped pieces that curve upwards at one or both ends, giving the trunk a shaggy appearance.

Silhouette. Many kinds of trees develop distinctive silhouettes when not crowded. Familiar examples include the columnar silhouette of the Lombardy poplar, the vase-shaped silhouette of the American elm, and the pyramidal silhouette of the pin oak and many conifers. Figure 3.4 shows the various distinctive silhouettes.

FIG. 3.4. TREE SHAPES

Columnar

Round

Pyramidal

Oval

Oblong

Vase-Shaped

Irregular or Asymmetric

4: TREES OF IOWA

THE FOREST UNDERSTORY COMMUNITY consists of trees adapted to living in the shade of the forest canopy. Important providers of wildlife habitat, dogwood, ironwood, redbud, serviceberry, pawpaw, and other understory species are also familiar landscaping trees.

THE FOLLOWING PAGES contain descriptions of; illustrations of; and information about the distribution, natural history, and uses of our native and common introduced trees. In most cases only one species is discussed, but in a few instances two or more are discussed together.

The common name of the tree appears first with the botanical name directly following it. Nomenclature, with a few exceptions, follows Little (1953) and Rehder (1940).

Following the common and botanical names of each tree is a paragraph listing the distinctive features of the tree's leaves, winter twigs, buds, flowers, fruits, and bark. In most cases this is followed by a description of similar trees, which contrasts the features of the tree with the features of other trees that might be mistaken for it.

The next paragraph describes the geographical distribution of the tree in Iowa. Most trees are described as *native,* meaning they grew here before the arrival of white settlers. The geographic ranges of native trees are described as precisely as possible, but much remains to be learned about the distributions of some species. Range maps are not included because of our incomplete knowledge of species distributions; the relative abundance of a species often varies considerably from one part of its range to another, and some species have been widely planted outside their natural ranges. Thus, maps have the potential to mislead more than to clarify.

Other terms of distribution are cultivated, planted, escaped, and naturalized. *Cultivated and planted* refer to trees that have been intentionally planted in an area, whether they are native or not. If wind, birds, or some other natural agent disperses the seeds of a non-native tree to a vacant lot, fencerow, or similar spot and these seeds grow into new trees, the species is said to have *escaped* from cultivation.

If an escaped species begins to reproduce in the wild as if it were native, it is said to be *naturalized*.

At this point appears a discussion of the tree's natural history, its cultural characteristics, and its desirability for various uses. The term *conservation plantings* in the discussion refers to plantings for the purposes of reforestation, wildlife habitat, erosion control, and watershed protection in rural areas. The term *pioneer* describes species that will establish themselves in bare or barren areas.

The arrangement of the trees in this book is based on a classification of plants proposed by the German botanists Adolf Engler and Karl Prantl in the late nineteenth century. Although this classification is now out of date, it is still followed in most botanical manuals and is used here for the sake of consistency with those publications.

In the classification of Engler and Prantl, as well as in more modern classifications, the trees found in Iowa are placed into two distinct groups: *conifers* and *broadleaf* trees.

CONIFERS

"PINE" AND "EVERGREEN" are often used as general terms for trees having cones and needlelike leaves, but botanists prefer the word *conifer,* which is Latin for "cone-bearing." Pines actually compose only one genus, or group, of conifers, and evergreen refers to any tree, conifer or broadleaf, that remains green during the winter. Most conifers are evergreen, of course, but some, such as the larches and baldcypress, have leaves that turn color and drop every autumn.

Besides the obvious dissimilarities in foliage and the method of branching, conifers differ from broadleaf trees in that their reproductive organs are borne in cones instead of flowers. Both the male, or pollen, cones and the female, or seed, cones are produced in spring, and in some species they are brightly colored when they first emerge. Usually both types occur on the same tree, but in a few species, such as the redcedar, they appear on separate trees. The male cones fall from the tree not long after they have shed their pollen, but the female cones continue to grow and develop and may remain on the tree for several years.

Conifers are the largest and most important surviving branch of an ancient line of seed plants called the gymnosperms. Yews and the ginkgo, which are planted as ornamentals in Iowa, represent two other branches of the gymnosperm line. Their pollen is produced in small cones, as is the case with conifers, but their seeds are attached individually to the branches. Representatives of other gymnosperm lines occur in deserts and tropical forests, and others are known only from fossils.

Conifers are a prominent part of the landscape in most parts of Iowa today, but this was not always so. When the settlers arrived in Iowa from the east, only three coniferous trees occurred here—white pine, redcedar, and balsam fir. The redcedar was distributed along river bluffs throughout most of the state, though in smaller numbers than today; the other two species were native to northeastern Iowa. Most of the conifers found in Iowa today were introduced from Europe, the Rocky Mountains, and the Great Lakes region.

In Iowa conifers are used primarily for ornamentals, Christmas trees, windbreaks, wildlife plantings, and reforestation. Another promising use for some conifers is the reclamation of strip-mined land. Seeds of conifers are eaten by many kinds of birds and small mammals, and their evergreen foliage is an important source of winter cover.

PINES

WHEN one considers the abundance and importance of pines, it is not surprising that the terms "pine" and "evergreen" are synonymous to so many people. No other group of conifers is more valuable for landscaping and conservation.

As a group, pines are easy to recognize. Unlike spruces, firs, and other familiar conifers, the leaves of pines are grouped in small bundles called *fascicles.* Each fascicle has from 2 to 5 leaves, depending upon species.

The seed cones of pines are also distinctive. Most conifers mature their cones in a single growing season but pine cones do not mature until the end of the second year. The terminal portion of each cone scale is thickened and often quite different in color from the remainder of the scale. This thickened area, called the *apophysis,* bears a small diamond-shaped protuberance called the *umbo.* In many species the umbo is tipped by a short prickle. When the cone is mature but has not yet opened, the apophysis and umbo are the only parts of the scales that are visible. The characteristics of the apophysis and umbo are used in distinguishing species.

The five pines most commonly seen in Iowa are illustrated and discussed on the following pages. Several additional species are discussed on page 26.

White Pine, *Pinus strobus* L.

Distinguishing characteristics: *Leaves* in fascicles of 5, very slender, 2 to 5 (usually about 3) inches long, marked with fine white lines (seen with magnifying glass), very flexible. *Terminal buds* ovoid; about ⅜ inch long; abruptly tapered to short, slender tips, with light brown scales. *Twigs* flexible, often drooping, about ⅛ inch in diameter. *Cones* elongate, 4 to 5 (rarely to 8) inches long, apophysis brown, umbos without prickles. *Bark* smooth and light gray on young trees; becoming dark gray to nearly black with flat plates separated by shallow fissures; eventually dark and deeply furrowed with scaly, blocky plates.

Similar trees: No other pine commonly planted in Iowa has leaves in fascicles of 5.

Distribution: Native in northeastern Iowa and along Pine Creek in Muscatine County and the Iowa River in Hardin County; widely planted throughout the state. Natural stands are found on bluffs, ridges, and wooded slopes, usually in well-drained soils.

WHITE PINE has long been one of America's most valuable and celebrated trees. Large specimens were abundant and widespread in the Northeast and the Great Lakes states at the time of European settlement, but their numbers were soon depleted to satisfy a growing nation's demand for wood. Majestic trees 150 feet tall were felled, transported south on rivers and streams, and used for everything from lumber and shingles to furniture and paneling.

When settlers arrived in Iowa, they found this species to be the only native pine. At that time it was confined largely to the northeastern corner of the state, with outlying populations in central and southeastern Iowa. It has since proved popular for landscaping, windbreaks, wildlife plantings, and reforestation and has been planted widely outside its natural range.

The white pine is one of our most distinctive conifers. Its leaves, which are lighter in color and much more slender than those of other pines, tend to droop in dense tufts at the ends of the twig, giving its foliage a soft, delicate look. When viewed from a distance, a tree can be easily recognized by its irregular shape. Most conifers have a cone-shaped crown that tapers neatly from the bottom to the top, with branches of gradually decreasing length. In the white pine, however, the length of the limbs may vary considerably from one whorl to the next, especially in old trees.

White pine grows well in eastern and central Iowa when planted on well-drained upland soils and is one of the most desirable conifers for planting in those parts of the state. Plantings in western Iowa sometimes fail, especially in highly calcareous soils, although good growth has been recorded on sheltered sites where the soil is fertile and slightly acidic. Young trees transplant easily and grow quickly, eventually reaching a height of 50 to 80 feet. Dwarf, columnar, and weeping cultivars are available for landscape use.

The wood of the white pine is light, soft, and easily worked. It shrinks and swells very little, making it ideal for foundry patterns, doors, and window sash. It is used also for boxes and crates and at one time was the principal source of wooden kitchen matches. In the days of the great sailing ships, it was highly esteemed for masts; one of the contributing causes of the Revolutionary War was the British Crown's decree that the biggest and straightest white pines in the colonies be reserved for the Royal Navy.

Scots Pine, *Pinus sylvestris* L.

Distinguishing characteristics: *Leaves* in fascicles of 2, slender, 1 to 4 inches long, usually twisted and often marked with fine white lines (seen with magnifying glass). *Terminal buds* ovoid to ovoid-elongate, ⅜ to ½ inch long, with sharp- or blunt-pointed tips and red-brown scales. *Twigs* flexible, about ⅛ inch in diameter. *Cones* 1 to 2 inches long, falling intact (i.e., basal scales not missing); apophysis yellow-brown; umbos flattened or (more commonly) raised and pyramidal, prickles minute or absent. *Bark* scaly and light orange on larger branches and upper trunk, divided into large gray plates covered with orange scales on lower trunk.

Similar trees: Austrian and red pines have longer leaves; jack pine has the two leaves of each fascicle strongly divergent from one another. Mature Scots pines can be easily distinguished from these species by the orange bark of their upper trunk and limbs.

Distribution: Planted throughout the state.

AMONG the many kinds of conifers planted in Iowa, the Scots pine has the most unpredictable habit of growth. Young trees look much like other species of pines, but as they mature, each takes on a personality of its own. The crown may vary from round, compact, and symmetric to irregular and picturesque, but it seldom fails to be interesting. Planting a seedling Scots pine can be a real adventure, because one can never be certain what the outcome will be.

Another striking feature of the Scots pine is the flaky orange bark that clothes its upper trunk and largest limbs. Many other common pines have at least some orange color in their bark, but always on a background of gray or black. The more uniform orange of the Scots pine's bark is visible from quite a distance and provides the easiest and quickest means of identifying the tree.

Scots pine is hardy throughout Iowa and has long been popular for shelterbelts, farm groves, and ornamental use. More recently, it has become the favorite conifer for Christmas tree plantings. It has proved more adaptable in western Iowa than many other pines, perhaps because it tolerates drought and calcareous soils. Dwarf and columnar cultivars are available for landscaping.

Scots pine was for many years a rather trouble-free species, but in recent years it has proved susceptible to pine wilt disease and Zimmerman pine moth. Pine wilt has several causes including pine wood nematodes, blue-stain fungi, shothole beetles, and unfavorable environmental conditions. Affected trees may decline and die suddenly. There is no known cure, but spread of the disease can be slowed through proper cultural practices (see Chapter 2) and by promptly removing and destroying dead trees. (For information about the pine moth, see under *Austrian pine*.)

Scots pine is one of the world's most broad-ranging trees. It is native from Scotland east through most of central and southern Siberia, south to Spain, the Balkan Peninsula, the Caucasus region, Mongolia, and Manchuria. The many geographic races are adapted to different soils and climates, and they cannot all be expected to grow equally well in Iowa.

In its native range the Scots pine may grow to heights of 100 feet or more, but in the Midwest it is usually only 30 to 60 feet tall. At the time of this writing, the largest known Scots pine in the United States was a 73-foot giant in Nevada, Iowa.

Austrian Pine, *Pinus nigra* Arnold

Distinguishing characteristics: *Leaves* in fascicles of 2, stout, 4 to 6 inches long, rather stiff but resistant to breakage when bent in two. *Terminal buds* subglobose to ovoid; ½ to ¾ inch long; abruptly tapered to short, slender tips, with brown scales coated with a white, waxy substance. *Twigs* stiff, about ⅜ inch in diameter. *Cones* 2 to 3 inches long, falling intact (i.e., basal scales not missing); apophysis yellow-brown; umbo usually armed with a tiny prickle. *Bark* divided into large, dark gray plates; more or less covered with lighter colored scales.

Similar trees: Red pine and ponderosa pine are the only other pines planted in Iowa that regularly have leaves over 4 inches long. Red pine has brown buds, and ponderosa pine has at least some fascicles with 3 needles. Fallen cones of both species have missing basal scales. Red and ponderosa pines are used primarily for conservation plantings in Iowa and are seldom seen as ornamentals.

Small individuals sometimes have needles that are shorter than 4 inches. Such trees might be mistaken for Scots pine, but Austrian pine has fat, whitened buds and Scots pine has slim, red-brown buds.

Distribution: Planted throughout the state.

LIKE the Scots pine and several other European conifers, the Austrian pine has proved to be an adaptable and useful tree for planting in the United States. it will grow in a variety of soils, including heavy clays, and resists salt, heat, drought, and difficult urban conditions. Long, dark green needles make it attractive in landscape plantings and as a Christmas tree.

Unfortunately, Austrian pine in Iowa is susceptible to needle and shoot diseases. These cause the leaves to turn brown and die and in severe cases may cause extensive defoliation. Trees can be protected by spraying their foliage with a suitable fungicide in spring, but this must be repeated annually to achieve good results. For information on what and when to spray, contact a local extension office.

Austrian pine is also susceptible to the Zimmerman pine moth. Damage is caused by the insect's larvae, which bore into the stems and feed on the inner bark and sapwood. Infested shoots turn brown and die, curving downward to form a "shepherd's crook." The trees also exude a white pitch that accumulates on the bark where the branches join the stem. Control is accomplished by pruning infested wood and by applying an appropriate insecticide at the correct time.

Young Austrian pines have dense crowns and a broadly pyramidal shape like spruces and firs. At this stage they are most attractive if their lower branches are retained. The trees later develop more open crowns, but the tops typically remain compact and often become flattened. Eventually the lower branches can be removed. Height at maturity is usually 50 to 60 feet.

Austrian pine is native from central Europe to western Asia. Most of the trees planted in Iowa are the variety *nigra*, which ranges from the Austrian and Italian Alps to the Carpathians and Balkans. Other varieties occur in the Pyrenees and southern France, in Corsica, and in Turkey and the Crimea.

Red Pine, *Pinus resinosa* Ait.

Distinguishing characteristics: *Leaves* in fascicles of 2, slender, 4 to 6 inches long, fairly flexible but breaking readily when bent in two. *Terminal buds* ovoid; ½ to ¾ inch long; gradually tapered to long, slender tips, with brown scales. *Twigs* about ¼ inch in diameter. *Cones* 1½ to 2¼ inches long; basal scales remaining on the twig when the cone falls, leaving a small depression in the base of the cone; apophysis brown or gray; umbos without prickles. *Bark* gray and flaky on younger trees, eventually dividing into flat plates separated by shallow furrows and covered with red-orange scales.

Similar trees: Austrian pine has strongly whitened buds and larger, yellow-brown cones that retain their basal scales when falling from the twigs. Ponderosa pine has some fascicles with 3 needles and larger cones with sharp prickles. Scots pine has shorter, twisted leaves.

Distribution: Planted throughout the state, but more common in the east than in the west.

MANY people know this tree as the "Norway pine," although it is native to North America, not Europe. Apparently, some eighteenth-century explorers mistook it for the Norway spruce, which is an important timber tree in Europe, or the Scots pine, which is common in Norway. Their misnomer was adopted by the lumberjacks and settlers who followed and has persisted to the present day.

The red pine closely resembles the Austrian pine when young and the two species are frequently confused. The bark of both is a rather somber gray at first, but as the trees age, the bark of the Austrian pine acquires a whitish cast while that of the red pine becomes a mottled orange-red. The trees can be identified even when small by bending a leaf in half: the leaf will break cleanly in two if the tree is a red pine but will remain unbroken if from an Austrian pine.

The principal uses of the red pine in Iowa are for reforestation, wildlife habitat, and other conservation plantings. It requires a well-drained, acid soil and grows poorly or dies when planted in wet or calcareous soils. Like the white pine, it is more reliable in eastern and central Iowa than in the western part of the state. Mature trees are usually 50 to 80 feet tall.

Red pine is native to the Great Lakes states, New England, and southern Canada. Its geographical range extends as far south as southeastern Minnesota, southwestern Wisconsin, and northeastern Illinois, but does not quite reach Iowa. It is the state tree of Minnesota and a conspicuous feature of the northern lakes region there.

Red pine is an important timber tree where native and is often sold as a Christmas tree in Iowa. Its pale reddish wood is straight grained, moderately soft, and moderately heavy. Its principal uses are poles, posts, paper pulp, doors, window sashes, and interior and exterior finish.

Jack Pine, *Pinus banksiana* Lamb. (*P. divaricata* Du Mont)

Distinguishing characteristics: *Leaves* in fascicles of 2, moderately stout, strongly divergent from one another, ¾ to 1½ inches long. *Terminal buds* ovoid to ovoid-elongate, ¼ to ⅜ inch long, with blunt tips and light brown scales. *Twigs* flexible, about 3/16 inch in diameter. *Cones* 1½ to 2 inches long, asymmetric with a slight to quite pronounced curve, typically remaining closed for several years; apophysis light yellow or brown on young cones, gray and weathered on older cones; umbos unarmed or armed with a tiny prickle. *Bark* dark gray or brown, divided into irregular ridges separated by shallow furrows.

Similar trees: Short-needle varieties of the Scots pine are the only other pines with leaves consistently less than 1½ inches long. They can be distinguished by their nondivergent leaves and symmetric cones. Jack pine is sometimes mistaken for a spruce or fir because of the short length and extreme divergence of its leaves.

Distribution: Planted throughout the state.

IN comparison to the other pines commonly planted in Iowa, the jack pine looks like a poor relation. It is typically a small and rather unattractive tree, with unusually short leaves and a crown that is sparse and misshapen. Appearances can be deceiving, however, for this homely and seemingly unhealthy pine is one of the hardiest trees native to North America. It grows farther north than any other pine and tolerates dry, sterile soils that are inhospitable to most other trees.

Jack pine is not recommended for general conservation plantings in Iowa because most Iowa soils are fertile enough to support larger and more valuable conifers, but it is sometimes used for reforestation projects on severely eroded lands. It grows faster than most of the other pines planted for conservation in Iowa but is the smallest, usually attaining a height of only 35 to 50 feet.

Jack pine has the broadest geographic distribution of any North American pine, ranging from New England and the Canadian maritime provinces on the east to the Great Lakes and Rocky Mountains on the west and north to the limit of tree growth. A pioneer species, it rapidly invades lands that have recently been burned or logged and often forms pure stands. It is common in mixed stands with red pine, quaking aspen, and paper birch in the canoe country of northern Minnesota.

The unusual cones of the jack pine are its most interesting feature. They are asymmetrically shaped and may remain closed long after the seeds are mature. Unopened cones sometimes persist on the trees for so long—20 years or more—that they become embedded in the wood of the branches. These cones seem oblivious to alternate freezing and thawing, wetting and drying, and the other natural cycles that initiate changes in nature; but if scorched with fire they will slowly open. This strange behavior is an adaptation to the tree's environment, which is subject to devastating forest fires during dry years, and allows it to rapidly reseed burned-over areas. Jack pine, like most other pioneer species, is intolerant of shade and requires an open, sunlit area to reproduce itself.

The wood of jack pine is moderately light and soft. It is used for pulp, posts, poles, and mine timbers.

Other Pines

MOST of the pines in Iowa belong to one of the five species discussed on the previous pages, but several other species are planted for landscaping or conservation. Four of these are described below.

PONDEROSA PINE, *Pinus ponderosa* Laws. *Leaves* in fascicles of both 2 and 3, stout, 4 to 11 inches long, flexible. *Cones* 2½ to 6 inches long; basal scales remaining on the twig when the cones fall, leaving a depression in the base of each cone; apophysis brown; umbo armed with a sharp prickle.

THIS native of the western United States is recommended for ornamental and conservation plantings in western Iowa, as it grows well in calcareous soils and is tolerant of dry conditions. Attempts to grow this species in eastern Iowa often fail because its more humid climate favors the development of needle blight diseases. Mature trees reach heights of 60 feet or more.

Ponderosa pine is one of the most important timber trees in the Rocky Mountain and Pacific Coast states. Its wood is manufactured into plywood, paneling, millwork, boxes and crates, and many other products.

VIRGINIA PINE, *Pinus virginiana* Mill. *Leaves* in fascicles of 2, moderately stout, usually twisted, 1½ to 3 inches long. *Cones* 1½ to 3 inches long, often remaining on branches for many years, their scales purplish on the inner (upper) edge; apophysis brown on young cones, gray and weathered on older cones; umbos armed with sharp prickles ¹⁄₁₆ to ⅛ inch long.

THIS straggly little tree has a number of common names, including such descriptive if unflattering titles as "scrub pine" and "poverty pine," but the name most frequently seen in print is Virginia pine, the English version of its botanical name. It is of minor importance in Iowa as it has little ornamental value, is inferior to other species for most types of conservation plantings, and is not reliably hardy in the northern and western parts of the state. However, it grows very well on coal spoils and on heavy clay soils, making it useful for reforestation and strip-mine reclamation in southern Iowa. Some Virginia pines planted on abandoned Iowa coal mines are reproducing naturally from seed.

Virginia pine is native to the Appalachian Mountains in the eastern United States. It has little value as a timber tree but is becoming increasingly important as a source of paper pulp.

MUGO PINE, *Pinus mugo* Turra. *Leaves* in fascicles of 2, moderately stout, 1½ to 3 inches long. *Cones* ¾ to 1½ inches long, apophysis brown; umbos without prickles.

THIS attractive little pine is easy to recognize, as it branches freely near the ground instead of having a single main stem like other pines. It is often planted around homes and other buildings because it withstands pruning well and is naturally small in size.

Mugo pine is native to the mountains of central and southern Europe and is hardy in all parts of Iowa.

LIMBER PINE, *Pinus flexilis* James. *Leaves* in fascicles of 5, moderately stout, 1½ to 3 inches long. *Cones* elongate, 3 to 10 inches long, with extremely thick scales; apophysis yellowish-brown; umbos lacking prickles.

THIS little-known tree resembles our native white pine and is easily mistaken for it, because both species have needles in fascicles of five. The leaf tips of limber pine are smooth, however, whereas those of white pine bear many tiny teeth that make them feel rough. Limber pine further differs from white pine in having much thicker twigs and cone scales. The unusual flexibility of its twigs has given it both its common and botanical names.

Limber pine grows slowly but is long lived and remarkably windfirm, eventually attaining a height of 25 to 50 feet. It has been successfully cultivated on the Iowa State University campus for many years and the authors have observed it growing well in northwestern Iowa. It is native to high elevations in the Rocky Mountains and the Black Hills.

Pinus flexilis variety *reflexa,* often called the southwestern white pine, differs from typical limber pine in having its cone scales strongly reflexed. Though native to the southwestern United States and northern Mexico, it has proved hardy at the Iowa Arboretum. Some botanists consider it to be a distinct species, *P. strobiformis* Engelm.

blue spruce ►

white spruce

Spruces, *Picea* A. Dietr.

Distinguishing characteristics: *Leaves* linear, four-sided, evergreen, with woody, peglike bases that remain on the twig when the green portions fall; spirally arranged and extending from the twig in several directions. *Buds* small, with overlapping, recurved scales. *Cones* pendant, falling intact. *Bark* thin, dark, scaly.

Similar trees: Firs and Douglas-fir resemble spruces and are often confused with them but differ in having flattened leaves that lack woody, peglike bases. Fir cones are held upright on the branches and disintegrate at maturity; cones of Douglas-fir have protruding bracts.

Distribution: Three introduced species commonly planted across the state.

SPRUCES are among the hardiest of conifers and their compact, symmetrical silhouettes are familiar sights across Iowa. The popularity of individual species has changed through the years, but spruces as a group have long rivaled pines as the most important of the large conifers for landscaping.

Spruces develop a columnar crown under forest competition and their lower branches prune naturally; but when the trees are grown in the open their lower branches persist and spread horizontally, producing a broadly pyramidal crown. The presence of these branches near the ground enhances the beauty of the tree, although they take up considerable space. If the presence of lower branches is likely to be objectionable, one of the pines is a better choice as an ornamental, for lower limbs can be removed on most pines without detracting from the beauty of the tree.

Spruces are often planted in windbreaks but are seldom used in other types of conservation plantings. Pines grow faster and more vigorously and are preferable for reforestation and wildlife habitat in most instances.

Although spruces are usually trouble-free if properly sited and maintained, they may be bothered by any of several diseases and insects, especially when stressed by old age, overcrowding, or drought. Pests include spider mite, spruce needle miner, scale insects, and gall adelgids. The most widespread and serious diseases are Cytospora canker, which kills the branches, and Rhizosphaera needlecast, which causes the older, inner needles to turn reddish brown or purplish brown and fall prematurely. Both of these diseases usually start near the base of the tree and progress upwards. Neither is easy to control, and they are best presented by promoting tree health through proper cultural practices.

The spruces most commonly planted in Iowa are described and discussed below. Several other species show promise as ornamentals and are being tested at arboretums.

NORWAY SPRUCE, *Picea abies* (L.) Karst. *Leaves* ⅜ to 1 inch long, dark green. *Twigs* drooping, distinctly orange on new growth. *Cones* 4 to 6 inches long; scales dull brown, very rigid, with finely toothed margins.

THE Norway spruce was once very popular as an ornamental in Iowa, but today it is less commonly planted than the blue and white spruces. It is the fastest growing and most gracefully shaped of the three, developing long, drooping branchlets as it ages. More than 100 cultivars have been selected, including some that are columnar, weeping, or dwarf in habit.

◄ Norway spruce

◄ blue spruce

white spruce

Norway spruce is the tallest native tree in Europe and is an important constituent of Germany's famed Black Forest. Its wood, which is called "whitewood" or "white deal" in England, is similar to that of the white spruce and used for many of the same purposes. Burgundy pitch, a resin obtained from the bark of this species, is used in the manufacture of certain varnishes and medicinal compounds.

WHITE SPRUCE, *Picea glauca* (Moench) Voss. *Leaves* ⅓ to ¾ inch long, green or light blue-green. *Twigs* gray on new growth. *Cones* 1 to 2 inches long; scales dull light brown, flexible, with entire, rounded margins.

WHITE SPRUCE lacks the colorful foliage of the blue spruce and the distinctive drooping habit of the Norway spruce, but it is a handsome ornamental in its own right. Its dense foliage and ability to withstand extremes of heat and cold make it desirable for windbreaks and it is often planted in Iowa for this purpose.

White spruce is an important timber tree in the coniferous forests of Canada and the northern United States. Its wood is light and soft but fairly strong for its weight. Its principal use is for paper pulp; it is also used for lumber, boxes, crates, and many other products.

The Black Hills spruce, *Picea glauca* var. *densata,* is a variety of the white spruce that is often sold in nurseries. It develops into an attractive, conical tree that is smaller and more compact than typical white spruce, and it grows more slowly. It is native to the Black Hills of South Dakota and Wyoming.

BLUE SPRUCE, *Picea pungens* Engelm. *Leaves* ¾ to 1¼ inches long, blue-green, sharp pointed. *Twigs* distinctly orange on new growth. *Cones* 2¼ to 4 (usually 3 to 3½) inches long; scales light yellow-brown, shiny, very flexible, with irregularly toothed margins.

THIS attractive tree has become the most popular of the spruces used for landscaping in Iowa. Its popularity is due in large part to the striking blue-green color of its foliage, which is caused by a white, waxy material on the surface of its leaves. However, individual trees vary considerably in the intensity of this color and some may even be dark green. To ensure uniformity in color, many of the trees sold in nurseries are propagated by grafting rather than by seed. Several of the best cultivars can be seen at the Iowa Arboretum near Boone.

Blue spruce is native to the Rocky Mountains and is the state tree of Colorado and Utah. Its wood resembles that of white spruce but is knotty, brittle, and of little importance.

European   tamarack
Larch

European Larch, *Larix decidua* Mill.

Distinguishing characteristics: *Leaves* linear but very slender, without petioles, ¾ to 1¼ inches long, deciduous; spirally arranged on twigs, tufted at ends of spur shoots on branchlets. *Twigs* long, slender, drooping. *Terminal bud* about 1/16 inch long, with brown, overlapping scales. *Cones* ¾ to 1½ inches long, with 40 to 50 thin scales, held upright on the twigs and persisting for several years. *Bark* separating into irregular plates covered with gray and red-brown scales.

Similar trees: Tamarack is the only other conifer planted in Iowa whose leaves are tufted at the ends of spur shoots. Its cones are ½ to ¾ inch long and have only 12 to 15 scales (see cone on right in above photograph).

Distribution: Planted throughout the state.

THE European larch, the only deciduous conifer commonly planted in Iowa, has as many faces as there are seasons. In winter it is as bare and lifeless as any broadleaf tree; but its small, upright cones; tall, tapered trunk; and horizontal branches are distinctly coniferous. When spring arrives, its branches are decorated with tiny, bright red cones, which nicely complement the soft, light green leaves that emerge from overwintering buds. In summer the larch's foliage takes on a darker hue and its pyramidal crown resembles that of other cone-bearing trees; but its long drooping twigs and slender leaves give it a graceful, fine-textured appearance that can be easily recognized from a distance. Finally, in late October or early November, long after most broadleaf trees have lost their leaves, the larch turns a brilliant gold, providing a last blaze of color before the onset of winter.

The European larch has many qualities that recommend it for landscaping and conservation plantings. It grows faster than most other conifers when planted in the open on moist, well-drained soils, often exceeding a height of 40 feet in 20 years. Larch is also windfirm, is relatively free of disease, and grows well on moderately calcareous soils. However, it should not be planted on wet, extremely dry, or highly calcareous soils; and it is sensitive to soil compaction and drought. Its height at maturity may be 75 feet or more.

The larch is native to the mountains of central and eastern Europe and has been widely planted elsewhere in Europe as well as in the United States. Its wood is hard, heavy, strong, and durable; in Europe it is used for poles, posts, vats, and boats.

The tamarack or eastern Larch [*Larix laricina* (Du Roi) K. Koch] is occasionally planted in Iowa, but it is not as attractive as the European larch. It is native to the coniferous forests of Canada and the northern United States, where it is a common inhabitant of bogs.

Douglas-fir, *Pseudotsuga menziesii* (Mirb.) Franco

Distinguishing characteristics: *Leaves* linear, flattened, petiolate, evergreen, ¾ to 1¼ inches long, blue-green above and marked with two white lines below; spirally arranged and extending from the twig in all directions. *Buds* ovoid-elongate, pointed, ¼ to ⅜ inch long, with brown or red-brown overlapping scales. *Cones* 2 to 3 inches long, pendant, falling intact, with three-pronged bracts protruding between the scales. *Bark* gray and scaly on young trees, eventually becoming red-brown and deeply furrowed.

Similar trees: Spruces have woody, peglike leaf bases that persist on twigs when the leaves fall. Leaves of true firs lack petioles. None of these trees have large, sharp-pointed buds or protruding cone bracts.

Distribution: Planted throughout the state.

EXPLORERS who first encountered this tree in the western United States did not know whether to call it a spruce, a fir, or a hemlock, for it has some characteristics of all three. Its leaves superficially resemble those of true firs, but they have short petioles like the leaves of hemlocks and diverge from all sides of the twigs like the leaves of spruces. Botanists now realize that the tree is not closely related to any of these conifers and consider it to be in a genus by itself. However, the tree has been known as a fir for so many years that the word is still accepted as part of its common name.

The most distinctive feature of the Douglas-fir is its cone. All conifers have a dry, chaffy bract at the base of each of their cone scales; but in most species the bract is small, inconspicuous, and seldom noticed. In the Douglas-fir this structure is elongated and forklike and protrudes conspicuously between the scales. Cones are often pro-

duced when the tree is very young and can usually be found on the ground beneath the tree, if not on its branches, so the Douglas-fir is usually easy to identify. When cones are absent, it can be distinguished from similar conifers by its large, pointed buds.

Douglas-firs found in the West occur in two distinct forms, Rocky Mountain and Pacific Coast, but authorities disagree as to whether the two types are different enough to be considered two species. Other than range, cones are the most reliable means of distinguishing the types. Cones of the Rocky Mountain trees are rather small, averaging 2 to 3 inches in length, with strongly reflexed bracts pointing toward the base of the cone. Pacific Coast trees have cones 3 to 4 inches long with straight bracts pointing toward the tip of the cone.

The Pacific Coast form of Douglas-fir is not reliably hardy in Iowa, but the Rocky Mountain form is often planted for landscaping, windbreaks, and wildlife habitat. It resembles the blue and white spruces, having blue-green foliage and a compact, pyramidal crown. Although usually rather trouble-free, it is sometimes attacked by Swiss needlecast and Cytospora canker. Trees usually grow at a moderate rate, maturing at heights of 40 feet or more.

Douglas-fir is one of the most important timber trees in the world. It is the source of much of the plywood and construction lumber sold in the western and central states and is also heavily used for paper pulp, railroad ties, tanks and vats, and barrels. Another important use of this valuable tree is for Christmas trees, especially in the West.

Firs, *Abies* Mill.

Distinguishing characteristics: *Leaves* linear, flattened, blunt, without petioles, evergreen; spirally arranged on the twig but often twisted at the base and appearing two-ranked. *Buds* small, with blunt or rounded tips and tightly overlapping scales with a waxy covering. *Cones* upright on branches, disintegrating when mature.

Similar trees: Spruces have four-sided leaves with woody, peglike bases that remain on the twig after the needlelike portion has fallen. Douglas-fir has petioled leaves and elongated, pointed buds. See also discussion below.

Distribution: One species native in the northeastern corner of the state and another planted throughout the state as an ornamental.

FIRS, like spruces, are trees of high mountains and cold, northern regions. They superficially resemble the spruces in foliage and general appearance and are often confused with them, but a careful comparison of the leaves of spruces with those of firs reveals several differences. Perhaps the easiest way to distinguish between the two is to place a detached leaf firmly between finger and thumb and attempt to roll it. If the tree is a spruce the leaf will roll easily; if it is a fir, it will refuse to budge.

Firs are attractively shaped and relatively free of diseases and insect pests, but most species are sensitive to heat and drought and do not grow well in Iowa. Of the many species native to the United States, the balsam and white firs are the only firs one is likely to encounter in Iowa. The Douglas-fir, which is often planted as an ornamental in Iowa, is not closely related to the true firs.

BALSAM FIR, *Abies balsamea* (L.) Mill. *Leaves* ¾ to 1½ inches long; dark green above and marked with two white lines below. *Buds* ⅛ to ¼ inch long. *Cones* 2 to 4 inches long, scales longer than wide. *Bark* smooth and gray on young trees; separating into thin, red-brown scales on large trees.

BALSAM fir is native in northeastern Iowa but is very rare, occurring only on steep, sheltered slopes in Allamakee, Clayton, Winneshiek, and Howard counties. (The photograph above left shows a native stand along the Upper Iowa River near Bluffton, in Winneshiek County.) Its sensitivity to heat and drought limits its value for general landscape or conservation use, although individual trees sometimes grow very well if carefully sited and maintained.

Balsam fir is common in the coniferous forests of Canada and the northeastern United States. Its wood, though light, soft, and weak, is excellent for pulp; and this species is one of Canada's most commercially important trees. Balsam fir was once very popular as a Christmas tree, but plantation-grown pines have largely replaced it for this purpose today. It is the source of Canada balsam, a resin used in the manufacture of optical instruments and prepared microscope slides.

WHITE FIR, *Abies concolor* (Gord. and Glend.) Lindl. *Leaves* ¾ to 3 (usually 1½ to 2) inches long, usually blue-green on both surfaces. *Buds* ⅛ to ¼ inch long. *Cones* 3 to 5 inches long, scales wider than long. *Bark* smooth, gray on young trees, eventually dark and furrowed.

THIS attractive tree tolerates dryness better than most firs and is used for landscaping and windbreaks in Iowa. It grows at a slow to moderate rate, developing a dense, pyramidal crown and attaining a height of 50 feet or more. It is often sold in nurseries under the name "concolor fir."

White fir is native to the Rocky Mountains. Its wood, which is similar to that of balsam fir, is used for pulp, lumber, boxes, crates, doors, and window sash.

Eastern Redcedar, *Juniperus virginiana* L.

Distinguishing characteristics: *Leaves* evergreen, of two types, both usually (but not always) present on the same tree: (*a*) scalelike, opposite, dull pointed, closely appressed to twig, about ¹⁄₁₆ inch long, each pair overlapping the pair immediately above it and oriented at right angles to it; and (*b*) needlelike, opposite or occasionally in whorls of three, sharp pointed, divergent from twig, ¼ to ½ inch long. Foliage with a dark green, blue-green, or reddish cast. *Twigs* four sided. *Buds* tiny, naked, hidden by leaves. *Cones* blue, berrylike, ¼ to ⅓ inch in diameter; dioecious. *Bark* light gray or red-brown; separating into long, narrow, vertically oriented strips.

Similar trees: Leaves of common juniper are all needlelike and in whorls of three. Arborvitae has light green, scalelike leaves; flattened branchlets; and small woody cones.

Distribution: Native throughout the state and widely cultivated.

IF entered in a contest with our other conifers, the redcedar would not win any prizes for size or beauty, but it would easily take first place for versatility and adaptability. It has been widely used in landscaping, soil conservation, windbreaks, and wildlife plantings; and although it is not the best for each of these purposes, few trees can claim to be valuable for so many applications. Wild cedars cling to rocky cliffs; colonize eroded, overgrazed land; and thrive in poor, gravelly soils in which few other trees will grow. They are the only native conifers throughout most of the state.

The redcedar and other junipers are unique among our conifers in that their cones are fleshy and berrylike instead of woody. Thus they are popular with songbirds and rodents, and one small bird is so fond of them that it is called the cedar waxwing or cedarbird. The cones are digested by the animals that eat them, but the hard seeds pass through unharmed. This accounts for the presence of solitary seedlings in ditches, pastures, fencerows, and other out-of-the-way places. Many more reach maturity now than in presettlement times when prairie fires regularly swept across the landscape.

If asked to name the oldest Iowa tree, many people

would choose cottonwood or oaks because of their massive trunks and tall, spreading crowns. Nevertheless, botanists now believe that the oldest living trees in Iowa are relatively small cedars growing on river bluffs in eastern Iowa. An age of 200 years is very old for a cottonwood and the oldest known oaks in Iowa are slightly over four centuries old, but a redcedar has been discovered in Linn County that is nearly 450 years old. Botanists believe that older trees may yet be found.

Because they are evergreen and easy to grow, the redcedar and other junipers are widely used in landscaping. No group of woody plants varies more in size, color, or habit of growth; some are trees with columnar or pyramidal crowns, others are low and shrubby. A complete treatment of all the types grown in Iowa would require a small book in itself. Besides the redcedar, commonly planted species include the Chinese juniper, *Juniperus chinensis;* the Rocky Mountain juniper, *J. scopulorum;* the savin juniper, *J. sabina;* and the creeping juniper, *J. horizontalis.* For information on the most desirable cultivars, see Olson's "Landscape Plants for Iowa" or Dirr's *Manual of Woody Landscape Plants.*

Redcedar is recommended for conservation plantings on thin, droughty, highly calcareous soils; but pines grow faster on most other soils. A degree of caution should be exercised in planting redcedar as it is the alternate host of various rust diseases of apples, crab apples, hawthorns, and serviceberries.

The distinctive red-brown heartwood of the redcedar is hard and moderately heavy. It is manufactured into chests, wardrobes, and closet linings because of its fragrance and reputed ability to repel moths. Its natural durability makes it especially useful for untreated fence posts and it has also been used for shingles. At one time most of the redcedar cut was used for making pencils, but the incense cedar of the Pacific Coast has largely replaced it for this purpose today.

Arborvitae (Northern White Cedar), *Thuja occidentalis* L.

Distinguishing characteristics: *Leaves* scalelike, opposite, evergreen, closely appressed to the side of the twig, light green in color, about ⅛ (occasionally up to ¼) inch long; leaf pairs alternating at right angles, with the members of each lateral pair folded in half and tightly overlapping the flattened facial pair immediately above them. *Twigs* and branchlets decidedly flattened. *Buds* naked, tiny. *Cones* erect, ⅓ to ½ inch long; scales 8 to 12, of which only 4 bear seeds. *Bark* gray to red-brown, shreddy, with shallow furrows and interconnecting ridges.

Similar trees: Redcedar has four-sided twigs, berrylike cones, and at least some needlelike leaves.

Distribution: Planted throughout the state.

NO ONE is certain why this handsome tree was named *arborvitae,* a Latinized form of the French *l'arbre de vie,* or "tree of life." Some attribute the name to the tree's longevity (400 years or more); others attribute it to a story that a tea made from its bark and leaves cured scurvy among the members of Cartier's expedition to North America in the early sixteenth century. Another possible explanation is the tree's evergreen foliage—evergreens have long symbolized eternal life and are frequently planted in cemeteries.

The principal use of the arborvitae in Iowa is in landscaping, although it is sometimes planted in farm windbreaks, especially in northeastern Iowa. It grows slowly and withstands pruning well, making it ideal for hedges and plantings around the foundations of buildings. A medium-sized tree, 40 to 50 feet tall, the arborvitae normally develops an irregularly oblong crown of short, horizontal branches. It prefers a moist, well-drained, moderately calcareous soil but is tolerant of both wet and acidic soils. Though hardy and relatively free of diseases, it is susceptible to winter injury when planted in dry locations (see page 9).

The arborvitae is native to the Great Lakes states, New England, and southeastern Canada. It can be found on a variety of sites but usually grows in swamps; along lakeshores; and in other moist, low-lying areas, frequently forming large thickets. Its foliage is an important source of food for deer during the lean months of winter and its seeds are a favorite item in the diet of the pine siskin.

Foresters know the arborvitae as the "northern white cedar." The word "cedar," like "fir" and "pine," is used in the names of a large number of trees that are not necessarily related. All the trees called "cedar" in the United States belong to the cypress family, a group characterized by tiny, scalelike, evergreen leaves and soft, light, durable, aromatic wood. The arborvitae and eastern redcedar are the only trees of this family commonly seen in Iowa, but many species occur in western North America and eastern Asia. True cedars, including the famed cedar of Lebanon, belong to the pine family. They have tufted, needlelike leaves resembling those of larches.

The wood of the arborvitae is used for poles, posts, siding, shingles, fishnet floats, and fishing lures. Native Americans valued it for the frames of their canoes because it is easy to split and work, resists decay, and is very light in weight.

BROADLEAF TREES

BROADLEAF TREES comprise the larger of the two principal groups of trees on earth today and account for all but a handful of the tree species native to Iowa. Broadleaf trees provide shade for our homes, fuel for our fireplaces, lumber for the manufacture of fine furniture, and much of our locally grown fruit. Their colorful blossoms liven the Iowa landscape in spring and their turning leaves attract thousands of admirers to the outdoors every autumn.

Leaves of broadleaf trees have a variety of shapes and sizes, but all are much broader than the needlelike leaves of the conifers. They also differ from conifer needles in having a conspicuous network of branching vascular bundles or *veins*. Conifer leaves have vascular bundles too, but theirs are unbranched and best seen with the aid of a microscope. These structures serve as the "plumbing" of the leaf, transporting water and mineral nutrients into the leaf and sugars out of it.

All broadleaf trees native to Iowa are deciduous; that is, they lose their leaves every autumn. However, the terms *broadleaf* and *deciduous* are not necessarily synonymous. For example, species of oaks, hollies, magnolias, and other genera with evergreen leaves appear in the southern states; and one conifer widely planted in Iowa, the European larch, is deciduous. Even some of our most common trees, notably the white oak and ironwood, tend to retain their dried, brown leaves throughout the winter.

Broadleaf trees are often called *hardwoods* since the wood of most species is harder and heavier than that of the conifers, or *softwoods*. However, the woods of several common species of broadleaf trees, including the cottonwood, black willow, and basswood, are considerably lighter and softer than the wood of some conifers. A more reliable distinction between the two groups of trees is the presence of *vessels* or *pores,* as they are commonly known, in the woods of broadleaf trees. Coniferous wood never has vessels.

Though the broadleaf trees are not universally deciduous or hardwooded, all bear flowers sometime during the growing season. Most species bloom in spring, either before or at about the same time their leaves appear. Many of our smallest trees, such as the redbud and crab apple, bloom so spectacularly that they are cultivated solely for that purpose. On the other hand, the flowers of most large shade and forest trees are so tiny, drab, and inconspicuous that few people notice them. This disparity in the size and color of tree flowers is due to the different ways in which their pollen is spread. Showy, fragrant blossoms are pollinated by bees and other insects whereas small, drab flowers are usually pollinated by the wind.

Another common feature of broadleaf trees is the production of fruit. Botanists consider a fruit to be the ripened, seed-bearing ovary of a flower. According to the botanical definition, the pod of the honey locust and acorn of the oak are fruits just as are apples and plums. Similarly, the "seeds" of ashes and maples, the nuts of walnuts and hickories, and the tiny capsules of willows and poplars are all properly considered to be fruits. The cones of conifers and the plumlike seed of the ginkgo, despite their similarity to fruits, do not qualify as such because they are not derived from flowers.

The checkerboard rule in the photographs of bark is 12 inches long.

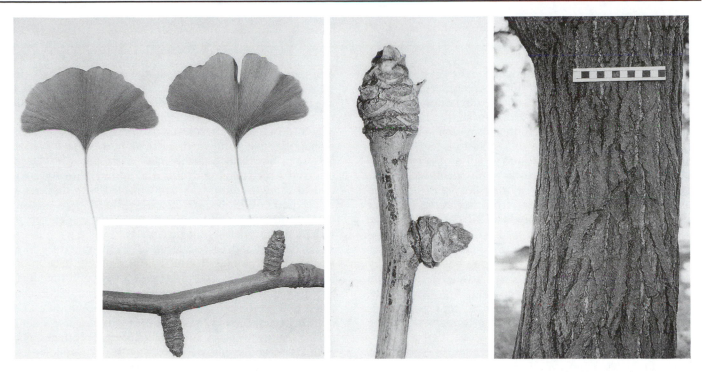

Ginkgo, *Ginkgo biloba* L.

Distinguishing characteristics: *Leaves* simple, alternate on twigs but clustered at the ends of spur shoots on branchlets, fan shaped, lobed or not, entire, with numerous veins forking into pairs of equal, parallel branches. *Winter twigs* moderate in diameter, with shreddy outer bark; leaf scars small, half round, each with 2 bundle scars. *Buds* subglobose, with brown, overlapping scales, about 3/16 inch long; terminal bud present. *Flowers* absent (see discussion of reproductive structures below). *Seed* plumlike; stalked; about 1 inch long; with fetid, yellow flesh and nutlike center. *Bark* gray-brown, with long scaly ridges and shallow furrows.

Similar trees: No other tree has fan-shaped leaves with dichotomously branching veins. Winter: larches have small cones; all other trees with spur shoots on their twigs have 3 or more bundle scars.

Distribution: Planted throughout the state, but more common in cities than small towns.

THE ginkgo is an ancient and remarkable tree. It is often called a "living fossil" because it has changed very little for millions of years and is the last surviving member of a family that flourished in the age of the dinosaurs. It is almost pest-free, having apparently outlasted any diseases or insects that may once have afflicted it. It will grow in many different soils and withstands drought and other environmental adversities. There are ginkgos in the Orient reputedly more than 1,000 years old.

Like pines and other conifers—and unlike most broadleaf trees—ginkgos lack pores (vessels) in their wood and do not have true flowers. Their tiny male and female reproductive structures occur on separate trees, appearing with the leaves in spring. The male structures, or microsporangia, resemble the stamens of flowers and occur in catkinlike clusters. Their pollen is dispersed by the wind. The female structures, or ovules, are borne in pairs at the ends of short stalks. Following pollination and fertilization, they develop into seeds resembling small plums.

These seeds apparently gave the tree its name. The word "ginkgo" is usually attributed to the Chinese words *gin-yo* or *gin-go,* meaning "silver apricot." Another ancient Chinese name of the tree was *ya chio* meaning "leaf of a duck's foot." Today the ginkgo is sometimes called *maidenhair tree* because its leaves resemble those of the maidenhair ferns.

Because of its hardiness, adaptability, and handsome appearance, the ginkgo is planted as a street and yard tree throughout Iowa. It usually grows rather slowly in the Midwest, eventually attaining a height of 50 to 80 feet. When young it has ascending branches and a pyramidal shape, but as it ages its branches grow more horizontally and its shape becomes more irregular. Its trunk, like conifer trunks, tapers gradually and often runs unforked to the top of the crown. The leaves turn bright yellow in late autumn.

Female ginkgos are undesirable as ornamentals, because the fleshy, outer layer of the seed gives off a foul odor as it decays. The inner, nutlike portion of the seed has long been roasted and eaten by Asians, who consider it a delicacy. The raw seeds are reputedly poisonous, and even the cooked seeds may be slightly toxic if eaten in excess.

Ginkgos were once native throughout the northern hemisphere but became extinct in North America and Europe during the Pleistocene Ice Age. Fortunately, the trees found a refuge in mountain valleys near the Yangtze River in eastern China and have persisted in the forests there to the present day. Ginkgos also have been cultivated for centuries in China and Japan.

Willows, *Salix* L.

WILLOWS are to the lowlands what oaks are to the uplands. It would be difficult to find a watercourse in Iowa, whether tiny creek or major river, that did not have at least one species of willow growing along its shore; and in low-lying areas willows are often the dominant vegetation. When the settlers first arrived on the vast prairies of western and central Iowa, they found small streambank willows to be the only native trees in many localities.

The long, narrow, finely toothed leaves of our common willows are quite different from the leaves of other trees, allowing them to be easily identified as willows. The leaves of some less common species, however, are relatively short and broad with untoothed margins. Whatever shape its leaves might be, any willow can be recognized by its small, single-scaled buds that are arranged alternately and often tightly appressed to the twig. The twigs themselves are typically long and slender and sometimes brightly colored, a further aid in identification when the leaves are absent in winter.

Although it is usually easy to recognize a tree as a willow, identifying individual species is normally difficult and often impossible, even for botanists. Species are seperated by small differences in the leaves and twigs and cannot always be identified by these features alone. The tiny flowers and fruits, which are often essential to confirm identity, are present for just a short time in spring. Identification is further complicated by pronounced variation within species, by frequent hybridization between species, and by the occurrence of the male and female flowers on separate trees.

More than a dozen species of willows are reported as native to Iowa. Only three of these—the black, peachleaf, and Missouri River willows—typically attain tree size. Four others are usually large shrubs but may become small trees 15 to 25 feet tall. The remaining species are shrubs. Some of the smaller willows are very rare, occurring in only a few bogs, marshes, or prairie remnants in eastern or northern Iowa.

In addition to our native species, several Eurasian willows have been introduced to Iowa for landscaping. At least four of these have escaped locally from cultivation and can be found growing in the wild. Although these trees grow quickly and make beautiful ornamentals, the larger species have numerous disadvantages that should be carefully considered before planting: (1) They tend to be messy, dropping numerous twigs and even small branches during ice- and windstorms. (2) They are short-lived and lose their youthful attractiveness with age. (3) They are notorious for clogging drains and sewers with their roots and in some localities they are troubled with diseases and insect pests. Willows are excellent choices for wet soils where other trees will not grow, but for well-drained sites more suitable species can be chosen.

The tiny, short-lived seeds of willows mature in late spring or early summer and require a moist, bare mineral soil for germination. Fresh deposits of silt and sand left by receding spring floodwaters provide an ideal seedbed and are rapidly colonized by seedlings of these sun-loving, fast-growing trees. However, such willow thickets are a temporary phenomenon, for the trees cannot reproduce in their own shade and eventually give way to silver maple, hackberry, boxelder, ashes, and other more shade-tolerant trees.

Willows have little commercial importance because most species are too small to provide merchantable timber and their wood is less valuable than that of other species. However, willows play an important role in the conservation of our soil and wildlife. Most species can be propagated quickly and inexpensively by simply cutting twigs and placing their ends in moist soil. The plants that grow from these cuttings produce networks of interlacing roots that prevent stream banks from washing away; and their foliage provides shelter, food, and nesting cover for many birds and mammals.

The bitter bark of willows contains salicin, a chemical precursor of aspirin. Its medicinal properties were discovered by an eighteenth-century British scientist who used an extract of willow bark for treating malaria. This drug is now manufactured synthetically.

Willows reaching tree size in Iowa are described and discussed on the following pages.

Black Willow, *Salix nigra* Marsh.

Distinguishing characteristics: *Leaves* simple, alternate, narrowly lanceolate, gradually tapered to sharp-pointed tips, 3 to 6 inches long with petioles ⅛ to ¼ inch long, finely and closely toothed (teeth usually 18 to 25 per inch of margin at midleaf), lower surface light green and glabrous (sometimes minutely hairy along the midvein). *Stipules* usually conspicuous and persistent on vegetative shoots. *Winter twigs* very slender, glabrous, gray-brown to brown, very brittle at base; leaf scars small, linear, or crescent shaped with 3 bundle scars. *Buds* ovoid, ¹⁄₁₆ to ³⁄₁₆ inch long, the terminal absent; bud scale glabrous, its edges freely overlapping on the back (twig) side of the bud, often with a distinct basal band different in color from its brown upper portion. *Catkins* similar to those of peachleaf willow (see also discussion below). *Bark* dark brown to nearly black, deeply furrowed with thick scaly ridges.

Similar trees: Sandbar willow, the only other species having very narrow, short-petioled leaves with green undersurfaces, is a much smaller tree with distantly toothed leaf margins and deciduous stipules. Winter: peachleaf willow is very similar, though usually distinguishable by color of twigs and buds and shape of the leaf scars. Other large willows have buds with fused scales.

Distribution: Native as far west as the Missouri River and the natural lakes district of northwestern Iowa.

BLACK WILLOW, probably the best known of our native willows, is a medium-sized tree 30 to 60 feet tall. It is common on stream banks, floodplains, lake shores, and low-lying meadows throughout most of Iowa. Trees are usually multistemmed and often lean out over the water, but erect, single-stemmed individuals can also be found.

Willows are notoriously difficult to identify to species but the black willow can usually be recognized easily. Among the willows that commonly reach tree size, it is the only species whose leaves are green underneath rather than blue-green or white. Its leaves have shorter stalks and are narrower than those of other large willows. The conspicuous stipules on its vegetative shoots are another distinctive feature. Stipules occur in other willows, too, but are usually tiny or early deciduous.

Black willow is the only American willow of any commercial importance. Its wood is widely used for artificial limbs because it is flexible, is light in weight, and resists splitting and warping. It is used also for rustic furniture, polo balls, boxes, crates, construction lumber, paper pulp, charcoal, and firewood.

Black willow was once widely planted for farm groves and shelterbelts because it grows quickly and is easily propagated, but this use is now being discouraged since it is very short lived and susceptible to wind damage. It is a poor choice as a shade or ornamental tree for the same reasons.

The tiny flowers of black willow (and other willows) appear during spring in dense, elongate clusters called catkins. The staminate and pistillate flowers normally occur in separate catkins on separate trees, so individual willows are either male or female. Willow flowers lack petals and are rather drab compared to the blossoms of many other flowering trees, but the bright yellow stamens of young male flowers are surprisingly attractive when examined closely. Both types of flowers are rather simple in structure, with the staminate consisting of 3 to 5 stamens, 2 reddish basal glands, and a yellowish bract and the pistillate composed of a single flask-shaped pistil, one gland, and a yellowish bract that falls before the seeds have matured. The tiny seeds are equipped with long silky hairs that facilitate their dispersal by wind.

Peachleaf Willow, *Salix amygdaloides* Anderss.

Distinguishing characteristics: *Leaves* simple, alternate, lanceolate to ovate-lanceolate; gradually or abruptly tapered to long, slender, often taillike tips; 2 to 5 inches long with slender, frequently twisted petioles ¼ to ¾ inch long; margins finely and closely toothed; lower surface glabrous and pale blue-green to white. *Stipules* usually minute or absent. *Winter twigs* very slender, glabrous, usually light yellow or yellowish-gray; leaf scars small, U shaped, with 3 bundle scars. *Buds* 1/16 to 3/16 inch long, similar to black willow except upper portion of scale often yellow or black. *Catkins* appearing in spring at the ends of expanding leafy shoots; flowers apparently whorled on the catkin axis, each subtended by a greenish-yellow, deciduous bract; stamens 4 to 7; pistils stalked, glabrous. *Bark* brown, deeply furrowed with flat, scaly ridges.

Similar trees: See below and under *Black Willow,* page 37.

Distribution: Native throughout the state.

PEACHLEAF WILLOW is less familiar to most people than the black willow, our only other native willow of comparable size. The two species are frequent companions along the banks of rivers and streams across many parts of Iowa and other midwestern states; but the peachleaf willow ranges farther to the north and west and replaces the black willow entirely in northwestern Iowa, Nebraska, and the Dakotas. Like the black willow, its trunks often lean far out over the water. Both its common and botanical names refer to the similarity of its leaves to those of the peach.

Peachleaf willow is closely related botanically to the black willow. The staminate flowers of the two species are quite different from those of other willows but very similar to one another. Their buds are also unlike those of other willows, having scales with overlapping instead of fused margins.

Despite these and other similarities, black and peachleaf willows can be easily distinguished by their leaves. Peachleaf willow leaves are much broader relative to their width than black willow leaves, with longer petioles and long, frequently taillike tips. When fully grown, the leaves of peachleaf willow differ from those of black willow in that their lower surfaces are coated with a thin, waxy material that imparts a definite blue-green or white color. Another difference between the two species is the presence of conspicuous stipules on the vegetative shoots of black willow. Stipules are usually lacking or very tiny in peachleaf willow.

Peachleaf willow is unimportant as a timber tree because it does not occur in merchantable stands, but its wood is very similar to that of black willow and not distinguishable from it when harvested. It is useful for holding eroding stream banks but is not especially desirable for other kinds of conservation plantings in Iowa. It is a poor choice as an ornamental tree, having the same faults as the weeping willow and lacking its attractive shape.

The peachleaf and other willows are the closest known relatives of the cottonwoods and poplars. The leaves and buds of the two groups are quite different and give no clue to the relationship; but their flowers are very similar and their small, flask-shaped fruits are practically identical. The tiny seeds of the trees also resemble one another very closely, having tufts of cottony hairs that aid their dispersal by wind—cottonwood is not solely responsible for the abundant quantities of "cotton" floating through the air in spring!

Sandbar Willow, *Salix interior Rowlee (S. exigua* Nutt.)

Distinguishing characteristics: *Leaves* simple, alternate, linear to linear-lanceolate, gradually tapered to sharp-pointed tips, 2 to 6 inches long with petioles up to ⅛ inch long; margins distantly toothed (teeth 3 to 11 per inch of margin); lower surface green and either glabrous or sparsely hairy. *Stipules* usually minute or absent. *Winter twigs* very slender, glabrous, or finely hairy; usually reddish-brown in color; leaf scars small, linear, with 3 bundle scars. *Buds* ovoid, 1/16 to 3/16 inch long, frequently paired above some of the leaf scars, terminal absent; bud scale glabrous, yellow or brown, caplike with no free edges. *Catkins* solitary or paired at the ends of long leafy shoots; flowers spirally arranged, each subtended by a greenish-yellow, deciduous bract; stamens 2; pistils stalked, either glabrous or sparsely hairy. *Bark* gray to brown, smooth, becoming scaly at the base of larger trees.

Similar trees: See following and under *Black Willow,* page 37.

Distribution: Native throughout the state.

THE lowly sandbar willow is the most abundant and widely distributed of our native willows. Deposits of sand and silt in the floodplains of rivers and streams are its typical habitat; but it can be found in a variety of wet places including ditches, low-lying prairies, shores of lakes and marshes, and even the edges of woods. Though usually a slender, thicket-forming shrub only 5 or 6 feet high, it occasionally becomes a small tree 20 to 25 feet tall with a narrow, sparsely branched crown.

Sandbar willow is always easy to identify, a quality not shared by many willows. Its leaves are narrower and have shorter petioles than leaves of any other tree in Iowa, and their teeth are unusual in being widely spaced along the margin. Its winter twigs superficially resemble those of black willow, but its bud scales have no visible edges. The buds themselves are often paired above the leaf scars, another characteristic not normally seen in black willow. Other distinctive features are its polelike stems, thicket-forming nature, and habit of flowering well into summer.

Sandbar willow is of no consequence as a timber or ornamental tree but plays an invaluable role in erosion control and wildlife conservation. It quickly invades moist, bare mineral soil along rivers and streams and produces a network of dense, fibrous roots that holds the soil until larger and more valuable trees can become established. Thickets of sandbar willow also provide shelter and nesting sites for many small birds and animals and food for deer, beaver, and rabbits.

Weeping Willows, *Salix* spp.

Distinguishing characteristics: *Leaves* simple, alternate, lanceolate, gradually tapered to sharp-pointed tips; bluish-green to whitened beneath; finely and closely toothed, usually with small black glands on the upper portion of the petiole near the base of the blade. *Winter twigs* slender, variously colored, long and drooping; leaf scars small, linear to crescent shaped, with 3 bundle scars. *Bud scale* caplike with no visible edges. *Catkins* appearing with the leaves on expanding leafy shoots; flowers spirally arranged on the axis, each subtended by a greenish-yellow, deciduous bract; stamens 2; pistils sessile or short stalked, glabrous. *Bark* gray to brown, furrowed.

Similar trees: No other trees have the long, drooping twigs that are distinctive at all times of the year.

Distribution: Cultivated throughout the state, rarely escaping to stream banks and other moist places.

A TREE that is fast growing, easily propagated, and beautifully shaped is certain to be a popular ornamental, and the many types of weeping willows fit these specifications very well. Like most other rapidly growing trees, however, weeping willows are short lived and weak wooded and their attractiveness is seldom maintained for very long. They also grow to be large trees—a wise thing to keep in mind when landscaping a small yard. The ideal spot for one is a large, open space along a pond or natural drainageway where it will have plenty of room to spread and its habit of dropping twigs during stormy weather will not be a problem. In most other situations, another tree might be a better choice.

Weeping willow is actually a general term for a number of closely related hybrids and clones, not for a single species. All have narrow, lance-shaped leaves and long, slender, drooping branchlets. Unfortunately, the nomenclature of these willows is very confused and different clones may be sold under the same name. A few of the more common types are described below.

The best known of the weeping willows is *Salix babylonica* L. According to Santamour and McArdle (1988), all the Babylon willows planted in the United States are female and probably represent the same clone, for which they have proposed the cultivar name 'Babylon.' These trees are not reliably hardy in the northern United States and have been crossed with the crack willow (*S. fragilis* L.) and white willow (*S. alba* L.) to produce hybrids that will tolerate our harsh winters.

Salix ×*blanda* Anderss. is the botanical name for crosses between the Babylon and crack willows. Individual clones are often sold under the names Wisconsin or Niobe. Their branchlets are dull green or brown.

Salix ×*sepulcralis* Simonkai is the botanical name for crosses between the Babylon and white willows. These trees vary in habit; some are quite pendulous, while others have ascending branches with only the tips drooping. Their branchlets are usually greenish or yellow.

The Golden Weeping Willow, often sold under the names Tristis and Niobe, is a hardy tree with long, pendulous branches and bright yellow twigs. It has become very popular for landscaping in Iowa and other midwestern states. This tree is often listed as a cultivar of the white willow, but Santamour and McArdle believe it to be a hybrid of the Babylon and white willows (*S.* ×*sepulcralis*).

The Thurlow Weeping Willow, listed in Rehder's manual under the name *Salix elegantissima* K. Koch, is of unknown origin but is thought by some botanists to be a hybrid of the Babylon and crack willows (*S.* ×*blanda*). It has lustrous brown branchlets.

Pussy Willow, *Salix discolor* Muhl.

Distinguishing characteristics: *Leaves* simple, alternate, variable in shape but usually elliptic to elliptic-lanceolate, 2 to 4 inches long with petioles ¼ to ⅝ inch long; margins entire or distantly toothed; lower surface white and glabrous. *Stipules* large, often persistent. *Winter twigs* moderate in diameter, brown or reddish-purple, usually glabrous; leaf scars small, crescent shaped, with 3 bundle scars. *Buds* ovoid, ⅛ to ⅜ inch long, the terminal absent; bud scale caplike with no free edges, reddish-purple, glabrous or hairy at the base only. *Catkins* sessile or nearly so, appearing long before the leaves in early spring; flowers spirally arranged on the catkin axis, each subtended by a dark brown, persistent bract; stamens 2; pistils stalked and finely hairy. *Bark* gray to brown, scaly at the base of larger stems.

Similar trees: Other willows having broad leaves with entire or distantly toothed margins have gray-hairy leaf undersurfaces. Winter: not easily distinguished from rigid willow.

Distribution: Native throughout most of the state, but uncommon outside of northeastern and north central Iowa.

PUSSY WILLOW is widely distributed but rather uncommon in most parts of Iowa. Few people would know it even existed if it were not for the furry catkins or "pussies" that decorate its branches in early spring. They expand with the onset of warmer weather, revealing the tiny flowers that have been concealed within the buds throughout the winter. As in other willows, the male and female catkins are borne on separate plants. The female catkins are gray-green and rather unassuming but the male catkins are surprisingly colorful with their bright yellow stamens.

Pussy willow occurs in a wide variety of wet habitats, including marshes, bogs, low-lying prairies and meadows, springy wooded slopes, and soggy ground along streams. It is usually shrubby in both size and habit but sometimes becomes a small tree 15 to 25 feet tall with an open, rounded crown.

Pussy willow belongs to a group of shrubby native willows that is very complex botanically. All have sessile or short-stalked catkins that develop directly from overwintering buds after a brief pussy stage. Some species, notably the pussy and prairie willows, bloom in early spring long before any leafy shoots expand. Others, such as the Bebb willow, flower about the same time that leaves appear.

Pussy willow, like most other willows, is susceptible to many diseases and insect pests. Perhaps the most interesting of these is a midge, or tiny fly, that inserts its eggs into the expanding buds of willows during spring. The eggs, placed one to a bud, soon hatch into tiny grubs (larvae). Each parasitized bud then develops into a gall resembling a small pine cone (see photo above right). The grubs live in the galls during the ensuing summer, fall, and winter and emerge as adults the following spring.

Many "pussy willows" cultivated in Iowa are not our native species but the European goat willow (*Salix caprea* L.). It is not as hardy as the true pussy willow but is preferred as an ornamental because it has larger and more attractive catkins. The gray or florist's willow (*S. cinerea* L.) and rosegold willow (*S. gracilstyla* Miq.) are two other cultivated species producing pussies in spring. The stems will grow more vigorously and produce larger catkins if cut back to the ground every few years.

Other Willows of Tree Size

MISSOURI RIVER WILLOW, *Salix eriocephala* Michx. (*S. missouriensis* Bebb). *Leaves* lanceolate to oblong-ovate, closely toothed, 2½ to 6 inches long with petioles ⅓ to ⅝ inch long, pale or whitened beneath. *Winter twigs* brown, more or less covered with grayish hairs. *Catkins* appearing when the leaves are just beginning to unfold in spring; flowers spirally arranged on the catkin axis, each subtended by a persistent brown bract; stamens 2; pistils stalked, glabrous.

THIS small to medium-sized tree is apparently native throughout most of Iowa, but (as its name suggests) it is most common along the Missouri River in the western part of the state. Many authorities consider it to be nothing more than a large, vigorously growing variety of the rigid willow (*S. rigida* Muhl.), a wide-ranging shrubby species.

SHINING WILLOW, *Salix lucida* Muhl. *Leaves* lanceolate to ovate, thick and leathery, with long taillike tips, 2½ to 5 inches long; margins closely toothed; surfaces green and glossy; petioles ¼ to ½ inch long with conspicuous glands at their junctions with the blades. *Winter twigs* brown, glabrous, glossy. *Catkins* appearing at the ends of expanding leafy shoots in spring; flowers spirally arranged, each subtended by a deciduous, yellowish bract; stamens usually 5; pistils stalked, glabrous.

THIS rare native willow is a shrub or small tree up to 25 feet tall. It is known from only a few sites in north central and northeastern Iowa.

The bayleaf or laurel willow (*S. pentandra* L.) resembles the shining willow but its leaves have short-pointed tips. It is cultivated in Iowa and occasionally escapes to low, moist areas.

BEBB WILLOW, *Salix bebbiana* Sarg. (*S. rostrata* Rich.). *Leaves* highly variable in shape but usually elliptic or obovate, 1¼ to 3 inches long with petioles 3/16 to ½ inch long; margins entire or distantly toothed; lower surface pale or whitened with a prominent network of raised veins. *Winter twigs* reddish-brown, often hairy. *Catkins* sessile or short stalked, appearing with the leaves in spring; flowers spirally arranged, each subtended by a persistent yellowish bract; stamens 2; pistils stalked, hairy, with long, beaklike tips.

BEBB WILLOW is usually a shrub but occasionally becomes a small tree up to 25 feet tall. It is native in moist ground across most of northeastern and north central Iowa.

CORKSCREW WILLOW, *Salix matsudana* Koidz. 'Tortuosa.' *Leaves* lanceolate, closely toothed, 3 to 6 inches long with petioles ⅙ to ⅓ inch long, pale or whitened beneath. *Winter twigs* spirally twisted. *Catkins* appearing at the ends of expanding leafy shoots in spring; flowers spirally arranged, each subtended by a deciduous, yellowish bract; stamens 2; pistils short stalked, glabrous.

THIS medium-sized willow is named for its peculiar twigs that twist spirally in the manner of a corkscrew. A native of northeastern Asia, it is hardy throughout Iowa and occasionally planted here as a curiosity.

WHITE WILLOW, *Salix alba* L. *Leaves* lanceolate, 2 to 5 inches long, finely and closely toothed (teeth usually 18 to 25 per inch of margin); surfaces persistently hairy, the lower bluish-green or white; petioles 3/16 to ⅜ inch long with tiny glands near their junctions with the blades. *Winter twigs* green or greenish-brown, hairy. *Catkins* appearing at the ends of expanding leafy shoots in spring; flowers spirally arranged, each subtended by a yellowish, deciduous bract; stamens 2; pistils glabrous, nearly sessile.

THIS large European willow was introduced to colonial America as a fast-growing source of shade, timber, and gunpowder charcoal. It has since become naturalized across most of the eastern United States, including Iowa. Clones having yellow twigs and nearly hairless leaves, often referred to this species under the names "vitellina" or "tristis," are probably hybrids with other species.

CRACK WILLOW, *Salix fragilis* L. *Leaves* lanceolate, 3 to 6 inches long, rather coarsely toothed (teeth usually 10 to 17 per inch of margin); surfaces glabrous, the lower green or bluish-green; petioles ⅜ to ⅝ inch long, with tiny glands near their junctions with the blades. *Winter twigs* green or greenish-brown, glabrous, glossy, very brittle at the base. *Catkins* appearing at ends of expanding leafy shoots in spring; flowers spirally arranged, each subtended by a yellowish, deciduous bract; stamens 2; pistils short stalked, glabrous.

THIS European species was introduced to colonial America for the same purposes as the white willow and it has likewise become naturalized across most of eastern North America, including Iowa. Both its common and botanical names refer to its twigs, which are very brittle at the base and easily broken from the tree.

Eastern Cottonwood, *Populus deltoides* Bartr.

Distinguishing characteristics: *Leaves* simple, alternate, broadly triangular in shape, 3 to 6 inches long, glabrous, toothed; petiole flattened, 1½ to 3 inches long, with two or three tiny glands at its junction with the blade. *Winter twigs* moderate in diameter, glabrous, gray or gray-green; pith star shaped in cross section; leaf scars variably shaped and sized, with 3 bundle scars. *Buds* ovoid, the terminal bud ⅜ to ¾ inch long and the lateral buds often of two sizes, the lowermost scale of each centered directly over the leaf scar; bud scales yellow or brown, glabrous, slightly sticky. *Flowers* dioecious, in catkins, appearing before the leaves in spring. *Fruit* a flask-shaped capsule about ⅓ inch long, opening in early summer. *Seeds* tiny, with long cottony hairs. *Bark* thin, smooth and light gray-green on young trees, eventually thick and deeply furrowed with long, light gray ridges.

Similar trees: Aspens have rounded leaves and brown twigs; Lombardy poplar has smaller terminal buds and sharply ascending branches.

Distribution: Native throughout the state.

THE cottonwood, with its tall, massive trunk and tall, broad-spreading crown, is one of our most impressive native trees. It was widely planted by the farmers and townspeople who settled the treeless prairies of Iowa, as it is fast growing, adaptable, and was readily available along rivers and streams. Today many people do not like the cottonwood because its prodigious cottony seeds can be a nuisance downwind. As in other poplars, however, the cottonwood's male and female flowers occur on separate trees and only the latter produce seeds. Thus, some trees never release the objectionable "cotton."

Cottonwood is probably our most rapidly growing native tree and it is certainly the largest. Young trees grow 2 to 4 feet per year in moist, well-drained soils; under ideal conditions they may grow as much as 5 feet annually. Mature trees are usually 80 to 100 feet tall and 3 to 4 feet in diameter, although trees bigger than this are not uncommon. The largest known tree in Iowa is a cottonwood, 92 feet tall and more than 10 feet in diameter, in Crawford County. The maximum life span of the cottonwood is believed to be 200 years, though a 75-year-old tree is considered an old-timer.

Cottonwoods grow well when transplanted to dry upland sites: but wild trees are almost always found along streams, lakes, and other wet places. The tiny seeds require a moist, exposed mineral soil in which to germinate, and they will die if they do not land on such a seedbed soon after being shed from the tree. One can often find a long row of cottonwood seedlings on the beach of a lake or a mud flat in a river, clearly marking the location of the shoreline the previous June.

The wood of the cottonwood is light, soft, and generally pale in color. It is used for paper pulp, excelsior, pallets, boxes, crates, and plywood for the manufacture of furniture.

The plains cottonwood (*P. sargentii* Dode) has been reported from several counties in western Iowa and from a few scattered localities in the eastern part of the state. It differs from the eastern cottonwood chiefly in having yellow twigs and hairy-margined bud scales. Some consider it to be a variety of the eastern cottonwood, *P. deltoides* var. *occidentalis* Rydb.

Lombardy Poplar, *Populus nigra* var. *italica* Muenchh.

Distinguishing characteristics: *Leaves* simple, alternate, triangular to broadly diamond shaped in outline, 1½ to 4 inches long, glabrous, with toothed margins and flattened petioles. *Winter twigs* slender, glabrous, yellow or gray-green; leaf scars half-round to nearly round, small, with 3 bundle scars. *Buds* ovoid, the terminal ³⁄₁₆ to ¼ inch long and the laterals slightly smaller, each with its lowermost scale centered directly over the leaf scar; bud scales brown, glabrous, slightly sticky. *Flowers,* when present, in catkins. *Fruits* and *seeds* absent. *Bark* thin, light gray, smooth on branches and upper trunk, shallowly and irregularly furrowed on lower trunk. *Crown* columnar, with ascending branches.

Similar trees: Cottonwood has larger terminal buds and spreading branches. Petioles, leaf undersurfaces, and twigs of bolleana poplar are covered with white, matted hairs.

Distribution: Planted throughout the state.

THE tall, spirelike Lombardy poplar is one of our most distinctive trees. Its rapid growth and narrow, compact crown have long made it popular for borders, screens, and wind breaks, although its usefulness is limited by its short life span. Trees seldom reach an age of 50 years even under ideal circumstances, and they are sometimes killed or disfigured at a much earlier age by cankers. The attractiveness of an unbroken row of Lombardy poplars is seldom maintained for very long.

Lombardy poplar is perhaps the mostly commonly planted tree having a columnar crown, but it is by no means the only one. Horticulturists have selected columnar cultivars from several species of poplars and a variety of other trees including elm, maple, oak, birch, crab apple, pine, and ginkgo. Names such as 'Columnaris,' 'Erecta,' and 'Fastigiata' are often given to these trees.

Lombardy poplar is variously classified as variety *italica* or cultivar 'Italica' of the black poplar, *Populus nigra* L., which is native to Europe and west Asia. Like cottonwoods, aspens, and willows, its male and female flowers are borne on separate trees. Most of the Lombardy poplars used in landscaping are infertile males, propagated clonally from cuttings. Female trees, which reportedly have a somewhat broader crown, are rarely seen in cultivation.

Poplars belong to the same genus, *Populus,* as our native cottonwood and aspens. A number of exotic species, hybrids, and cultivars of this genus have been introduced for landscaping. The Lombardy and white poplars are the most commonly cultivated types, but the following trees are also worthy of note.

The balsam poplar or tacamahac (*P. balsamifera* L.) is characterized by smooth, finely toothed, ovate leaves with slender, rounded petioles; fragrant terminal buds about 1 inch long; and a narrow, open crown. It is native to moist lowlands in the north woods of Canada and in the Great Lakes states. Wild-growing trees, either natives or escapes, have been reported from Osceola, Emmet, Mitchell, Howard, and Winneshiek counties.

The Balm-of-Gilead is a tree of uncertain origin that reportedly has escaped from cultivation in northern Iowa. It resembles the balsam poplar but has broad, heart-shaped leaves, slightly hairy beneath, with hairy petioles. Some botanists consider it to be a clone of *P. balsamifera* var. *subcordata* Hylander.

Siouxland poplar is a male or cottonless clone of the eastern cottonwood. It is resistant to leaf rust but susceptible to stem cankers.

Quaking Aspen, *Populus tremuloides* Michx.

Distinguishing characteristics: *Leaves* simple, alternate, nearly round in outline, 1½ to 3 inches in diameter, glabrous, with 20 to 40 small teeth on each side; petiole flattened, 1½ to 3 inches long. *Winter twigs* slender, glabrous, dark brown; leaf scars half-round or crescent shaped, small, with 3 bundle scars. *Buds* ovoid, the terminal ¼ to ⅜ inch long and the laterals often of two sizes, closely appressed to the twig, each with its lowermost scale centered directly over the leaf scar; bud scales shiny dark brown, glabrous, slightly sticky. *Flowers* dioecious, in catkins, appearing before the leaves in early spring. *Fruit* a flask-shaped capsule about ¼ inch long, opening in late spring. *Seeds* tiny, with long cottony hairs. *Bark* smooth, thin, white or greenish-white, with black warty thickenings; becoming dark and furrowed at the base of the tree.

Similar trees: Leaves of bigtooth aspen have fewer and larger teeth. Cottonwood leaves are triangular in outline; and leaves of paper birch are ovate with short, rounded petioles. Winter: cottonwood has gray or greenish twigs; bigtooth aspen and white poplar have dull hairy buds that angle away from the twigs; paper birch has exposed catkins and false terminal buds.

Distribution: Native. Common in eastern Iowa; rare and local along the principal river valleys in southern and western Iowa.

THE quaking aspen is appropriately named, as its leaves seem to quiver and rustle incessantly. It is not the only tree with trembling leaves—cottonwood, bigtooth aspen, and several poplars also have the long flattened leaf stalks that cause this motion—but its small, rounded leaf blades seem to flutter more easily and gracefully, as if they were specially designed for that purpose.

This species has a wider range than any other North American tree. It is native from New England and Labrador on the Atlantic to Alaska on the Pacific and south along the Rocky Mountains to Mexico. Aspen occurs on a variety of sites within its range, but in Iowa it is most commonly encountered in dry, upland woods.

The quaking aspen grows rapidly, tolerates a wide variety of soils, and has ornamental value at all times of the year so that one might expect it to be a useful and popular tree for landscaping. Unfortunately, it has a number of faults that discourage its use for street and yard plantings. Like other aspens, it often reproduces rapidly by root suckers that form dense thickets if not cut repeatedly. It is short lived, with an average life span of only 50 years; is subject to attack by a number of diseases and insect pests; and its small, open crown provides meager shade. It seems wise to leave the aspen in its natural haunts and appreciate it there.

From a distance quaking aspen is often confused with the paper birch, since both trees frequent upland woods and have chalk-white bark with patches of black, warty thickenings. They can be distinguished easily if one remembers that birch bark separates into papery strips and appears somewhat rough-hewn, while aspen bark is very smooth and tight fitting. Also, birch leaves have short, rounded stalks and do not tremble in the wind.

Quaking aspen is an important forest tree in Canada and the northern United States. Its wood is light, soft, weak, and usually pale in color. It is used for pulp, excelsior, boxes, crates, pallets, matches, and many other products. The wood of the bigtooth aspen is similar, and the two species are not distinguished from one another in the forest products industry.

Bigtooth Aspen, *Populus grandidentata* Michx.

Distinguishing characteristics: *Leaves* simple, alternate, broadly ovate, 2 to 5 inches long, glabrous when mature, with 5 to 15 large blunt teeth on each side; petiole flattened, 1½ to 2½ inches long. *Winter twigs* moderate in diameter, brown, either glabrous or finely gray-hairy; leaf scars similar to quaking aspen. *Buds* ovoid, the terminal ³⁄₁₆ to ¼ inch long and the laterals often of two sizes, slightly divergent from the twig, the lowermost scale of each centered directly over the leaf scar; bud scales brown, partially covered with fine gray hairs. *Flowers* dioecious, in catkins, appearing before the leaves in early spring. *Fruit* a flask-shaped capsule ⅛ to ³⁄₁₆ inch long, opening in late spring. *Seeds* tiny, with long cottony hairs. *Bark* thin, smooth, dull yellow-green on upper trunk; dark brown with broad, flattened ridges and narrow furrows on lower trunk.

Similar trees: Quaking aspen has glossy, dark brown buds and smaller, more numerous leaf teeth. Leaf undersurfaces, petioles, and twigs of white poplar are covered with matted white hairs.

Distribution: Native as far west as the Des Moines River valley (west fork); also reported in woods along the Little Sioux River in Clay County.

OUR two native aspens closely resemble one another and can be found in the same woods, but anyone who takes time to observe them carefully can learn to identify the two with little difficulty. The most obvious difference is the margin of the leaves—in quaking aspen the margin is composed of many small teeth; in bigtooth aspen, as the tree's name suggests, it is made up of a few large teeth. Another dissimilarity is in the buds, which are smooth, shiny, and dark brown in quaking aspen and dull, hairy, and light brown in bigtooth aspen.

The bigtooth aspen grows somewhat faster than the quaking aspen, reaches a larger size, and is more resistant to disease. The ecological characteristics of the two species are otherwise similar. Botanists speak of them as pioneer trees because their small seeds are blown great distances by the wind and germinate readily in open, sunny areas resulting from fire or human disturbance. Young trees grow rapidly and often form large clones through the production of root suckers. What appears to be a large group of individual trees growing close together may actually be proliferation from a single seedling.

Aspens cover large tracts of land in Canada and the Great Lakes states. The composition of these aspen woodlands changes rapidly with time, for aspens are short lived and cannot reproduce in their own shade. Seedlings of conifers, oaks, hickories, maples, and other trees that are more tolerant of shade grow well in the shelter and humus the aspens have provided and readily invade the understory. In a hundred years or less the forest will be dominated by these trees, with only a few old, solitary aspens remaining to provide a clue to the forest's beginning. Eventually even these monarchs succumb to disease or old age, and then the forest remains aspenless until fire or logging starts the cycle anew.

Aspens are an important source of both food and cover for wildlife. Their foliage and twigs are eaten by deer and rabbits, and their buds are a mainstay of the ruffed grouse's winter diet. Beavers relish the inner bark and use the trunks in their dams.

Aspens are important in one other respect. They turn a brilliant gold while the maples are losing their faded leaves and the reddish hues of the oaks are changing to brown, providing a last spectacle of color for those who frequent the woods of autumn.

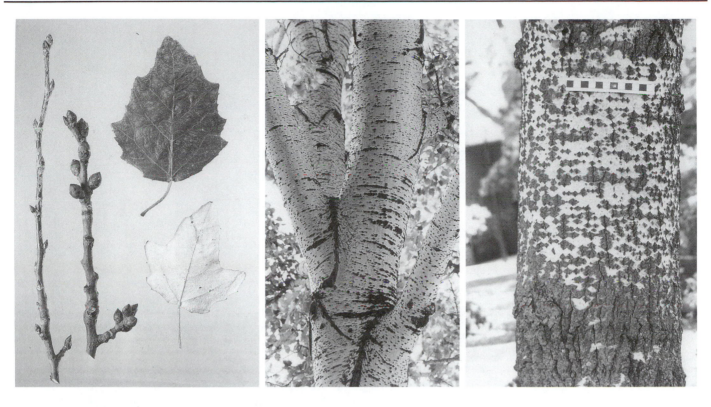

White Poplar, *Populus alba* L.

Distinguishing characteristics: *Leaves* simple, alternate, oval to nearly round in outline, 3 to 5 lobed or with a few irregularly sized teeth, 2 to 5 inches long; lower surface and petiole having a white, feltlike coating. *Winter twigs* slender to moderate in diameter, olive-green to gray, densely covered with a white, feltlike material that can easily be rubbed off; leaf scars similar to quaking aspen. *Buds* ovoid, the terminal ⅛ to ¼ inch long and the laterals often of two sizes, divergent from the twig, the lowermost scale of each centered directly above the leaf scar; bud scales brown, partially to completely covered with matted white hairs. *Flowers* dioecious, in catkins, appearing before the leaves in spring. *Fruit* a flask-shaped capsule about ⅛ inch long, opening in late spring. *Seeds* tiny, with long cottony hairs. *Bark* on upper trunk and larger branches thin, smooth, white, with numerous black warty outgrowths, black and furrowed at base.

Similar trees: Mature leaves of bigtooth aspen are glabrous beneath. Winter: no other white-barked tree has a white, feltlike coating on its twigs.

Distribution: Planted throughout the state, commonly escaping from cultivation in some localities.

THIS European import has many of the qualities one looks for in a shade or ornamental tree, but unfortunately it has an equally large number of shortcomings that limit its value for landscaping. It grows rapidly, reaches a large size, and has a broad, spreading crown; but like most other poplars it is very short lived. Although its bark and foliage are among the most attractive of our introduced trees, its brittle branches are often broken during storms, marring its appearance. It adapts well to city life, but its roots often clog drains and sewers. Perhaps its most serious flaw is its tendency to spread aggressively by root suckers, especially after the above-ground portion of the tree has died. One can sometimes find abandoned farmsteads that have been completely overrun by this species.

As in other poplars, the tiny, inconspicuous flowers of this species are arranged in elongate clusters called catkins.

These appear in early spring, long before the leaves. An individual catkin is composed of either male or female flowers but never both, and the male (staminate) and female (pistillate) catkins occur on separate trees. Most white poplars found in Iowa are female. Each of their flowers develops into a tiny, flask-shaped capsule containing numerous cottony, wind-blown seeds. The seeds often become a nuisance when they are dispersed in late spring and early summer, clogging screens, vents, and air conditioners. The relatively innocuous catkins of male trees release pollen and fall from the trees before the leaves are full grown.

The following varieties and hybrids of white poplar are worthy of note.

BOLLEANA POPLAR, *P. alba* 'Pyramidalis.' This cultivar is characterized by sharply ascending branches and a columnar crown. It is less susceptible to cankers than Lombardy poplar and is often touted as a substitute for it, but it has the same faults as typical white poplars.

SILVER POPLAR, *P. alba* var. *nivea* Ait. This variety has prominently whitened lower leaf surfaces.

GRAY POPLAR, *P.* ×*canescens* (Ait.) Sm. This tree is believed to be a hybrid of the white poplar and the European aspen, *P. tremula* L. It resembles the white poplar but has unlobed leaves with heart-shaped bases.

P. alba × *P. grandidentata.* This tree is a hybrid of the white poplar and the bigtooth aspen. Four clones were found growing wild in southeastern Iowa in the 1950s. They grow very quickly and have been of interest to foresters.

Black Walnut, *Juglans nigra* L.

Distinguishing characteristics: *Leaves* once-pinnately compound, alternate, 1 to 2 feet long, usually tipped by a pair of leaflets smaller than those near the middle of the leaf; leaflets 11 to 23 in number, ovate-lanceolate, 2½ to 4 inches long, finely toothed, glabrous above and hairy below. *Winter twigs* moderate to rather stout, gray-green or light brown; pith chambered; leaf scars large, heart shaped, with 3 bundle scars. *Buds* globose to subglobose, with 2 or 4 visible scales covered with tiny gray hairs; the terminal bud 3/16 to 1/3 inch long, the laterals smaller. *Flowers* similar to butternut. *Fruit* a round nut, 1½ to 2 inches in diameter; composed of a single seed enclosed by a hard, corrugated shell and a green, indehiscent, semifleshy husk that eventually turns black. *Bark* dark gray or black, deeply furrowed, with interconnecting ridges that become thick and blocky on large trees.

Similar trees: Butternut is the only other tree having the combination of compound leaves, chambered pith, and true terminal buds. It has long, yellowish terminal buds, a conspicuous fringe of hairs along the top of each leaf scar, oblong fruits, and light gray bark. Its leaves end in a single leaflet.

Distribution: Native throughout the state.

FEW people need an introduction to the black walnut. Its beautiful heartwood has long been regarded as the choicest American wood for gunstocks, veneer, and fine furniture. Its savory nuts, which retain their distinctive taste after cooking, are valued for baking and flavorings. Anyone who has a walnut tree in the backyard knows that squirrels also prize the nuts, despite their hard outer shells—research has shown that walnuts comprise about 10 percent of a squirrel's diet.

The rich brown color and attractive grain of the black walnut's wood are only two of the qualities that make it such a precious commodity. Walnut is also strong, hard, durable, resistant to shock and warp, and easy to machine and finish. The largest and finest logs may bring several thousand dollars. Even old stumps are valuable for their beautiful figure.

Iowa is a leading producer of black walnut timber. Oaks surpass walnut in the total volume of timber cut annually, but walnut is our single most important tree in terms of income received from sale. Most walnut harvested here is shipped out of state for processing.

Native black walnut occurs in a variety of habitats; but is most commonly found on the rich, well-drained soils of bottomlands, terraces, and lower slopes. On such sites it often grows 70 to 90 feet tall with a trunk 2 to 3 feet in diameter, and sometimes even larger.

Not surprisingly, walnut is an excellent choice for reforestation and woodlot improvement in Iowa. Most landowners plant it primarily for timber, but its valuable nuts are another crop that should not be overlooked. Members of the Iowa Nut Grower's Association (I.N.G.A.) are actively selecting and testing black walnuts for improved kernel quality, ease of cracking, and other characteristics. For more information on growing black walnut for timber or for nuts, contact the Iowa Department of Natural Resources or I.N.G.A., both at the Wallace State Office Building, Des Moines 50319.

Despite its value as a forest and orchard tree, black walnut is not especially desirable for landscaping. Its leaves drop early, often with little change in color; its nuts tend to be messy; and its roots and nut husks release a substance that is antagonistic to some kinds of garden and ornamental plants.

Butternut, *Juglans cinerea* L.

Distinguishing characteristics: *Leaves* once-pinnately compound, alternate, 1 to 2½ feet long, usually tipped by a single leaflet equal to the others in size; leaflets 11 to 17 in number, oblong-lanceolate, 2 to 4 inches long, finely toothed, hairy below. *Winter twigs* moderate to rather stout, green or red-brown; pith chambered; leaf scars large, lobed, each with 3 bundle scars and a fringe of yellow-brown hairs along its upper margin. *Buds* with 2 or 4 visible scales covered with tiny, usually yellow-brown hairs; the terminal bud ovoid-elongate, ⅜ to ¾ inch long, much larger than the globose lateral buds. *Flowers* monoecius, appearing with or shortly after the leaves in spring, the staminate in catkins and the pistillate in short spikes. *Fruit* similar to black walnut but decidedly oblong in shape. *Bark* smooth on young trees, eventually furrowed with broad, flat, ashy gray ridges.

Similar trees: Black walnut terminal buds are globose to subglobose, and scales are covered with tiny gray hairs. Its fruit is round and its leaf scars lack a fringe of hairs along the upper margin.

Distribution: Native as far west as the Des Moines River and its principal tributaries; also reported from scattered localities in the southwestern part of the state.

BUTTERNUT is closely related to black walnut and is sometimes called "white walnut"; but it is a smaller, less valuable, and relatively uncommon tree. Saplings of butternut and black walnut are often confused because their foliage is so similar, but they can be reliably distinguished by their buds, fruits, and leaf scars.

Butternut is widely distributed in eastern and central Iowa woodlands but is rarely an abundant tree. It grows best and is most commonly found in the moist, rich soils of ravines and stream valleys. Unfortunately, mature trees are dying out in many places because of butternut canker, which produces sunken, black lesions that eventually girdle the trunks and branches.

The light brown heartwood of butternut is light, soft, easily worked, and resistant to warp. Its principal use is for veneer for furniture, paneling, and cabinets; and it is also used for window sash, doors, and instrument cases. The tree sap yields a sweet syrup when boiled down and the husks of its fruits contain a dye that was once used to give clothing an orange or yellow coloring.

Although they are difficult to crack open, the aromatic nuts of butternut and black walnut have a much richer flavor than the walnut commonly available in stores, the so-called English or Persian walnut (*J. regia* L.). Ironically, the rough, bony shells of our native nuts, which seem such a nuisance when the kernels are extracted, have value themselves as an industrial abrasive. The nuts are less valuable to wildlife than one might expect, since few animals other than squirrels are able to open them. Dispersal of the trees depends on squirrels, which forget some of the nuts they bury.

Most people consider the fruits of walnut and butternut to be nuts, but in many ways they are more like the stone fruit (drupe) of peach or plum. The inner portion resembles a peach pit in that it consists of a single seed encased within a bony, corrugated covering. The green outer husk, though not as fleshy as the pulp of a typical drupe, softens when ripe and certainly could be described as "semifleshy." Some authorities prefer the term "drupaceous nut" (which is at least descriptive if not technically precise) to either drupe or nut.

Shagbark Hickory, *Carya ovata* (Mill.) K. Koch

Distinguishing characteristics: *Leaves* once-pinnately compound, alternate, 8 to 14 inches long; leaflets 5 in number (occasionally 7), finely toothed, glabrous, the terminal 3 leaflets 4 to 7 inches long and the other 2 smaller. *Winter* twigs moderate to rather stout, red-brown or dark gray-green; leaf scars large, half-round to heart shaped, with numerous bundle scars. *Buds* ovoid, the terminal ½ to ¾ inch long and the laterals smaller; outer bud scales dark brown and nearly glabrous, inner scales yellow-brown and finely hairy. *Flowers* monoecious, appearing when the leaves are nearly full grown in spring, the staminate in branched catkins and the pistillate in short spikes. *Fruit* a nut 1 to 2½ inches long; husk unwinged, ⅛ to ½ inch thick, splitting completely open at maturity, green at first but turning nearly black. *Bark* slate gray, smooth on young trees, eventually dividing into irregularly shaped, vertically oriented strips that curve away from the trunk at one or both ends, giving the tree a shaggy appearance.

Similar trees: Other trees with alternate, once-pinnately compound leaves have more than 5 leaflets. Winter: shellbark hickory has similar bark but its twigs are pale orange. Other hickories have shallowly furrowed bark.

Distribution: Native west to the Des Moines and Raccoon rivers in central Iowa to the Missouri River in southern Iowa, but only locally common along the western edge of this range; old reports from Dickinson County.

THE shagbark hickory is one of our easiest native trees to identify. Its bark separates into large, irregularly shaped strips that curve up at one or both ends, giving the trunk a rough, shaggy appearance. The bark is tough and hard like the wood of the tree and the pioneers are said to have used the strips for making boxes.

The wood of shagbark and other hickories is the principal source of handles for hammers, axes, and other striking tools because of its exceptional strength and shock resistance. It is also used for skis and other sporting goods, ladder rungs, agricultural implements, and charcoal. Sawdust and chips from green hickory have long been prized for smoking meats. People who use fireplaces or wood-burning stoves know it is one of the best firewoods available; a cord of hickory (4,240 pounds) produces as much heat as 1.12 tons of anthracite coal.

The nuts of the shagbark hickory have an excellent flavor, but their shells are difficult to crack open. They are appreciated by squirrels, chipmunks, raccoons, turkeys, grosbeaks, woodpeckers, blue jays, nuthatches, and many other kinds of wildlife. One can often find young shagbarks in pastures and other uncultivated areas bordering woods, a sure sign that the squirrels did not recover all the nuts they stashed away in previous autumns.

Shagbark hickory occurs on a variety of sites but is most commonly found in upland woods with white, bur, red, and black oaks. (It is such a constant companion of oaks in the Midwest that our drier upland woods are called *oak-hickory*.) The shagbark is sometimes used for reforestation and woodlot improvement in Iowa but grows more slowly than oaks and most other native trees.

Shagbark hickory grows to a height of 70 to 80 feet and develops an open oblong crown. Its picturesque appearance, relative freedom from diseases and insect pests, and delicious nuts make it desirable for landscaping, although it is seldom planted because it grows so slowly and is difficult to transplant. Shagbarks often reach an age of 250 to 300 years.

Bitternut Hickory, *Carya cordiformis* (Wangenh.) K. Koch

Distinguishing characteristics: *Leaves* once-pinnately compound, alternate, 6 to 10 inches long; leaflets 7 to 11 in number, glabrous above and either glabrous or hairy below, finely toothed, the terminal leaflet 3 to 6 inches long and the others slightly smaller. *Winter twigs* slender to moderate in diameter, gray-green or gray-brown; leaf scars moderately large, half-round to heart shaped, with numerous bundle scars. *Buds* with 2 bright yellow scales that meet along their edges without overlapping; the terminal bud ovoid-elongate, ⅓ to ¾ inch long, the laterals smaller. *Flowers* similar to shagbark hickory. *Fruit* a nut about 1 inch long; husk winged above the middle, less than ⅛ inch thick, splitting halfway open at maturity, yellow-green at first but becoming brown. *Bark* light gray, smooth on young trees, eventually very shallowly furrowed with narrow, interconnecting ridges.

Similar trees: Shagbark hickory has fewer leaflets, thinner-husked nuts, shaggy bark, and plump buds with overlapping brown scales. Ashes have opposite leaves.

Distribution: Native west to valleys of the Missouri and Little Sioux rivers; also present in woods around the Spirit-Okoboji lakes chain and along the Big Sioux River north to Plymouth County.

THE bitternut hickory is not as well known as its cousin, the shagbark, but it ranges over a larger geographical area and is the only native hickory in most of northwestern Iowa. Though differing from shagbark in leaf and fruit, it is most easily distinguished by its bright yellow buds. Its bark is relatively smooth and its twigs are more slender than other native trees with compound leaves—two useful aids in identification when the buds and foliage are out of reach.

Bitternut hickory can be found on both wet and dry sites but prefers a moist, well-drained soil. It is usually found on stream terraces, the back portions of floodplains, and sheltered slopes with hard maple, basswood, red oak, elms, and ashes. Young bitternuts tolerate shade and are a common sight in the woodland understory across much of the state. The seeds are apparently unpalatable to rodents, the principal means of dispersal for most nut trees, so dissemination is thought to occur largely by gravity and water.

The wood of the bitternut is similar to that of the shagbark, but it is not quite so hard and heavy. Most of the timber cut is used for charcoal, tool and implement handles, and meat smoking. However, the best logs are reserved for furniture veneer and paneling and some poor, knotty timber is made into pallets. Bitternut hickory is also an excellent firewood.

The bitternut and other hickories are more difficult to transplant and slower to establish than many other native trees, which limits their popularity for landscaping. They are, nevertheless, very handsome, durable, and long-lived trees, and existing specimens are worth preserving when wooded sites are developed. Bitternuts grow somewhat faster than most other hickories and are normally more attractive in autumn, their leaves turning a bright, clear yellow rather than brown or yellow-brown. Mature trees are usually 50 to 60 feet tall.

Other Native Hickories

THE shagbark and bitternut hickories are the only native hickories in most parts of Iowa, but three other species are native along the principal river valleys in the southeastern corner of the state. Their flowers, foliage, twigs, and fruits resemble those of the shagbark and bitternut but differ in the characteristics listed below.

MOCKERNUT HICKORY, *Carya tomentosa* Nutt. *Leaves* 9 to 14 inches long; leaflets 7 to 9 (rarely 5), soft-hairy below, the terminal three leaflets 3 to 6 inches long and the others smaller. *Twigs* red-brown. *Terminal buds* ⅜ to ¾ inch long; inner scales densely covered with fine yellow-brown hairs; outer scales dark red-brown, deciduous in late autumn. *Nut* 1½ to 2 inches long; husk unwinged, ⅛ to ¼ inch thick, red-brown, splitting nearly to the base. *Bark* dark gray, shallowly furrowed with interconnecting ridges.

MOCKERNUT HICKORY is distributed from Lee County north to Scott and Cedar counties and northwest along the Des Moines River valley to Wapello County. It is usually found in dry upland woods with white and black oaks and shagbark hickory. This species was reportedly native in southwestern Iowa when the settlers arrived, but there have been no authenticated reports of it from that part of the state since the turn of the century.

The wood of the mockernut hickory has a greater crushing and bending strength than shagbark hickory and is considered the finest of the hickories. However, this species is of little importance in Iowa because of its limited distribution and the small size of much of the timber.

The seeds of the mockernut hickory are sweet and edible like those of the shagbark. The name *mockernut* has been attributed to the fact that the meat is much smaller than one would expect from examining the nut and hardly worth the effort needed to crack the hard outer shell.

SHELLBARK HICKORY, *Carya laciniosa* (Michx. f.) Loud. *Leaves* 15 to 22 inches long; leaflets 7 (sometimes 5 or 9), glabrous above and finely soft-hairy below, the terminal three leaflets 4 to 9 inches long and the others smaller. *Twigs* pale orange-brown. *Terminal buds* ½ to 1 inch long (usually about ¾ inch); scales loose, the inner covered with pale yellow-brown hairs and the outer dark brown. *Nut* 1¾ to 2½ inches long; husk unwinged, ¼ to ½ inch thick, brown, splitting completely open. *Bark* slate gray, shaggy.

THIS handsome tree resembles the shagbark hickory but it has much larger leaves and fruits, as suggested by its other common names of *bigleaf shagbark* and *kingnut*. Its seeds are sweet and edible.

Shellbark hickory is found in floodplains along the Mississippi River and its principal tributaries north to Jackson and Iowa counties, and locally in south central Iowa. It has become rare in most places because of the extensive clearing of bottomland timber for agriculture, but it is still fairly common along the Chariton River downstream from Lake Rathbun.

PECAN, *Carya illinoensis* (Wangenh.) K. Koch. *Leaves* 12 to 20 inches long; leaflets 9 to 17, prominently curved, glabrous or nearly so, 4 to 8 inches long, the terminal the same size as the laterals. *Twigs* brown or red-brown. *Terminal bud* ¼ to ½ inch long; scales meeting at the edges without overlapping, brown or yellow-brown. *Nut* 1 to 2½ inches long; husk winged, very thin, dark brown, splitting to the base. *Bark* light brown or reddish-brown; divided into irregular, scaly ridges and narrow furrows.

MOST people think of the pecan as a tree of the South, but it grows wild along the Mississippi River bottoms as far north as Jackson County, Iowa. It has been suggested that our northern trees were planted by native Americans and thus should not be considered native. This cannot be proven but would account for pecans found along the Des Moines River in Kossuth County and other locations remote from the Mississippi.

Although pecans are not an important crop in Iowa, our native trees are of interest to horticulturists because they are able to mature their nuts in our relatively short growing season. Thus, they may prove useful for breeding new cultivars that can be grown farther north, with nuts that retain the size and cracking ability of existing cultivars.

Pecan is the largest and fastest growing of the hickories, often attaining a height of more than 100 feet and a trunk diameter of 2 to 4 feet. Its wood is used for furniture, flooring, and cabinetry.

The pignut hickory [*Carya glabra* (Mill.) Sweet] has been reported to be native in Iowa, but these reports have not been authenticated. This species is characterized by 5 (occasionally 7) glabrous leaflets, slender twigs, terminal buds ⅜ to ½ inch long with deciduous outer scales, shallowly furrowed bark, and thin nut husks that split about halfway to the base.

Ironwood (Hop Hornbeam), *Ostrya virginiana* (Mill.) K. Koch

Distinguishing characteristics: *Leaves* simple, alternate, oblong-ovate, 3 to 5 inches long with petioles about ¼ inch long, toothed; some of the veins forking, others running unforked to the teeth. *Winter twigs* very slender, brown, often hairy; exposed catkins sometimes present; leaf scars very small, half-round, with 3 bundle scars. *Buds* ovoid, ⅛ to ¼ inch long, the terminal absent; bud scales usually 6 to 9 in number, spirally arranged, glabrous or hairy, their surfaces creased with fine vertical lines (seen with magnifying glass). *Flowers* monoecious, in catkins, appearing with the leaves in spring. *Fruit* a nutlet about ⅓ inch long enclosed in a small papery sac; sacs overlapping one another in hoplike clusters 1½ to 2 inches long. *Bark* gray or brown, unbroken on young trees but eventually separating into vertically spiraled rows of small rectangular plates that are typically appressed to the trunk but sometimes loose and shaggy.

Similar trees: Other trees with similar leaves have leaf veins all running unforked to the teeth (elms, hornbeam, yellow birch) or ending before reaching the margin (cherries, serviceberries). The hoplike fruit clusters are also distinctive. Winter: bud scales of other trees are not creased with vertical lines.

Distribution: Native throughout the state.

IF a census of our native trees were ever undertaken, it would probably reveal that the ironwood is our most common species. A naturally small tree that seldom exceeds a height of 30 feet, it may completely dominate the understory of upland woods. Though apparently preferring the shade provided by oaks, maples, and other large trees, it also grows well in full sun and sometimes invades uncultivated land bordering woods. In some woodlands it outnumbers all other species of trees put together.

A tree this common should also be well known, but the ironwood attracts little attention. Unlike most other small trees, it has no showy flowers, beautiful autumn color, or other eye-catching features. Mature trees can be easily recognized by their distinctive bark, fruits, and catkins; but ironwoods take many years to mature, so mature trees are few and far between. Moreover, the ironwood's leaves and buds are quite ordinary and can be easily mistaken for those of elms, cherries, or a half-dozen other trees. Many people do not know that the ironwood exists.

Ironwood is appropriately named. Its wood is harder than any other native tree, tougher and stronger than white oak, and second only to hickory in weight. It is too small to be of much commercial importance, but its wood was once used for a variety of products including mallets; levers; wedges; tool handles; sled runners; ox yokes; kitchen utensils; and wheels, axles, and tongues of wagons. It is also an excellent fuelwood.

Ironwood is often called *hop hornbeam*. The first part of this name refers to the resemblance of its fruiting catkins to those of hops and the second to its tough wood. The botanical name *Ostrya* is taken from a Greek word for "tree with tough wood."

It is unfortunate that the ironwood is so seldom used for landscaping in Iowa. Although it is often slow to establish after transplanting, it develops into a handsome and very durable small shade three that is seldom bothered by diseases or insects. When grown in the open, it usually develops a broad, rounded crown. Its leaves turn yellow in autumn, then fade to pale brown and persist through much of the winter, especially on the lower branches of the tree.

Hornbeam, *Carpinus caroliniana* Walt.

Distinguishing characteristics: *Leaves* simple, alternate, ovate to oval, 2 to 4 inches long with petioles about ⅓ inch long, toothed; veins running directly to the teeth. *Winter twigs* very slender, red-brown, glabrous; leaf scars very small, half-round, with 3 bundle scars. *Buds* ovoid, about ⅛ inch long, the terminal absent; bud scales about 12, arranged in four vertical rows, brown or red with white margins, glabrous or nearly so. *Flowers* monoecious, in catkins, appearing with the leaves. *Fruit* a nutlet about ⅓ inch long attached to the base of a leafy, 3-lobed bract 1 to 1½ inches long; bracts overlapping one another in a dense cluster 2 to 4 inches long. *Bark* light gray, very smooth. *Trunks* with a distinctive twisted or muscled appearance, often growing in clumps.

Similar trees: Ironwood has rough, platy bark, exposed staminate catkins, and spirally arranged bud scales creased with fine vertical lines. Its principal leaf veins tend to fork near the margin. The bark of downy serviceberry resembles that of hornbeam; but serviceberry has elongate buds with spirally arranged scales, its leaf veins form a network near the margin, and its trunks lack a muscled appearance.

Distribution: Native through most of the eastern third of Iowa, also in the Iowa and Des Moines River valleys in the central part of the state.

THIS attractive little tree has so many names, it is difficult to keep track of them all. *Hornbeam* combines "horn," meaning toughness, with "beam," an old name for tree. However, some people call it "bluebeech" because its bark is very smooth like that of the American beech, whereas others prefer "musclewood" or "ironwood." Botanists call the tree by its ancient Latin name, *Carpinus*.

Most of the English names of this tree refer to its hard, heavy, peculiarly twisted wood. This gives its smooth-barked trunks a characteristic muscle-bound appearance, a useful aid in recognizing a species that is otherwise little different from several other, more common understory trees. The wood is occasionally used for homemade mallets, levers, tool handles, and other articles requiring exceptional strength and toughness; but the hornbeam is too small to be important commercially. It makes an excellent firewood, although it seems a shame to cut it for such a mundane purpose when oak, ash, and other equally suitable woods are plentiful.

Hornbeam, which often grows in clumps of several stems, is seldom over 30 feet tall or 1 foot in diameter. Most Iowa hornbeams are smaller. Like the ironwood, hornbeam is very tolerant of shade and is usually found beneath a canopy of other trees. It sometimes grows side by side with ironwood but prefers a moister site such as a stream terrace or the lower part of a north-facing slope.

Hornbeam has a good deal of ornamental value and could be more widely planted in eastern and central Iowa. It is relatively free of diseases and insect pests, though somewhat difficult to transplant. Trees do best when placed in a moist, sheltered location where the soil is fertile and slightly acid in reaction. The ornamental value of its twisted trunks is enhanced by encouraging the trees to form clumps. The leaves turn a handsome reddish-orange in autumn if the tree is growing on a favorable site.

Paper Birch, *Betula papyrifera* Marsh.

Distinguishing characteristics: *Leaves* simple, alternate on twigs but paired at the ends of short spur shoots on branchlets, ovate to oval, 2 to 3 (rarely 5) inches long with petioles ½ to ¾ inch long; margins toothed; bases rounded or truncate; veins running directly to the teeth. *Winter twigs* slender, glabrous, red-brown, dotted with conspicuous white breathing pores (lenticels); exposed catkins usually present; leaf scars small, half-round to crescent shaped, with 3 bundle scars. *Buds* ovoid, the terminal present on spur shoots but absent from twigs, the laterals about ¼ inch long with 3 or 4 brown, glabrous scales. *Flowers* monoecious, in catkins, appearing with or shortly before the leaves in spring. *Fruit* a tiny winged nutlet borne in a conelike catkin 1 to 1½ inches long. *Bark* smooth, white, peeling into papery strips.

Similar trees: European white birch has drooping twigs and triangular or diamond-shaped leaves. River birch has wedge-shaped leaf bases and scaly bark that is orange or orange-brown on young trees and dark gray on older trees. (See also *Quaking Aspen.*)

Distribution: Native from Allamakee County west to Mitchell County and south to Linn, Delaware, and Jackson counties; also along the Iowa River in Hardin County. Occasionally planted throughout the state.

PAPER BIRCH is one of the most characteristic trees of the north woods. One does not associate it with the prairies and deciduous woods of Iowa; but like the white pine and several other northern trees, it grows naturally in the northeastern corner of the state. The cool, moist climate and thin, well-drained soils there provide the environment it requires; and its gleaming white trunks are a familiar sight on hilltops and wooded slopes in many locales. It is also native on sheltered bluffs along the Iowa River in Hardin County.

The beautiful, chalky white bark of this tree is its most distinctive feature. The bark's strength, light weight, and ability to repel water were greatly appreciated by native Americans in the Great Lakes states, who used it for making birchbark canoes. The bark is also prized because it can be used to start a campfire when everything is wet. However, peeling the bark from living birches makes their trunks turn black and may injure the trees.

Although the paper birch is the only native birch with white bark, several Eurasian species also have this characteristic. Some of these are planted in Iowa as ornamentals, especially the European white birch, *Betula pendula* Roth, which is prized for its graceful, drooping branchlets. The Japanese white birch, *B. platyphylla* var. *japonica* (Miq.) Hara is another frequently planted tree.

Unfortunately, most white-barked birches have a short life span in cultivation. The trees are stressed when planted outside their native habitats, making them susceptible to attack by the bronze birch borer. Through its feeding on the tree's inner bark, this insect may girdle branches and even trunks, causing the foliage to wilt and the stems to die. Infested trees are eventually killed or so badly disfigured that their ornamental value is destroyed.

Borers are difficult to control, and damage is best prevented by replacing susceptible birches with resistant ones, such as our native river birch. 'Whitespire,' a cultivar of the Japanese white birch, also has shown resistance in trial plantings. Resistant cultivars should be propagated by cuttings rather than seed to ensure that resistance is maintained.

The wood of paper birch resembles that of yellow birch but is somewhat lighter, softer, and weaker. It is used for pulp, lumber, toothpicks, tongue depressors and other medical sticks, and small, turned articles such as spools and handles. It is an excellent firewood.

River Birch, *Betula nigra* L.

Distinguishing characteristics: *Leaves* simple, alternate on twigs but paired at the ends of spur shoots on branchlets, ovate with a wedge-shaped base, 1½ to 3¼ inches long with petioles about ½ inch long; margins toothed; veins running directly to the teeth. *Winter twigs* slender, glabrous, red-brown to orange-brown, dotted with conspicuous white breathing pores (lenticels); exposed catkins usually present; leaf scars small, half-round to crescent shaped, with 3 bundle scars. *Buds* ovoid, the terminal present on spur shoots but absent from twigs, the laterals about ¼ inch long, with 3 or 4 brown scales that may be either hairy or glabrous. *Flowers* similar to paper birch. *Fruit* a tiny winged nutlet borne in a conelike catkin 1 to 1½ inches longs. *Bark* on young trees flaking into thin, papery pieces that are at first orange and white and later orange-brown; bark of mature trees scaly and dark red-brown to nearly black.

Similar trees: Paper and European white birches have chalky white bark with no trace of orange. The bark of large river birches is very similar to that of black cherry, which has oblong-lanceolate leaves, glandular petioles, and red buds with more than 4 scales.

Distribution: Native through most of the eastern third of Iowa and in scattered localities in south central and southwestern parts of the state west to Adams County; planted elsewhere.

WHEN the word *birch* is mentioned, most people think of white-barked trees and cold northern lakes, but several species of birch have dark colored bark and grow in more temperate climes. One such tree is the river birch, the most widely distributed of the birches native to Iowa and in many ways the most suitable species for landscaping here.

Birches are most easily distinguished from one another by bark. In some species, including the river birch, the bark changes markedly as the trees mature. The outer bark of saplings is sometimes white like paper birch, but it

flakes off and reveals the orange inner bark. As they grow, their shreddy outer bark becomes light orange-brown. Eventually it turns dark gray and scaly and more closely resembles the bark of black cherry than another birch.

The river birch is an attractive tree and is being increasingly planted as a substitute for the white-barked birches. Its bark is less striking, but it is a more reliable tree in its resistance to borers and tolerance of heat and poorly drained sites. It prefers a moist, slightly acid soil and sometimes suffers from chlorosis (leaf yellowing) when grown in alkaline soils. The ornamental effect of its bark is enhanced by planting multiple-trunked trees and removing their lower branches as the trunks grow. Trees commonly develop an oval to pyramidal crown and attain a height of 40 to 70 feet.

River birch prefers a warmer climate than most birches and is widely distributed in stream bottoms throughout the southern and central states. It is very common along some eastern Iowa rivers, particularly the Mississippi and the Wapsipinicon, but it is only a minor constituent of forests in most other parts of its Iowa range. Its seeds mature in May or early June, long before those of other birches. They require a moist, bare, mineral soil in which to germinate, so early ripening permits them to take advantage of the fresh deposits of silt and sand left by receding spring floodwaters.

The wood of the river birch is similar to that of yellow birch but lighter, weaker, and often knotty. It is used for firewood and for the manufacture of inexpensive furniture, barrel staves, woodenware, and novelties. It was once used for ox yokes and wooden shoes.

Yellow Birch, *Betula alleghaniensis* Britton (*B. lutea* Michx.)

Distinguishing characteristics: *Leaves* simple, alternate on twigs but paired at the ends of short spur shoots on branchlets, ovate to oblong-ovate, 3 to 4½ inches long with petioles ¾ to 1 inch long; margins toothed; bases rounded and often unequal; veins running directly to the teeth. *Winter twigs* similar to river birch but with a distinct wintergreen taste. *Buds* ovoid, the terminal present on spur shoots but absent from twigs, the laterals about ¼ inch long with 3 or 4 brown scales hairy along the edges. *Flowers* monoecious, in catkins, appearing with or before the leaves in spring. *Fruit* a tiny winged nutlet borne in a conelike catkin 1 to 1½ inches long. *Bark* light gray or yellow-gold, smooth when young, then separating into scales or thin, rolled strips.

Similar trees: Small trees can be distinguished from ironwoods, elms, serviceberries, and other trees with similar leaves by the wintergreen taste of the twigs and the presence of spur shoots on the branchlets. The thin, scaly bark of mature trees is distinctive.

Distribution: Native in extreme northeastern Iowa west to Mitchell County and south to Dubuque County; also native along the Iowa River in Hardin County.

THE yellow birch is one of our most unusual native trees. Its outer bark is very thin as in other birches but differs markedly in color, being light gray or a dirty yellow-gold. Smooth and tight fitting at first, it soon becomes scaly or curls into distinctive rolled strips. The tree's inner bark contains oil of wintergreen, once widely used to flavor patent medicines and still used in candy. One can easily identify the tree at all times of the year by simply chewing a twig!

Finding a yellow birch in Iowa is not a simple task. It is native to only a few counties in the northern part of the state, where it is restricted to steep, usually north-facing bluffs and slopes bordering streams. Even where it is most common, such as Pikes Peak State Park near McGregor, the yellow birch is scattered in the forest, occupying only a minor part of the canopy.

Another intriguing aspect is its unusual distribution in Iowa. Although most of our yellow birches are found within a small area in the extreme northeastern corner of the state, an isolated population occurs along the Iowa River in Hardin County, over a hundred miles away. This peculiar distribution is also characteristic of paper birch and white pine.

The origin of the Hardin County birches and pines long puzzled Iowa botanists. However, studies of pollen grains buried in peat bogs have shown that pines, spruces, birches, and other northern trees were widely distributed in Iowa at the end of the last ice age, an indication that the climate then was cooler and moister. The birches and pines along the Iowa River are believed to be relics of these early post-glacial forests, surviving there only because the moist, shady bluffs provide a special set of environmental conditions, or microclimate, similar to that of northern regions.

Yellow birch is a valuable timber tree in the northeastern United States and southeastern Canada, but it is too scarce in Iowa to be of any importance. Its wood is hard, heavy, strong, and shock resistant. Its principal uses are for furniture and veneer; but it is also utilized for doors, interior trim, woodenware, and a variety of other goods.

Yellow birch is not recommended for landscaping in Iowa because it is very sensitive to heat and drought. It is also susceptible to birch borers when planted outside its natural range.

Oaks, *Quercus* L.

THE General Assembly declared the oak to be Iowa's state tree in 1961. This should not be surprising to anyone familiar with the forests of our state. It would be difficult to find a tract of natural woodland in Iowa that did not harbor at least one species of oak; most areas have several. No other group of trees here is more important to people and wildlife.

The commercial importance of oaks is due in part to their sheer abundance; but the hard, strong, heavy wood of oaks would be esteemed even if the trees were scarce. The list of products manufactured from oak is almost endless; its most important uses include furniture, veneer, flooring, railroad ties, mine timbers, and barrel staves. Oak is also an excellent fuel.

Acorns, the nuts of oaks, are a dietary staple of a great many game animals and songbirds. Turkeys, pheasants, quail, wood ducks, raccoons, squirrels, chipmunks, blue jays, nuthatches, grackles, and several kinds of woodpeckers are a few of the species that depend on acorns for a significant part of their diet. The prevalence of oaks in Iowa woodlands also makes these trees valuable as shelter and nesting cover.

Although some species of oaks commonly occur in bottomlands, most are trees of well-drained upland woods. On moist upland sites, such as north- and east-facing slopes and ravines, they grow with maples, basswoods, and many other trees. On dry sites, such as ridges and south-facing slopes, hickories are their most common associates. (Oaks and hickories are so often found together in dry upland woods that the name "oak-hickory" has been given to this forest type.)

Oak leaves come in a variety of shapes and sizes. Our most common species have the familiar lobed or "oak-leaf" shape, but two native species have toothed leaves resembling those of chestnut and another has entire leaves like a magnolia. Whatever shape its leaves might be, an oak can always be recognized by its buds and acorns. In oaks several buds are clustered at the tip of the twig and each is covered by numerous tiny scales arranged in vertical rows.

Shapes of oak leaves may also vary from tree to tree within a species and even on a single tree, so identification must often be based on buds and acorns. Identification is further complicated by hybridization (crossing) of species. Features of the offspring resulting from such crosses are usually intermediate between those of the parents.

The tiny green or yellowish flowers of oaks appear when the leaves are unfolding in spring. The male flowers are arranged in long, conspicuous catkins like those of birches and poplars. The female flowers, which are located in the axils of the leaves, occur singly or in small clusters. The small, bright red pistil of each female flower is surrounded by a series of minute scaly bracts that eventually become the acorn-cup. Both sexes of flowers may occur on the same twigs.

Oaks are normally long-lived, durable trees but they can be very sensitive to changes in their woodland environment. When buildings and roads are constructed in wooded areas containing oaks, it is especially important to minimize disturbance to the forest soil. Injury to the root system through digging, filling, or soil compaction can cause the decline and even death of a mature tree, even if no harm is done to the trunk and branches. For information on how to protect trees during construction, see Olson & Wray's "Preventing Construction Damage to Trees."

Oak wilt, a serious disease of oaks similar to Dutch elm disease, has caused concern in Iowa. Although it is a serious problem in certain parts of the state, past outbreaks of the disease have remained localized and it seems unlikely that it will cause a widespread epidemic. Oaks in a weakened condition from drought or injury may be more subject to attack by canker diseases, insect borers, and bark beetles; so it should not be assumed that any oak that dies suddenly was killed by oak wilt. Laboratory diagnosis is necessary to determine if oak wilt was responsible.

Our native oaks can be divided into two groups: red oaks and white oaks. The white oak group (subgenus *Leucobalanus*) includes the white, bur, chinkapin, swamp white, and post oaks. The lobes or teeth of white oak leaves do not have bristle tips and the inner surface of their acorn shells is smooth. The acorns of white oaks mature in one growing season, germinating soon after they are dispersed in autumn. White oak wood is light brown to dark brown in color, and its pores (*vessels*) are blocked with small plugs (*tyloses*) that make the wood watertight and desirable for use in the "tight cooperage" industry (the manufacture of barrels for holding liquids). In fact, federal law requires that all domestic whiskey be aged in casks made from white oak.

The red oak group (subgenus *Erythrobalanus*) includes red, pin, black, Hill's, blackjack, and shingle oaks. The most distinctive feature of this group is the short bristle that occurs at the tip of each leaf or leaf lobe. The inner surface of the acorn shells of red oaks is velvety hairy. Their acorns require two growing seasons to mature and do not germinate until the spring following their dispersal. The pinkish or reddish-brown wood of red oaks has open pores (vessels), lacking the small occlusions (tyloses) that are such a conspicuous feature of the wood of white oaks.

White Oak, *Quercus alba* L.

Distinguishing characteristics: *Leaves* 7 to 9 lobed, 5 to 9 inches long with petioles ½ to 1 inch long; lobes with rounded tips, variable in length from one leaf to the next but rather uniform in any given leaf; surfaces green and glabrous. *Buds* subglobose, blunt pointed, ⅛ to ³⁄₁₆ inch long, glabrous or nearly so. *Acorns* oblong, ½ to ¾ inch long, sessile or nearly so; cups bowl shaped with thick warty scales, covering the lower ¼ of the nut. *Bark* light ashy-gray, separating into small scaly plates; often furrowed with thick blocky ridges on old trees.

Similar trees: Bur oak has hairy buds, fringed acorn-cups, dark furrowed bark, and irregularly lobed leaves that are hairy beneath. Swamp white oak has long-stalked acorns and more shallowly lobed leaves that are hairy beneath.

Distribution: Native in eastern, central, and southern Iowa, also in the Pilot Knob vicinity in north central Iowa; old reports from the Spirit-Okoboji lakes region.

WHITE OAK has long been a symbol of strength and longevity. Its wood, which was used in constructing the famous warship *Old Ironsides,* has long been used as a standard against which other woods are compared. Iowa has white oaks more than 400 years old, and even older trees have been reported in the eastern states.

The strength, hardness, durability, and widespread availability of white oak wood have combined to make this species one of the most important timber trees in the United States. White oak is the principal wood for mine timbers, railroad ties, flooring, and whiskey barrels; and it is also used for boatbuilding, fencing, and posts. The attractive figure of quartersawn white oak has long made it popular for paneling and furniture, particularly for desks and tables. Many pioneer homes were constructed of beams, lumber, and shingles of white oak. White oak is also one of the best firewoods available.

White oak is one of the most abundant native trees throughout its broad Iowa range, often dominating the drier upland woods. Its common associates on such sites include other oaks, hickories, ironwood, black cherry, white ash, and aspens. It also occurs on moist slopes with trees such as maple, basswood, and bitternut hickory; but it is usually much less abundant there than on the higher ground.

White oak commonly attains a height of 80 to 100 feet and a trunk diameter of 3 to 4 feet. When grown in the open it develops a broad, rounded crown of rugged-looking branches casting dense shade. Its leaves turn a rich wine color in early October, eventually fading to a dull reddish-brown and finally to light brown. Like other oaks, the dried leaves often remain on the branches well into winter. The picturesque shape of this tree and its light ashy bark also make it one of our most attractive native trees during the winter months.

The white oak's beauty, longevity, and durability make it an excellent shade tree, although it is seldom planted because it grows slowly and is difficult to successfully transplant. Great care should be exercised when building homes in wooded areas, as the roots of this species and other native oaks are very sensitive to soil disturbance. (See previous discussion.)

The English oak (*Quercus robur* L.) is occasionally planted in Iowa as an ornamental. It resembles the white oak but has shallowly lobed leaves 2½ to 5 inches long with petioles less than ⅜ inch long, stalked acorns, and dark furrowed bark. It typically develops a short, massive trunk with a broad, rounded crown.

Bur Oak, *Quercus macrocarpa* Michx.

Distinguishing characteristics: *Leaves* quite variable in shape but commonly obovate, shallowly lobed except for a pair of deeply cut sinuses near the center, 6 to 10 inches long with petioles ⅓ to 1 inch long, dark green above, paler and finely hairy below. *Buds* subglobose to ovoid, ⅛ to ¼ inch long, densely covered with fine gray hairs. *Acorns* globe shaped, ⅗ to 2 inches long, sessile or short stalked; cup with a prominent fringe of soft bristles around its rim, covering ⅓ or more of the nut. *Bark* dark, thick, and deeply furrowed. *Corky outgrowths* often present on older twigs.

Similar trees: Leaves of white oak are hairless beneath with lobes of uniform size and the leaves of swamp white oak lack deeply cut sinuses. Neither has bristles around the rims of its acorn-cups.

Distribution: Native throughout the state.

THE General Assembly did not designate any species when they declared the oak to be Iowa's state tree, but the bur oak deserves the honor. A picturesque tree with stout, rugged branches, it is the most widely distributed native oak and the characteristic tree of the prairie-forest border.

Bur oak, though occasionally found on stream terraces and floodplains, is primarily an upland species. It is the most abundant forest tree in most of western and parts of north central Iowa, often forming pure stands. In other parts of the state it is a less conspicuous member of the flora, sharing dominance with a variety of trees such as hickories, aspens, and other oaks.

Bur oak played a dynamic role in shaping the presettlement landscape of midwestern states. While other trees were restricted to the slopes of river valleys, the bur oak's thick, fire-resistant bark and natural resistance to drought allowed it to compete successfully with the prairie grasses.

When the settlers arrived from the east, they found open, parklike stands of bur oaks to be a conspicuous feature of the landscape. These stands, which they called "oak groves" or "oak openings," were favored sites for homesteads. Later, when cultivation brought an end to the prairie fires, many of the uninhabited oak openings became overgrown with brush and trees of other species.

The bur oak's drought resistance is due in large part to its extensive root system. Seedlings produce a deep taproot even before their leaves have unfolded; by the end of their first growing season it may be 5 feet long. Mature trees have long branch roots that extend 20 to 60 feet horizontally before growing downward, and their entire root system weighs as much as the above ground part of the tree.

Bur oak develops a broad, rounded crown that provides excellent shade, and it should be more widely used for landscaping in Iowa. Young trees grow slowly and are difficult to transplant, but a mature specimen is well worth the wait. Its leaves are less colorful in autumn than most other native oaks, turning a dull yellow or brown.

The overcup oak (*Quercus lyrata* Walt.) closely resembles the bur oak but has unfringed acorn-cups and more deeply lobed leaves. Three trees of this species were reported from the Iowa River bottom near Amana by B. Shimek in 1922. It is unknown whether these trees are still in existence or why they were growing in a location so remote from their natural range. Overcup oak is native to the Atlantic coastal plain and the southern Mississippi valley, so the presence of native trees of this species along the Iowa River would be quite remarkable.

Swamp White Oak, *Quercus bicolor* Willd.

Distinguishing characteristics: *Leaves* obovate with shallow lobes or blunt teeth and 6 to 8 pairs of veins, 5 to 7 inches long with petioles ½ to ¾ inch long; upper surface dark green; lower surface paler and finely hairy. *Buds* subglobose with round or blunt-pointed tips, ¹⁄₁₆ to ³⁄₁₆ inch long, glabrous or nearly so. *Acorns* broad-ovoid, ¾ to 1¼ inches long, paired at the ends of stalks 1 to 4 inches long; cups bowl shaped, covering about ⅓ of the nut; cup scales slightly thickened, those around the rim of the cup pointing upward, forming a fringe. *Bark* of branches light ashy gray, separating into papery scales that peel off and reveal the greenish inner bark; trunk bark light gray to gray-brown, scaly, eventually furrowed with thick blocky ridges.

Similar trees: Leaves of white oak are deeply lobed and hairless beneath; leaves of chinkapin oak have 8 to 13 pairs of veins with an equal number of usually sharp-pointed teeth. Bur oak leaves have at least one pair of deeply cut sinuses near the middle. All three have sessile or short-stalked acorns.

Distribution: Native in eastern, central, and south central Iowa.

SWAMP WHITE OAK, as its name suggests, is usually found in moist, low-lying woods. It is native across most of the eastern half of Iowa but is much less abundant than our upland oaks, occurring here and there in the forest instead of being a dominant tree. Silver maple, hackberry, American elm, green ash, black walnut, shingle and pin oaks, and river birch are a few of the many trees with which it is associated.

Swamp white oak is frequently confused with other trees in the white oak group, particularly the bur and chinkapin oaks. Besides its usually reliable difference in habitat, it can be distinguished from these species by leaf margins and the shape and relative hairiness of the buds. The acorns of swamp white oak are also distinctive when present, having much longer stalks than those of other native oaks.

Swamp white oak makes a handsome shade tree, developing a broad, rounded crown of stout, spreading branches. Its dark green, glossy leaves are very attractive in summer, but their autumn color is less striking than other oaks. The foliage can also suffer from yellowing (chlorosis) when the trees are grown in alkaline soil.

The hard, heavy, durable wood of swamp white oak resembles that of white oak and is generally not distinguished from it in the market. However, the trees' tendency to retain their lower branches for many years often results in knotty, inferior logs. This habit and the relative scarcity of the species make the swamp white oak less important than other native oaks as a timber tree.

The botanical name of swamp white oak means "two color," a reference to the contrast between the dark green upper surfaces of the leaves and their usually white lower surfaces. However, the leaves are not always white beneath, so color itself is not a reliable means of identifying the tree. ("Bicolor" would be an equally suitable description for the bur oak, since its leaves also tend to be dark green above and white below.)

Swamp white oak grows to a height of 60 to 70 feet, with a trunk 2 to 3 feet in diameter. It is long lived like most oaks and may attain an age of 300 years or more.

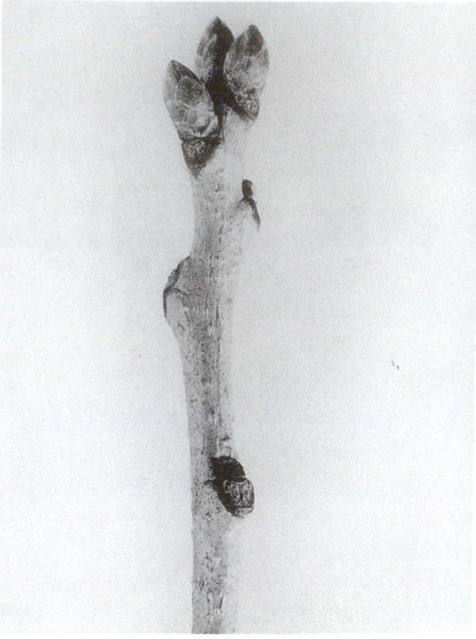

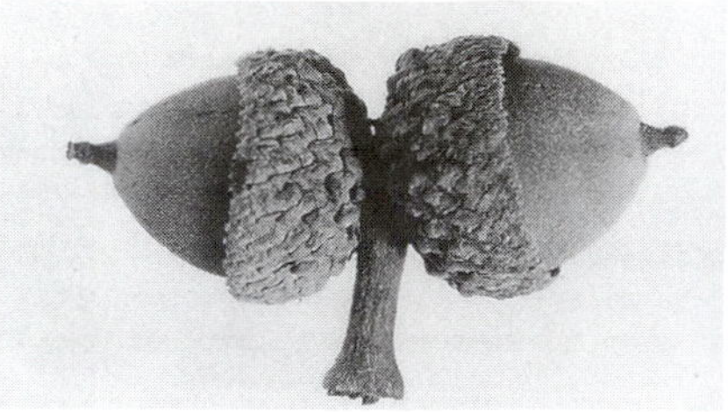

Chinkapin Oak, *Quercus muhlenbergii* Engelm. (*Q. prinoides* var. *acuminata* [Michx.] Gleason)

Distinguishing characteristics: *Leaves* oblong-lanceolate to obovate, with 8 to 13 pairs of veins and an equal number of large, usually sharp-pointed teeth; 4 to 7 inches long with petioles ¾ to 1½ inches long; glabrous and dark green or yellow-green above; paler and finely hairy below. *Buds* ovoid, sharp pointed, ⅛ to ¼ inch long; bud scales glabrous with pale, often slightly hairy margins. *Acorns* ovoid, ½ to ¾ inch long, sessile or nearly so; cups bowl shaped with thin appressed scales, covering the lower ⅓ to ½ of the nut. *Bark* scaly, light ashy gray.

Similar trees: Leaves of swamp white oak have blunt or rounded teeth and only 6 to 8 pairs of veins; swamp white oak also has blunt buds and larger, long-stalked acorns. Dwarf oak (see discussion following) has leaves with shorter petioles and only 3 to 7 pairs of teeth; its acorns are smaller than those of chinkapin oak and have thick cups. American chestnut lacks acorns and clustered end buds.

Distribution: Native south and east of a line extending from the loess hills in Mills County northeastward to Winneshiek County.

AT first glance, the chinkapin oak may not look much like an oak. Its leaves are not lobed like those of the white oak, pin oak, and other familiar species, but instead toothed like the leaves of a chestnut. Its acorns identify it as an oak, however, and when its leaves are absent, it closely resembles other oak species.

The chinkapin is, in fact, only one of several species of oaks whose leaves are toothed instead of lobed. Others are the swamp white and dwarf oaks, which are also native to Iowa; the chestnut and basket oaks of the eastern United States; and several species in eastern Asia. All can be recognized as oaks by their acorns and distinctive buds.

The range of chinkapin oak includes nearly half the state, but it is distributed sporadically within this area and is only locally common. Its usual habitat is well-drained, calcerous soils on dry bluffs; ridge tops; and rocky, south-facing slopes. Though sometimes the dominant tree on such sites, it is more often associated with a variety of other dry-soil species such as white, bur, and black oaks; shagbark hickory; ironwood; and redcedar.

Chinkapin oak is a very handsome shade tree and should be more widely planted. It grows faster than most white oaks, usually matures at a smaller size, and tolerates the heavy clay and alkaline soils that trouble some other species. Its autumn color is usually yellow but is sometimes a rich wine color like that of the white oak. Open-grown trees develop a rounded or oval crown 40 to 50 feet high.

Small chinkapin oaks closely resemble the ground or dwarf oak (*Quercus prinoides* Willd.), out only native oak that is shrubby in habit. The leaves of this species are somewhat shorter than those of the chinkapin (2½ to 5 inches long with petioles ⅛ to ⅜ inch long) and have only 3 to 7 pairs of teeth; its acorns are ⅖ to ⅗ inch long with thick, bowl-shaped cups composed of bumpy scales. It is native in uplands in southern Iowa and has also been reported from Allamakee County in the northeastern corner of the state.

The chinkapin and dwarf oaks may hybridize when they grow together, producing populations of oaks in which there is an intermingling of characteristics. Many authorities now consider them to be two varieties of a single species. If this view is accepted, the correct botanical name for the chinkapin oak is *Q. prinoides* var. *acuminata*.

Post Oak, *Quercus stellata* Wangenh.

Distinguishing characteristics: *Leaves* 5 lobed, the upper 3 lobes much larger than the others and forming a distinctive cross-shaped pattern, 4 to 6 inches long with petioles ½ to 1 inch long, dark green and roughened above, pale green to gray-green and finely hairy below. *Buds* blunt (rarely sharp pointed), ⅛ to ¼ inch long, sparsely hairy. *Acorns* ovoid, ½ to ⅔ inch long, sessile or nearly so; cups bowl shaped with thin scales, covering ⅓ to ½ of the nut. *Bark* gray-brown to light ashy gray, scaly; becoming furrowed on older trees.

Similar trees: Leaves of bur oak sometimes have 3 strongly developed upper lobes that suggest a cross, but the pattern is much more pronounced in the leaves of post oak. Bur oak also differs in having fringed acorn-cups and dark furrowed bark.

Distribution: Native in Lee, Henry, Van Buren, and Appanoose counties and possibly in other counties near the Missouri border.

POST OAK is one of our rarest native trees, being known in only a few localities in the southeastern corner of the state.

A dry-soil species, it occurs in small groves on gravelly ridges or as a minor associate of white oak, black oak, and shagbark hickory in upland woods. It is smaller than many oaks, rarely exceeding a height of 40 to 50 feet and a trunk diameter of 1 to 2 feet.

The unusual leaves of post oak make it easy to identify. Each leaf has 5 lobes—a small pair near the base and 3 large, squarish lobes aligned in a crosslike pattern at the end. In winter the trees are easily overlooked, resembling the white oak in bark and twig.

The hard durable wood of this tree was once widely used for posts, but it is of little importance today. In Missouri and other states where the post oak is common, its wood is sold as "white oak."

Blackjack Oak, *Quercus marilandica* Muenchh.

Distinguishing characteristics: *Leaves* obovate, shallowly 3 lobed, 5 to 7 inches long with stout petioles ⅜ to ¾ inch long; upper surface dark green and glossy, lower surface paler and more or less hairy. *Buds* ovoid, ¼ to ⅜ inch long, strongly angled in cross section, densely covered with light brownish hairs. *Acorns* oblong to subglobose, about ¾ inch long, sessile or nearly so; cups bowl shaped with loose, hairy, light brown scales, covering about ½ of the nut. *Bark* dark brown to nearly black; divided into thick, blocky plates.

Similar trees: The 3-lobed leaves and dark, blocky bark of the blackjack oak are distinctive. The only tree even remotely resembling it is its hybrid with black oak, which typically has 5-lobed leaves. (See discussion below.)

Distribution: The species (or its hybrid with black oak) is native locally from Lee County north to Louisa County and west to Marion, Union, and Decatur counties.

BLACKJACK OAK is native to extreme southeastern and south central Iowa, occurring locally in open, sandy areas and dry upland woods. It is a small, straggly tree, rarely exceeding a height of 30 feet or a trunk diameter of 1 foot. Its peculiar leaves and distinctive blocky bark easily distinguish it from the other oaks with which it is associated.

Blackjack oak hybridizes freely with black oak in Iowa. The resulting hybrids (*Quercus × bushii* Sarg.) are more common than the blackjack oak in many areas. Their leaves are quite variable in shape but usually have 3 large terminal lobes and a smaller pair near the base. The hybrids are generally similar to the blackjack oak in growth form.

The small size and poor form of the blackjack oak make it practically worthless as a timber tree. Its wood is used for fuel and charcoal in Missouri and other states where the species is common, but in Iowa it is too scarce to be of any importance even for these uses.

Red Oak, *Quercus rubra* L. (*Q. borealis* Michx.)

Distinguishing characteristics: *Leaves* 7 to 11 lobed, 5 to 9 inches long with slender petioles 1 to 2 inches long; lobes bristle tipped, usually no longer than the width of the central undivided portion of the blade (occasionally up to twice as long on leaves growing in full sun); sinuses U shaped; upper surface glabrous and dull green; lower surface paler and glabrous except for small tufts of hairs in the axils of the large veins. *Buds* ovoid, ⅛ to ⅜ (usually ³⁄₁₆ to ¼) inch long, rounded or slightly angled in cross section, glabrous or hairy just at the tip. *Acorns* ovoid, ½ to 1 inch long, sessile or nearly so; cups saucer shaped to bowl shaped with red-brown, closely appressed scales, covering no more than the lower ⅓ of the nut. *Bark* at base of trunk light gray to nearly black; thick and deeply furrowed; appearing "striped" on upper trunk; with dark, flattened ridges alternating with smooth light gray areas. Inner bark light red.

Similar trees: Pin and Hill's oaks have smaller buds and more deeply lobed leaves. Black oak has larger, strongly angled, densely hairy buds; yellow inner bark; and brown, hairy acorn-cups with a fringe of loose scales around their rims. Black oak leaves are usually 5 to 7 lobed, with one pair of lobes distinctly larger than the others.

Distribution: Native as far west as the Missouri and Little Sioux rivers and the Spirit-Okoboji Lakes chain.

RED OAK is one of our most common and widely distributed oaks; it is native in all but a few counties of sparsely wooded northwestern Iowa. It occurs on a variety of sites ranging from stream terraces to dry ridges; but it is most frequently found on moist, well-drained, sheltered slopes with hard maple, basswood, bitternut hickory, black walnut, elms, and ashes. On the drier upland sites, it often occurs as a minor associate of white oak and shagbark hickory.

The wood of red oak is hard, strong, and heavy like that of other oaks; but it is somewhat weaker, less durable, and harder to saw and machine than the wood of white oak. It is widely used for furniture, veneer, flooring, pallets, boxes and crates, agricultural implements, lumber, and firewood and, when treated with preservatives, for railroad ties, mine timbers, and fence posts. The large pores of this species are not occluded with tyloses as are the large pores of white oaks, so its wood is unsuitable for the manufacture of barrels for holding liquids.

Red oak is one of the best native oaks for landscaping. It grows faster than most other oaks, sometimes maintaining a rate of 2 feet per year when young. Eventually it attains a height of 70 to 80 feet and a trunk diameter of 2 to 3 feet, developing a symmetrical, rounded crown casting dense shade. Its leaves are handsome throughout the summer months and turn red, orange-red, or deep reddish-brown in autumn. Although susceptible to oak wilt, red oak is otherwise rather free of serious diseases and insect pests.

The red oak is in fact a more suitable tree for planting in Iowa than the pin oak, which is probably the most popular oak used in landscaping here. It does not develop the attractive pyramidal shape for which the pin oak is so well known but is an equally handsome tree and rarely develops the leaf yellowing (chlorosis) that so often afflicts the pin oak.

Although little variation occurs in the acorns of most oaks, red oak acorns have two distinct forms. Acorns of typical red oaks have a saucer-shaped cup that barely covers the base of the nut; acorns of the northerly race *Q. rubra* var. *borealis* have a bowl-shaped cup that covers the lower ⅓ of the nut. Both types of red oak are native to Iowa, but the relative extent of their ranges here is unknown.

Black Oak, *Quercus velutina* Lam.

Distinguishing characteristics: *Leaves* 5 to 7 lobed, 5 to 9 inches long with moderately stout petioles 2 to 6 inches long; lobes bristle tipped, with one pair much larger than the others; largest lobes 2 to 6 times longer than the width of the central, undivided portion of the blade; sinuses broadly U shaped or circular; upper surface dark green and glossy; lower surface paler and either glabrous or hairy. *Buds* ovoid, ¼ to ½ inch long, strongly angled in cross section, densely covered with light brown hairs. *Acorns* ovoid, ½ to ¾ inch long, sessile or nearly so; cups bowl shaped or cone shaped with loose, light brown, hairy scales forming a conspicuous fringe around the rim, covering ⅓ to ½ of the nut. *Bark* thick, dark, and furrowed on lower trunk, similar to red oak on upper trunk. Inner bark yellow.

Similar trees: Red oak has shallower and more evenly lobed leaves; reddish inner bark; and smaller, glabrous, slightly angled buds. Hill's oak and scarlet oak have smaller, slightly angled buds that are either sparsely hairy (Hill's oak) or hairy on the upper half (scarlet oak). The acorn-cups of all three species have tightly appressed scales.

Distribution: Native in the southern and eastern halves of Iowa, though rare and local through most of the central and north central parts of the state. Many of the "black oaks" along the edge of the range are not typical of the species (see discussion below).

BLACK OAK is one of the most common upland trees of southern and eastern Iowa as well as much of the southeastern United States. It is usually encountered on dry ridges and slopes with white oak, bur oak, chinkapin oak, and shagbark hickory and can occasionally be found on moist uplands with basswood and red oak. In eastern Iowa it also occurs on stream terraces and bottomlands where the soil is sandy and very well drained.

Black oak is seldom used in landscaping in Iowa. Its glossy leaves have a good deal of ornamental value, but small trees are difficult to transplant and large specimens are less attractively shaped than most of our other native oaks. The leaves turn red or reddish-brown in autumn.

Black oak is less important commercially than the red and white oaks (although its wood is similarly hard, heavy, and strong) because it often grows in fairly open stands on poor, coarse-textured soils—an environment conducive to slow growth, reduced size, and retention of lower branches. Dead, persisting branches cause the wood to be knotty and provide convenient routes for decay fungi and wood boring insects to enter the trunks. However, black oaks grown on good soils in dense forests often rival red and white oaks in size, developing tall straight trunks that are nearly free of branches. The wood of such trees is marketed as "red oak."

Black oak provides an excellent example of the problems frequently found in the identification and classification of oaks. Most trees in southern and east central Iowa are quite typical of the species, having large, strongly angled, densely hairy buds and acorn-cups with loosely attached scales. However, some of the trees called "black oak" along the edge of this species' range in northeast and north central Iowa have small, slightly angled buds that are incompletely hairy and acorn-cups with tighter-fitting scales. Their leaves also differ from the black oaks in southern and eastern Iowa. These trees may be geographical variants of *Q. velutina* or they may be hybrids between this species and red oak or Hill's oak. Further study is needed to clarify the status of these atypical trees.

Black oak hybridizes with blackjack oak in southeast and south central Iowa, producing a hybrid known as *Q.* × *bushii* Sarg.

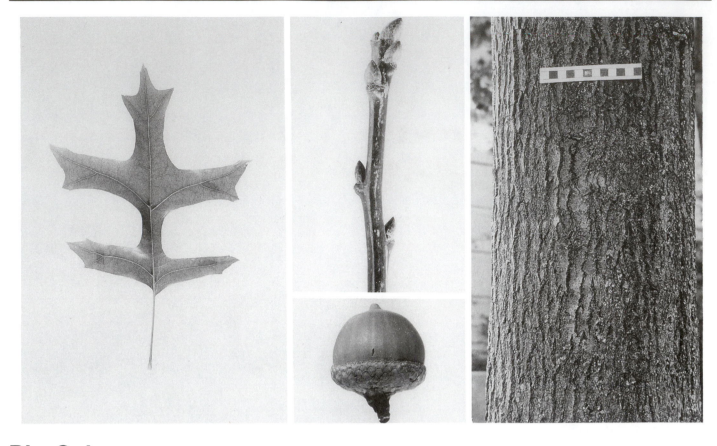

Pin Oak, *Quercus palustris* Muenchh.

Distinguishing characteristics: *Leaves* 5 to 7 lobed, 3 to 6 inches long with slender petioles ½ to 2 inches long; lobes bristle tipped, usually tapered to the tip, the larger ones 2 to 6 times longer than the width of the central, undivided portion of the blade, the lower pair curved downward and sometimes much smaller than the others; sinuses broadly U shaped or circular; upper surface dark green, glabrous, and glossy; lower surface paler, glabrous except for tufts of hairs in the axils of the large veins. *Buds* ovoid, ⅟₁₆ to ³⁄₁₆ (usually about ⅛) inch long, slightly angled, glabrous (sometimes with fine hairs along the edges of the scales). *Acorns* hemisphere shaped, ⅜ to ½ inch long, often striped with dark vertical lines, sessile or nearly so; cups saucer shaped with thin, appressed, red-brown scales, covering only the base of the nut. *Bark* on lower trunk gray-brown and shallowly furrowed, on upper trunk smooth and light gray, sometimes "striped" as in red oak.

Similar trees: Hill's oak has football-shaped acorns seated in cone-shaped cups that cover ⅓ to ½ of the nut. Red oak has larger buds and acorns, shallowly lobed leaves with narrow sinuses, and deeply furrowed bark. Scarlet and black oaks have larger buds that are either hairy above the middle (scarlet oak) or completely hairy (black oak). Their acorns are larger and have bowl-shaped or cone-shaped cups, with loose scales around the rim in black oak.

Distribution: Native along the Mississippi River and its lower tributaries north to Jackson County, including the drainages of the Wapsipinicon River to Jones County, the Iowa River to Johnson County, the Skunk River to Keokuk County, the Chariton River in Appanoose County, and the Thompson (Grand) River in Decatur County. Widely planted throughout the state.

PIN OAK is one of our most attractive native trees and the most popular oak for landscaping. Originally found only in eastern and southern Iowa, it has since been planted in every county.

The value of pin oak as an ornamental is due in large part to its handsome foliage and symmetric, pyramidal crown. Its glossy, finely dissected leaves are attractive throughout the summer and usually turn striking shades of red or purple in the fall. Like a conifer, its trunk often runs unforked to the top of the tree, producing many slender, lateral branches. The uppermost of these sweep skyward; the middle ones remain more or less horizontal; and the lowermost ones sweep downward, often touching the ground. Pin oak matures at a height of 70 to 80 feet, with a spread of 25 to 40 feet—not a tree for a small space!

Unfortunately, planted pin oaks are often afflicted with leaf yellowing, called chlorosis. This condition can greatly diminish a tree's ornamental value and in serious cases may lead to its decline and eventual death. Chlorosis is a complex problem that appears to be caused most often by nutrient deficiencies related to soil alkalinity. Certain nutrients, especially iron and manganese, are less soluble in alkaline soils and roots may be unable to absorb them in sufficient quantities. Poor drainage, drought, salt injury, excessive fertilizer application, and damage to the roots may also cause or contribute to chlorosis.

Where soil pH is above 7.5, the best solution is to consider trees other than pin oak. If an existing tree is chlorotic and a soil test has determined that soil alkalinity is probably the cause, consult a professional arborist to determine whether it is more practical to treat or replace the tree. The most lasting treatment involves acidification of the soil, soil application of any micronutrients that are deficient, and creation of a good environment for root growth by replacing turf under the tree with mulch. Another effective treatment is to implant nutrients directly into the trunk, but this wounds the tree and must be repeated every 2 to 4 years. Also, implantation treats only the symptoms and does not cure the cause of the problem.

Hill's Oak (Northern Pin Oak), *Quercus ellipsoidalis* E. J. Hill

Distinguishing characteristics: *Leaves* 5 to 7 lobed, 3 to 5 inches long with slender petioles 1 to 2 inches long; lobes bristle tipped, often broader at the end than the base, 2 to 6 times longer than the width of the central, undivided portion of the blade; sinuses U shaped or circular; upper surface bright green, glabrous, and glossy; lower surface paler, glabrous except for tufts of hairs in the axils of the large veins. *Buds* ovoid, ⅛ to 3/16 inch long, rounded to slightly angled in cross section, glabrous or sparsely covered with tiny pale hairs. *Acorns* broadly to narrowly football shaped, ½ to ¾ inch long, often striped with dark vertical lines, short stalked to nearly sessile; cups cone shaped with brown, hairy, tightly appressed scales, covering ⅓ to ½ of the nut. *Bark* similar to pin oak. Inner bark yellow.

Similar trees: Black oak has larger, strongly angled, densely hairy buds and acorn-cups with loose scales. Pin oak has squat acorns with saucer-shaped cups. Red oak has shallowly lobed leaves, larger buds, and reddish inner bark. (See also following discussion of scarlet oak.)

Distribution: Native in the northern half of the state west to the Little Sioux River, though rare in northwest Iowa.

THIS common but little-known tree is often mistaken for other oaks. Its leaves, twigs, and bark are so similar to those of pin oak that it is often called "northern pin oak," but its acorns are sufficiently distinct for most botanists to consider it a separate species. Hill's oak is also very similar to the scarlet and black oaks, and some botanists have suggested that it may be the product of hybridization of black oak and pin oak or merely a geographical variant of scarlet oak. It is known to hybridize with red oak in Minnesota and with black oak in eastern Iowa, and it may cross with these species in northern Iowa as well.

Hill's oak is named for E. J. Hill, who originally described it. It is primarily a tree of dry upland woods but it

can also be found on moist, sheltered slopes. Its common associates include bur, white, and red oaks; shagbark hickory; bigtooth and quaking aspens; chokecherry; and black cherry. Hill's oak usually attains a height of 60 to 70 feet and a trunk diameter of 2 to 3 feet but may be much smaller on sterile, sandy soil. It was apparently quite common along the prairie-forest border at the time of settlement, often becoming shrubby and invading the open prairie with bur oak, hazel, sumac, and other pioneer species.

Scarlet oak (*Quercus coccinea* Muenchh.) is an ornamental tree that closely resembles Hill's oak. It is common in the eastern United States but not native to Iowa. It is characterized by glossy leaves with 5 to 9 bristle-tipped lobes and deep circular sinuses, slightly angled buds ⅛ to ¼ inch long that are hairy on the upper half, and reddish inner bark. Its acorns, which are seated in bowl-shaped or cone-shaped cups with red-brown, closely appressed scales, are usually marked with distinctive concentric rings around their apices (see following figure).

Top and side view of scarlet oak acorn

Shingle Oak, *Quercus imbricaria* Michx.

Distinguishing Characteristics: *Leaves* oblong or elliptic, entire, tipped by a short slender bristle, 4 to 6 inches long with moderately stout petioles up to ¾ inch long; upper surface dark green, glabrous and glossy; lower surface paler and finely hairy. *Buds* ovoid, ⅛ to ³⁄₁₆ inch long, slightly angled, usually hairy, clustered at the twig tips. *Acorns* hemisphere shaped, ½ to ¾ inch long, short stalked; cups bowl shaped with tightly appressed brown scales, covering ⅓ to ½ of the nut. *Bark* gray-brown and shallowly furrowed on lower trunk, similar to pin oak above.

Similar trees: No other oak in Iowa has leaves that are neither lobed nor toothed. It is easily distinguished from magnolias, dogwoods, and other entire-leaved trees by its clustered end buds, acorns, and bristle-tipped leaf apices.

Distribution: Native from Lee County north to Muscatine County and west to Johnson, Marion, Union, and Taylor counties; also reported from Fremont County.

ONE would probably not guess this tree is an oak, if using its leaves alone for identification. Shingle oak leaves are not lobed like those of other native oaks, resembling more closely the leaves of a dogwood or magnolia. A careful inspection of each leaf, however, reveals that its midvein extends beyond its apex in the form of a short bristle, just as the veins do in the lobed leaves of the red oak and pin oak. The shingle oak's buds, acorns, and bark are also quite oaklike, leaving little doubt as to its identity.

Shingle oak is widely distributed across the southern third of Iowa but is common only in the eastern part of its range. It apparently tolerates a wider range of environmental conditions than other native oaks, as it occurs in several different habitats. Associated trees include hickories, other oaks, hawthorns, black cherry, and white ash in dry upland sites and elms, ashes, silver maple, hackberry, walnut, and pin oak in low-lying areas. It is also well adapted to and common on strip-mined soils in southeastern Iowa.

Shingle oak makes a handsome street and yard tree and could be more widely planted where it is hardy (southern half of Iowa). Growth is rather slow, as in most oaks, with the trees eventually attaining heights of 50 to 60 feet. Young trees have a pyramidal shape similar to pin oak, but the crowns of mature trees are often more open and rounded. The glossy, dark green leaves turn yellow or reddish-brown in late autumn, then fade to light brown and persist on the tree through most of the winter.

Shingle oak is relatively unimportant as a timber tree but its wood so closely resembles that of red oak that it is not distinguished from that species when sold. It has no distinctive uses today, but settlers discovered that it split easily and could be rived into shingles and shakes. Both the common and botanical names of the tree refer to this once widespread practice; *imbricaria* is Latin for "overlapping."

Several other oaks with unlobed, untoothed leaves occur in the southeastern United States. These trees are collectively known as "willow oaks" because the long, slender leaves of some species resemble those of willows and most species occur in low-lying, moist habitats. However, all have acorns; clustered end buds; and hard, heavy wood like other oaks. They are placed in the red oak group because their leaves have bristle tips, their acorns have hairy inner shells, and their wood is open pored.

American Elm, *Ulmus americana* L.

Distinguishing characteristics: *Leaves* simple, alternate, elliptic, 4 to 6 inches long with petioles about ¼ inch long, toothed; base unequal, surfaces glabrous or hairy; veins running directly to the teeth. *Winter twigs* similar to slippery elm, but typically glabrous and reddish-brown. *Buds* ⅛ to ¼ inch long, the flower buds larger and plumper than the ovoid leaf buds; scales 6 to 10, red-brown with dark margins, glabrous or nearly so, arranged in two vertical rows; the terminal bud absent. *Flowers* green, tinged with red, very small, perfect, without petals, on slender stalks up to 1 inch long, appearing in small umbellike clusters before the leaves unfold in early spring. *Fruit* an ovoid, 1-seeded samara about ½ inch long; wing glabrous with a hairy margin, broken at its apex by a deep notch extending nearly to the top of the seed cavity. *Bark* gray to gray-brown, divided into long, flat, scaly ridges separated by shallow to rather deep furrows; bark with alternating white and red-brown layers when viewed in cross section.

Similar trees: Leaves of other native elms closely resemble the leaves of American elm and their surfaces may vary from quite smooth to rough-hairy, so it is best distinguished from other species by buds and twigs. Ironwood, which also resembles this species, has leaves with equal or only slightly unequal bases. Its brown bud scales are spirally arranged and marked with fine parallel lines.

Distribution: Native throughout the state.

THE demise of American elms, once the most popular street and yard tree in America, ranks as one of the saddest chapters in botanical history. Fast growing, adaptable, and easily transplanted, the elm develops a graceful, vase-shaped crown that provides excellent shade. The accidentally introduced Dutch elm disease has now killed most of our larger trees, depriving future generations of the opportunity to appreciate the great beauty of elm-lined streets that were once taken for granted in our towns and cities.

Dutch elm disease is caused by a fungus parasite related to the organism responsible for oak wilt. It is spread over long distances by elm bark beetles and over short distances by natural root grafts between trees. Since elms cannot be cured once they have contracted the disease, the best solution is to prevent the fungus from becoming established in the trees. Infection can be reduced by community-wide survey, detection, and sanitation programs involving burning or burying infected and recently killed trees; treatment to prevent root graft transmission of the fungus; and preventing feeding by bark beetles. Another preventative measure is to inject trees with a systemic fungicide such as benomyl, a treatment that must be repeated periodically to be effective. Over the long run, the best solution is the development of hybrid elms that are resistant to the disease. However, this takes many years of selection and testing, and until such trees are widely available, it will be necessary to replace elms with other, disease-resistant species.

American elm is sometimes called *white elm* because its wood is so pale in color. The wood is hard, heavy, strong, and tough and is widely used for veneer; boxes; crates; barrel staves; and furniture, especially bent parts such as rockers and arms.

American elm was once a dominant tree in floodplain forests across most of Iowa. The death of the elms has opened up the forest canopy, providing space and sunlight for the growth of other species. Young elms are still common in many areas, being too small to attract the beetles that spread the disease.

Slippery Elm, *Ulmus rubra* Muhl.

Distinguishing characteristics: *Leaves* simple, alternate, elliptic, 4 to 7 inches long with petioles about ⅓ inch long, toothed; base unequal; upper surface dark green and rough-hairy, lower surface paler and hairy; veins running directly to the teeth. *Winter twigs* slender to moderate in diameter, ashy gray and often rough; bundle scars usually 3 (often compound into 4, 5, or 6), depressed within the surface of a pale brown, corky layer covering each of the small half-round leaf scars. *Buds* ⅛ to ¼ inch long, ovoid (leaf buds) to nearly globose (flower buds), the terminal absent; bud scales 6 to 10, dark purple, more or less covered with copper-colored hairs, overlapping in two vertical rows. *Flowers* green, very small, perfect, without petals, on stalks about 1/16 inch long, appearing in umbellike clusters before the leaves unfold in early spring. *Fruit* a 1-seeded, nearly round samara about ½ inch in diameter; wing glabrous, its apex shallowly notched; seed cavity distinct. *Bark* similar to American elm, but uniformly red-brown in cross section.

Similar trees: Siberian elm has smaller leaves and buds. Buds of American and rock elms are brown or red-brown and lack copper-colored hairs.

Distribution: Native throughout the state.

SLIPPERY ELM might seem an odd name for a tree whose leaves are as rough as sandpaper, but the adjective refers to the tree's mucilaginous inner bark. The inner bark has soothing properties and was once widely used as a wound dressing, poultice, and sore throat remedy. The species is also called *red elm* because its heartwood typically has a reddish cast.

Although it is not as well known as the American elm, slippery elm is as common and widely distributed in Iowa as its popular cousin. The leaves, outer bark, and growth form of the two trees are enough alike to cause them to be frequently confused, but in other characteristics the two are quite distinct: (1) The bud scales of American elm are smooth and red-brown with black margins, whereas those of slippery elm are dark purple to nearly black and have conspicuous copper-colored hairs. (2) The twigs of American elm are smooth and reddish-brown, while those of slippery elm are ashy-gray and often rough. (3) When the twigs are out of reach, a tree often can be distinguished by breaking off a chunk of the outer bark and cutting through a section of it. Slippery elm bark is uniformly red-brown in color, but American elm bark consists of alternating layers of red-brown and white.

Slippery elm, like the American elm, is very susceptible to Dutch elm disease. Large trees of both species were once common in floodplains and on moist, wooded slopes throughout the state. However, elms are prolific seeders and saplings of both species are still common in forest edges, waste places, and the woodland understory. They are not immune to the disease but survive because the bark beetles that spread the disease prefer to feed on larger trees.

Slippery elm was seldom used in landscaping even before the epidemic of Dutch elm disease. It is smaller than the American elm, typically attaining a height of 60 to 70 feet and a trunk diameter of 1½ to 2½ feet. It develops a vase-shaped crown similar to that of the American elm, but its twigs tend to point upward rather than droop. Its branching pattern thus lacks the graceful symmetry characteristic of the crown of its familiar cousin.

The wood of slippery elm is hard, heavy, strong, tough, and easier to split than that of American elm. It is used for boxes, crates, barrel staves, veneer, and bent parts of furniture such as rockers and arms.

Rock Elm, *Ulmus thomasii* Sarg.

Distinguishing characteristics: *Leaves* simple, alternate, elliptic to obovate, 2½ to 5 inches long with petioles about ¼ inch long, toothed; base equal or slightly unequal; upper surface glabrous; lower surface slightly hairy; veins running directly to the teeth. *Winter twigs* slender to moderate in diameter, glabrous to slightly hairy, light reddish-brown; branchlets gray-brown with thick corky outgrowths. *Buds* ovoid, ⅛ to ¼ inch long, gradually tapered to sharp-pointed tips, the terminal absent; bud scales 6 to 10, brown with dark margins, more or less hairy, arranged in two vertical rows. *Flowers* very small, perfect, without petals, on slender stalks up to ½ inch long, appearing in small racemes before the leaves in early spring. *Fruit* an obovate, 1-seeded samara about ½ inch long; wing hairy, shallowly notched at apex; seed cavity indistinct. *Bark* similar to American elm.

Similar trees: American and slippery elms have strongly unequal leaf bases and their branchlets lack corky outgrowths.

Distribution: Native throughout most of northeastern and north central Iowa; also rarely found in widely scattered localities in southern, western, and east central Iowa.

ROCK ELM would be easily overlooked if it were not for the corky outgrowths or "wings" on its small branches, for its bark, leaves, and buds are very similar to those of the more common American and slippery elms. It also differs from our other native elms in having a tall, straight trunk that remains unbranched for most of its length, even when grown in the open.

Large trees of rock elm, apparently uncommon even at the time of settlement, have become scarce because of timber clearing and Dutch elm disease. The species is usually found on floodplains, terraces, and the lower portion of moist slopes and can occasionally be encountered on rocky slopes and limestone bluffs. It grows slowly even on good sites, attaining a height of 50 to 80 feet and an age of 250 to 300 years (if not killed by Dutch elm disease). Common associates include hard maple, basswood, black ash, hackberry, black walnut, Kentucky coffee tree, swamp white oak, and other elms.

Rock elm would undoubtedly be an important timber tree if it were more common. Its wood is harder and stronger than that of other elms and it has a greater shock resistance than white oak. It was once widely used for iceboxes, washing machines, and kitchen furniture because it is so strong and easily cleaned and was the preferred material for the hubs and spokes of automobiles during the early days of the industry. Rock elm was highly esteemed for the manufacture of wooden sailing ships, as it is very durable in contact with water and is very difficult to split. Today it is usually marketed with American and slippery elms, though sometimes sold separately as "hard elm." Important uses include furniture, veneer, agricultural implements, hockey sticks, and ax handles.

The tiny flowers of rock elm, like other native elms, appear in early spring before the leaves. Each consists of a tiny greenish calyx, a single pistil, and 3 to 9 stamens with dark purple anthers. The flowers are arranged in an elongate cluster with a central axis, unlike those of American and slippery elms which occur in small bunches on the twigs. The pistil of each flower grows into a winged seed, or samara, about ½ inch long. The samaras ripen when the young leaves are about half-grown, whereupon they are dispersed by wind or water.

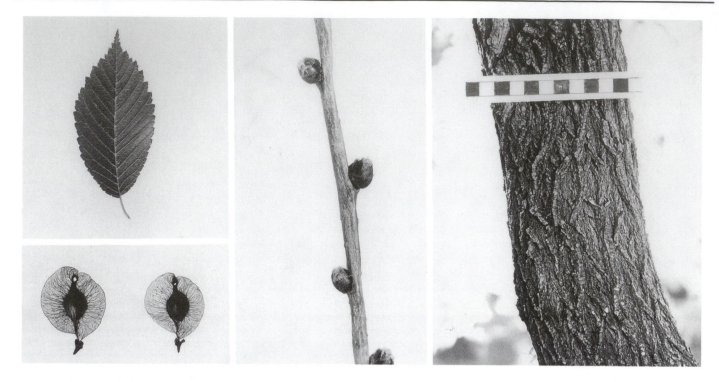

Siberian Elm, *Ulmus pumila* L.

Distinguishing characteristics: *Leaves* simple, alternate, elliptic to elliptic-lanceolate, 1 to 3 inches long with petioles $\frac{1}{16}$ to $\frac{1}{8}$ inch long, toothed; base slightly unequal; upper surface glabrous; lower surface glabrous or nearly so; veins running directly to the teeth. *Winter twigs* very slender, light gray or gray-green, glabrous or nearly so; leaf scars very small, otherwise similar to slippery elm. *Buds* ovoid or globose, $\frac{1}{16}$ to $\frac{3}{16}$ inch long, the terminal absent; scales 6 to 10, purple-brown, shiny, glabrous except for white hairs along their margins. *Flowers* green, very small, perfect, without petals, on stalks about $\frac{1}{16}$ inch long, appearing in crowded umbellike clusters before the leaves unfold in spring. *Fruit* a 1-seeded, nearly round samara about $\frac{1}{2}$ inch in diameter; wing glabrous, shallowly notched, seed cavity distinct. *Bark* gray-brown, shallowly furrowed with long scaly ridges, uniformly red-brown in cross section.

Similar trees: American, slippery, and rock elms have much larger leaves and buds.

Distribution: Cultivated throughout the state, often escaping to waste places.

THIS east Asian native has been widely planted and has even been advertised as the ideal shade tree, but its faults far outnumber its virtues. Like most fast growing trees, it has weak, brittle wood that breaks easily in storms. It is smaller and less attractively shaped than our native elms and is often troubled with wetwood, leaf-eating insects, and other pests that reduce its already limited usefulness as a shade tree. Also the Siberian elm produces large numbers of wind-blown seeds that begin new generations of trees in places where they are neither needed nor wanted. There seems little reason to plant this tree in Iowa, especially with so many native trees that are suitable for planting.

One redeeming feature of the Siberian elm is its resistance to Dutch elm disease and phloem necrosis, the two most serious diseases of our native elms. It is possible that the species could be used to develop hybrids that are desirable for landscaping, yet less susceptible to diseases. Crosses between this species and slippery elm have produced trees that are strong wooded and attractively shaped, though variable in disease resistance. The Siberian and American elms usually will not cross with one another.

All our common elms, native and introduced, are susceptible to a peculiar stem disease called wetwood. It is seldom fatal but can cause a chronic decline in the health of infected trees. It is caused by a bacterium that invades and ferments the sap in the trunk and larger branches. The gases resulting from this fermentation accumulate under pressure, causing the sap to exude or flux through wounds and run down the side of the tree. The fluxing sap is colorless; but it dries, leaving a pale-colored encrustation on the bark. Wetwood cannot be cured but its unpleasant effects can be lessened by installing small drain pipes below infected areas.

Siberian elm is often called "Chinese elm," a name more properly applied to another species of tree, *Ulmus parvifolia* Jacq. Its foliage resembles that of Siberian elm but its flowers and fruits appear in autumn instead of spring and it has brown buds. Its distinctive bark consists of irregularly shaped scales of orange, brown, and gray-green that fit together like the pieces of a jigsaw puzzle. Chinese elm is rarely planted in Iowa, but is a desirable medium-sized shade tree where it is winter hardy.

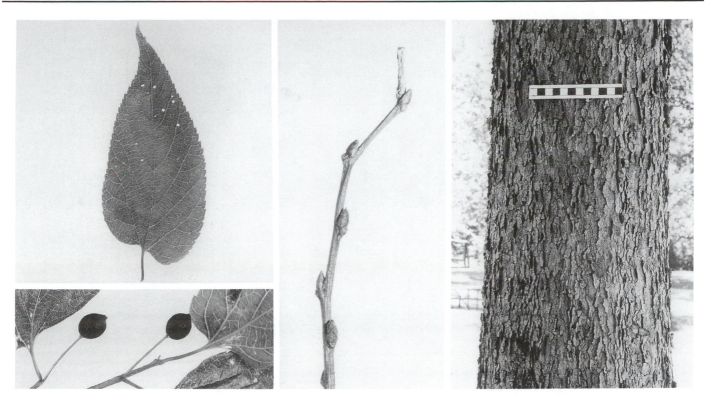

Hackberry, *Celtis occidentalis* L.

Distinguishing characteristics: *Leaves* simple, alternate, ovate, 2½ to 4 inches long with petioles ⅓ to ½ inch long; margins toothed (sometimes entire at base); veins forming a network near the margin, the largest three meeting in a single point at the base. *Winter twigs* very slender, light brown to gray-brown, usually glabrous; pith chambered at the nodes; leaf scars very small, half-round, with 3 (sometimes 1) bundle scars. *Buds* about ⅛ inch long, ovoid to triangular, closely appressed to the twig, the terminal absent; visible bud scales usually 3 or 4, light brown, finely and rather inconspicuously hairy. *Flowers* very small, greenish-yellow, either perfect or imperfect, apetalous, on slender stalks, solitary or in bunches of 2 or 3 from the axils of the newly unfolded leaves in spring. *Fruit* a dark purple drupe about ⅓ inch in diameter. *Bark* light to dark gray, with distinctive warty outgrowths.

Similar trees: No other tree has ovate leaves with strongly unequal bases. Winter: other trees with slender twigs have solid pith.

Distribution: Native throughout the state.

THE hackberry is one of our most common native trees, but it is unfamiliar to many people who easily recognize oaks, maples, and other common trees. Whatever the reason for this, it is certainly not due to a lack of distinctive features. No other tree has leaves quite like those of hackberry; and its rough warty bark, which is usually conspicuous even on saplings, is also unique. Few trees can be so easily recognized at all times of the year.

Hackberry makes a fine replacement for the American elm and is often grown as a street and lawn tree in Iowa. It grows moderately fast, tolerates poor soils and difficult urban conditions, withstands drought and windstorms, and develops a vase-shaped or rounded crown that casts excellent shade. It is usually a moderately large tree, 50 to 70 feet tall, with a trunk 1 to 2 feet in diameter; but it sometimes attains a height of nearly 100 feet and a trunk diameter of 4 feet when grown on fertile soils. Its leaves turn light yellow in autumn.

Hackberry has no serious diseases or insect enemies but is susceptible to several minor pests whose damage is mostly aesthetic. Nipple galls and witches' brooms are especially common. Nipple galls are small, nipple-shaped outgrowths from the leaves. They are caused by a tiny insect that can be controlled, if desired, by spraying at the appropriate time in spring. Witches' broom is a broomlike proliferation of short, stubby twigs, probably caused by as tiny gall mite and powdery mildew fungus. No cure is known, but the growths can be removed by pruning if desired.

Hackberry can be found in a wide variety of habitats, but it is primarily a tree of moist, low-lying woods. Its resistance to wind damage and its ability to grow well in poorly drained soils recommend it for windbreaks and conservation plantings on sites too wet for conifers.

The fruit of the hackberry is a small, hard, one-seeded pit surrounded by a thin flesh that tastes something like a prune or date. Hackberries are a favorite food of robins, flickers, cardinals, cedar waxwings, brown thrashers, and several other small birds. They are especially valuable as a wildlife food because they persist on the twigs into winter, long after other foods have become scarce. The pits pass unharmed through the digestive tracts of birds, which explains the prevalence of young hackberry trees in woods, fencerows, and thickets.

The wood of hackberry is flexible; shock resistant; and moderately strong, hard, and heavy. It resembles elm but typically has wider sapwood and distinctive yellow streaks. It is used for furniture, millwork, sporting goods, and veneer for plywood and containers.

White Mulberry, *Morus alba* L.

Distinguishing characteristics: *Leaves* simple, alternate, either lobed or unlobed (both types usually present on same tree), ovate-oval, 2½ to 4 (rarely up to 7) inches long with petioles ⅜ to 1 inch long; sap milky; margins with coarse and usually blunt teeth; base heart shaped or truncate, unequal; apex blunt or short pointed; upper surface glabrous and glossy; lower surface glabrous or with hairs restricted to the larger veins and vein axils. *Winter twigs* very slender, glabrous, gray-brown; leaf scars small, half-round to nearly round, concave, with 6 or more bundle scars. *Buds* globose or triangular, about ⅛ inch long, closely appressed to the twig, the terminal absent; scales 3 to 6, brown, glabrous. *Flowers* monoecious or dioecious, in catkins, appearing with the leaves in late spring. *Fruit* blackberrylike, ⅜ to 1 inch long, red or purple (rarely white) when ripe. *Bark* smooth and light orange-brown on young trees and branches of large trees, brown and furrowed on trunks of mature trees.

Similar trees: Red mulberry has larger leaves with hairy undersurfaces and long-pointed tips. Winter: red mulberry has ovoid buds that angle away from the twigs; all other trees with similar twigs have only 3 bundle scars.

Distribution: Naturalized throughout the state.

WHITE MULBERRY was not present in Iowa when the settlers arrived but is as firmly established in our flora today as any native tree. It is the traditional food for silkworms in its native China and was introduced into this country in the seventeenth century in an attempt to start a silk industry here. The venture failed because of high labor costs, but the white mulberry successfully adapted to its new environment and is now naturalized over most of the eastern United States.

The leaves of white mulberry are unusual in that they can be either lobed or unlobed, with both types usually present on the same tree and often on the same branch. The only tree whose leaves resemble them in shape is our native red mulberry, a relatively uncommon tree of southern and extreme eastern Iowa. However, the leaves of red mulberry are much larger with hairy surfaces and long-pointed tips, making it easy to identify the two species.

The blackberrylike fruit of the white mulberry is eagerly sought by robins, cardinals, orioles, catbirds, brown thrashers, waxwings, starlings, woodpeckers, raccoons, skunks, opossums, squirrels, and many other small animals. Many people also appreciate mulberries, fresh or in pies, jellies, and wines. The fruits vary in sweetness and color from one tree to the next; the usual color is red or purple but white-fruited trees can be found.

White mulberry is a weed tree in the true sense of the word. Its seeds are not harmed by passing through the digestive tracts of animals, so young trees are continually appearing in open woods, wood edges, fencerows, pine plantations, and other places frequented by birds. The trees grow quickly and tolerate a wide variety of soils and conditions, including difficult urban environments. Once established, mulberries are very difficult to eradicate; they sprout vigorously from the roots whenever the stems are cut down. The trees usually reach a height of about 30 feet at maturity but may grow as tall as 50 feet.

The dense, rounded crown of the white mulberry provides good shade and male trees can be used for street and yard plantings. Female trees should be avoided as their ripe fruits are very messy, staining sidewalks and driveways beneath the tree.

Red Mulberry, *Morus rubra* L.

Distinguishing characteristics: *Leaves* simple, alternate, broadly oval to nearly round, often 2 to 5 lobed on younger shoots, 3 to 9 inches long with petioles ¾ to 1¼ inches long; sap milky; margins toothed; base more or less heart shaped; apex abruptly tapered to a long slender point; upper surface either glabrous or rough hairy; lower surface finely hairy along veins and veinlets. *Winter twigs* slender, reddish-brown, glabrous; leaf scars small, nearly round, concave, with 6 or more bundle scars. *Buds* ovoid, ⅛ to ¼ inch long, the terminal absent; scales 3 to 6, greenish-brown with dark-colored margins. *Flowers* monoecious or dioecious, in catkins, appearing with leaves in late spring. *Fruit* blackberrylike, oblong, 1 to 1¼ inches long, dark purple when ripe. *Bark* dark brown with a reddish tinge, dividing into shallow furrows and scaly ridges.

Similar trees: Leaves of white mulberry or basswood are often mistaken for leaves of this species (see discussion below). Winter: white mulberry has appressed buds that are typically as wide as long; all other trees with similar twigs have only 3 bundle scars.

Distribution: Native across the southern half of the state, north along the Mississippi River to the Minnesota border and the Des Moines River to Webster County; also reported in Winneshiek and Delaware counties.

RED MULBERRY is the only species of mulberry native to Iowa, but in many parts of its range it is much less common than the introduced white mulberry. An understory tree of floodplains, ravines, and moist sheltered slopes, it rarely exceeds a height of 50 feet or a trunk diameter of 15 inches.

Red mulberry is similar to white mulberry but typically has much larger leaves, buds, and fruits. Its leaves also differ from white mulberry in having hairy undersurfaces and long-pointed tips. As in white mulberry, both lobed and unlobed leaves are often, but not always, present on the same tree; and individuals having leaves that are predominantly or entirely unlobed are quite common. Such trees are frequently mistaken for basswood, although a careful comparison of the two reveals several differences. Basswood leaves have smooth surfaces and noticeably lopsided bases, whereas those of red mulberry have hairy or rough surfaces and nearly equal bases. The leaves of basswood are also shorter relative to their width. Basswood buds have two bright red scales and those of mulberry have several greenish-brown scales with dark margins.

The juicy fruits of the red mulberry resemble those of the white mulberry but are larger and tastier. As in the blackberry, each "berry" is an aggregation of many tiny fruits packed together. However, a blackberry develops from a single flower with numerous pistils, whereas a mulberry is derived from a cluster of closely spaced flowers. The fruits of fig and osage orange trees are similar to those of mulberries in this respect and botanists consider them to be closely related. Male and female flowers often occur on separate trees, so not all individuals bear fruit.

Red mulberry is seldom used in landscaping in Iowa. It develops a dense, rounded crown casting good shade; but its fruits are very messy, staining sidewalks and driveways beneath the tree.

The wood of red mulberry is rather weak yet hard, heavy, and very durable in contact with the soil. It is unimportant commercially because of the scarcity and small size of the available timber, but it is used locally for fence posts, boatbuilding, and furniture.

Red mulberry has had several other uses that are of interest historically. Its bark contains tough fibers that can be used to make threads and cords. The Choctaws of the southeastern United States wove the fibers into cloaks and the Spanish conquistadors twisted them into ropes for their ships. The colonists in Jamestown used the leaves as food for silkworms in a futile attempt to start a silkworm industry in America.

Osage Orange, *Maclura pomifera* (Raf.) Schneid.

Distinguishing characteristics: *Leaves* simple, alternate, ovate to oblong-ovate, 3 to 5 inches long with petioles 1½ to 2 inches long, entire, with milky sap; leaf surfaces glabrous. *Winter twigs* moderate in diameter, brown, glabrous, usually with thorns ⅛ to ½ inch long and short spur shoots; leaf scars small, half-round or triangular, with 3 or more frequently consolidated bundle scars. *Buds* globose, about 1/16 inch in diameter, the terminal absent; scales 4 or 5, brown, glabrous. *Flowers* green, very small, monoecious or dioecious, without petals, appearing with the leaves in spring, the staminate in racemes and the pistillate in globe-shaped heads. *Fruit* ball shaped, 3 to 5 inches in diameter, composed of many tiny drupelike units; rind yellow-green and wrinkled, interior suffused with a milky, sticky sap. *Bark* orange and/or dark brown, divided into flat, often shreddy ridges separated by shallow furrows.

Similar trees: Russian-olive is the only other tree that combines entire leaves and thorny twigs. However, it is much different in appearance, with leaves that are linear to narrowly lanceolate in shape. Winter: honey locust, hawthorns, and wild crab apple have larger thorns.

Distribution: Once widely planted for living fences and shelterbelts across southern and parts of eastern Iowa; now escaped to pastures, ravines, woods, and other uncultivated areas.

THE osage orange is perhaps best known for its peculiar fruit, which often exceeds a grapefruit in size. These "hedge apples," as they are often called, are so large and produced in such abundance that it seems a shame to let them lie on the ground unused. Unfortunately, the fruit is filled with a sticky, milk-colored sap that makes the pulp unpalatable even to birds and other animals. Squirrels and quail eat the seeds, but the osage orange is more valuable to wildlife as a source of nesting and protective cover than as a source of food.

A close examination of an individual hedge apple re veals that what appears to be a single fruit is actually an aggregation of many tiny, one-seeded fruits packed together. Each of these constituent fruits is derived from a single pistillate flower that occurs with many others of its kind in a dense, ball-shaped cluster ¾ to 1 inch in diameter. The pistillate and staminate flower clusters appear when the leaves unfold in spring, usually on different trees. Thus, some trees never produce the large multiple fruits and must be recognized by other means.

Osage orange is native to a small area in eastern Texas, southeastern Oklahoma, and southwestern Arkansas but has been extensively planted across much of the Midwest. It was widely touted as a "living fence" during the midnineteenth century because it transplanted easily, withstood wind and extremes of temperature, tolerated both wet and droughty soils, had no serious diseases and insect pests, and (most important) its thorny branches provided an impenetrable barrier to livestock. However, hedges of osage orange had disadvantages as well. A living fence required several years of growth before becoming effective and the young trees were easily destroyed by fires, sheep, or small animals. Once established, a hedge could not be moved; and it took up considerable room and cast unneeded shade. Such drawbacks were acceptable to farmers where traditional fencing materials were unavailable, but once barbed wire was invented, the popularity of living fences declined abruptly. The original trees have persisted in fencerows across much of southern Iowa and their offspring can now be seen in pastures, ravines, and woods.

The wood of osage orange is extremely hard, heavy, tough, and durable; and it shrinks or swells very little compared to the wood of other trees. It is a golden yellow or bright orange when first cut but turns brown on exposure. Today it is used primarily for fence posts, insulator pins, and treenails; at one time it was extensively employed for archery bows. Both wood and bark contain a yellow dye that can be extracted by soaking in lukewarm water.

Saucer Magnolia, *Magnolia ×soulangeana* Soul.

Distinguishing characteristics: *Leaves* simple, alternate, obovate, 3 to 6 inches long, entire, glabrous above and more or less hairy below. *Winter twigs* moderate in diameter, dark red-brown or greenish-brown, glabrous or sparsely hairy; stipule scars forming a ring around the twig at each node; leaf scars crescent shaped, rather small, with a half dozen or more bundle scars. *Buds* ovoid; single scaled; densely covered with long, soft, greenish hairs; the terminal ½ to ¾ inch long and the laterals much smaller. *Flowers* very large; perfect; with 6 usually pinkish petals and 3 smaller, similarly colored sepals; solitary at the twig tips; appearing before the leaves in spring. *Fruit* a conelike aggregate of small follicles, each with 1 or 2 red, fleshy seeds suspended by slender filaments. *Bark* smooth, light gray.

Similar trees: No other tree having entire leaves or large, hairy terminal buds has stipule scars that completely encircle the twig.

Distribution: Cultivated across the southern two-thirds of the state.

MOST magnolias are trees of warm, southern climates but the saucer magnolia, a hybrid between two Asian species, is hardy across much of Iowa. It is cultivated primarily for its large, showy flowers that appear before the leaves in mid to late April. They vary from white to deep purple in color, depending on variety, but are rose-pink in most of the trees grown in Iowa.

Saucer magnolia often grows 20 to 30 feet tall, but its general appearance is more shrub- than treelike. Its trunk usually divides a few inches above the ground, giving way to a broad, rounded crown of numerous upward-curving branches. Trees should be grown in a protected spot, as the flowers are easily destroyed by spring winds and late frosts.

Star magnolia [*M. stellata* (Sieb. and Zucc.) Maxim.] and cucumber tree (*M. acuminata* L.) are two other magnolias that are occasionally cultivated in Iowa. Star magnolia, a native of Japan, is very similar to the saucer magnolia but has smaller leaves and buds and has flowers with 12 to 18 white sepals and petals. Cucumber tree, a large forest tree of the eastern United States, has green flowers that appear after its leaves in late spring.

Pawpaw, *Asimina triloba* (L.) Dunal

Distinguishing characteristics: *Leaves* simple, alternate, obovate-lanceolate, 6 to 12 inches long with petioles ¼ to ⅜ inch long, entire, very thin, glabrous except when young. *Winter twigs* moderate in diameter, red-brown, with diaphragmed pith; leaf scars crescent shaped, small, with 5 or 7 bundle scars. *Buds* densely covered with reddish-brown hairs but lacking scales, globe shaped and stalked (flower buds) or elongate and nearly sessile (leaf buds), the terminal ¼ to ½ inch long and the laterals smaller. *Flowers* large, perfect, appearing with the leaves in late spring, greenish at first but eventually brown or dark purple. *Fruit* an oblong, edible berry 2 to 5 inches long and 1 to 1½ inches in diameter, ripening in autumn. *Bark* smooth with small warty thickenings, light gray to brown.

Similar trees: Other trees with entire leaves have longer petioles and smaller leaf blades. Winter: no other tree has nonscaled buds clothed with reddish-brown hairs.

Distribution: Native in scattered localities along the Mississippi River north to Dubuque County, along the Des Moines River in Lee and Van Buren counties, and along the loess hills in Fremont County.

PAWPAW is one of our rarest and most unusual native trees. It is known in only a few counties in the eastern and southwestern parts of the state, where it forms thickets in wooded ravines, along the bases of bluffs, and in low-lying woods along streams. It is also one of our smallest native trees, seldom exceeding a height of 20 to 30 feet and a trunk diameter of 3 to 4 inches. Its unique leaves, buds, flowers, and fruits make it an easy species to identify at all times of the year.

Perhaps the most interesting feature of this tree is its fruit, a large, irregularly shaped, somewhat elongated berry called a pawpaw or custard apple. Its skin changes from green to greenish-yellow as the fruit ripens in autumn, then gradually turns black. Though not the most attractive of fruits, its sweet, yellow or orange flesh has a distinctive flavor that is appreciated by oppposums, raccoons, foxes, and many people.

Sycamore, *Platanus occidentalis* L.

Distinguishing characteristics: *Leaves* simple, alternate, 4 to 7 inches long, palmately 3 to 5 lobed with the margins of the lobes coarsely toothed. *Winter twigs* moderate in diameter, glabrous, orange-brown to light brown; stipule scars forming a narrow ring around the twig at each node; leaf scars ring shaped, completely encircling the buds, each with 5 to 9 bundle scars. *Buds* cone shaped, ¼ to ⅜ inch long, hidden within the base of the petiole, each covered with a single glabrous, brown scale; the terminal bud absent. *Flowers* very tiny; monoecious; crowded in small, ball-shaped heads that appear when the leaves are unfolding in late spring. *Fruit* ball shaped, about 1 inch in diameter, on a slender stalk 3 to 6 inches long, composed of numerous tiny achenes. *Bark* of branches and upper trunk either smooth and chalk white or mottled with thin, irregularly shaped patches of white and tan; on lower trunks composed of small light gray or reddish-brown plates.

Similar trees: Leaves of maples are arranged oppositely on the twigs. Winter: no other tree except the closely related London plane (see discussion below) has both twig-encircling stipule scars and bud-encircling leaf scars.

Distribution: Native or naturalized across most of the southern one-half to two-thirds of the state; cultivated throughout.

THE sycamore is one of our largest and most distinctive native trees. It grows faster than any native tree except the cottonwood and silver maple, developing a massive trunk 3 to 8 feet in diameter and a broad, spreading crown up to 100 feet tall. Its unusually large leaves, attractive mottled bark, and persistent seedballs allow it to be easily recognized at all times of the year.

Sycamore is often planted as a yard and street tree in Iowa because of its rapid growth and handsome appearance. It has stronger wood and is much longer lived than most other fast-growing trees. Sycamore is only marginally hardy in northern Iowa and trees planted on exposed sites in that part of the state may suffer twig dieback in severe winters.

The principal disadvantage of sycamore in landscap-ing is its susceptibility to anthracnose, a fungus disease. Anthracnose is ubiquitous on sycamore in Iowa, although the severity of infection varies greatly from year to year. Problems can be expected when the weather is wet and the average daily temperature is lower than 55°F during the two-week period following leaf emergence in spring. The disease is rarely fatal but may temporarily reduce the shade a tree provides in spring by killing its young leaves and shoots. (When this happens, new leaves will be produced by early summer.) Anthracnose may also weaken the tree, making it more susceptible to other diseases, insect pests, and winter injury. Control programs should include sanitation and spraying with a suitable fungicide when the weather is favorable for growth of the fungus in spring.

Native sycamores can be found along stream banks and river bottoms across most of southern, central, and east central Iowa. Though sometimes a dominant component of the forest canopy, sycamore occurs more often as a minor associate of cottonwood, silver maple, willow, and other trees.

The wood of sycamore is moderately hard and heavy, strong, and resistant to shock; but it rots quickly when exposed to conditions favoring decay and is rather difficult to work. It is used largely for veneer, flooring, boxes and crates, concealed parts of furniture, sugar and flour barrels, and pallets. It is also used for butcher blocks because it is very difficult to split.

The London plane tree [*Platanus* ×*acerifolia* (Ait.) Willd.] is a hybrid between the American and oriental sycamores that is sometimes planted as an ornamental in Iowa. It differs from the native sycamore in having more deeply lobed leaves and 2 or 3 seedballs per stalk instead of 1.

prairie crab apple ▶

apple

Crab Apples, Apples, and Pears, *Pyrus* (including *Malus* Mill.)

Distinguishing characteristics: *Leaves* simple, alternate, usually toothed, lobed in some species; veins usually ending or forming a network near the margin (running into the lobe tips in our native species). *Winter twigs* moderate in diameter, thorny in some species; spur shoots usually present; leaf scars linear or crescent shaped, small, with 3 bundle scars. *Buds* subglobose to ovoid, usually with 3 or more scales, usually hairy at least along the edges of the scales. *Flowers* showy, perfect, variously colored, in corymb- or umbellike cymes at the ends of the spur shoots, appearing either shortly before, with, or shortly after the leaves in spring; petals 5 or more, obovate or round; stamens numerous; ovary inferior with 2 to 5 styles. *Fruit* a pome, the seeds separated from the outer flesh by a thin, cartilaginous partition. *Bark* smooth or scaly, gray to reddish-brown in color.

Similar trees: Serviceberries and hawthorns are the only other simple-leaved trees with fruits that are pomes. Serviceberries have elongate buds; hawthorns have ball-shaped, glabrous buds and smooth thorns with no attached leaves or visible leaf scars.

Distribution: One native and several introduced species are common (see discussion below).

APPLES and pears are familiar to everyone, and one might expect the trees to be as dissimilar as their fruits. Instead, the various species so resemble one another in foliage, bud, flower, wood, and other features that most botanists place them in a single genus. Even fruits can lead one astray, with some pears resembling apples and vice versa. The so-called Asian pear, now available in many supermarkets, is a good example.*

Similarly, the difference between apples and crab apples is more commercial than botanical. Horticulturists usually define an apple as a tree having a fruit more than 2 inches in diameter and a crab apple as any tree with a smaller fruit. In fact, several of the wild Eurasian crab apples are more closely related to the apple (*Pyrus malus* L.) than they are to the American crabs.

For purposes of discussion, the following text separates the apples, crab apples, and pears into three artificial categories: 1) wild species, 2) ornamental crab apples, and 3) ornamental pears. Apples and pears grown primarily for fruit are not considered in this book; for more information on these trees, contact your local extension office.

Wild Species

The only member of the genus definitely native to Iowa is the prairie or Iowa crab, *Pyrus ioensis* (Wood) Carruth. This small, often thorny tree grows 25 to 30 feet tall with an open, rounded crown. It can be found in open woods, fencerows, wood edges, prairie remnants, and abandoned pastures throughout all but extreme northwestern Iowa. The botanist who named this species described it from an Iowa specimen, hence the name *ioensis*, meaning "of Iowa."

Prairie crab is characterized by oblong-ovate leaves 2¼ to 4 inches long that are shallowly lobed, toothed, and persistently hairy on their lower surface and petioles; by densely hairy sepals and flower stalks; and by green fruits ¾ to 1 inch in diameter. It is sometimes mistaken for a hawthorn because of similarities in leaf, branch, and habit of growth, but can be distinguished by its larger fruits, hairy buds and twigs, and the presence of leaves on its thorns.

Prairie crab can also be mistaken for the common apple, *P. malus,* which can sometimes be found growing wild in old orchards and near abandoned farmsteads. It resembles the prairie crab in having hairy buds and twigs, but its leaves are rolled (rather than folded) in the bud and are unlobed.

---

*Some authorities disagree with the "lumping" of all these species into a single genus and segregate them into two genera. According to this interpretation, *Malus* is composed of species having the styles united at base and the fruits containing few or no stone cells (i.e., the apples and crab apples); *Pyrus* (pears) has separate styles and abundant stone cells.

flowering crab apple

Ornamental Crab Apples

Crab apples have long been the most popular of our small flowering trees. Hardy and adaptable, they put on a floral display that no other tree can match. They are also unmatched in variety; one can find a crab having flowers of almost any desired shade between white and red, and fruits of any size between a pea and a small apple. A complete discussion of all the types grown in Iowa would require a book in itself.

Crab apples are planted primarily for their flowers, but many have attractive fruits that add ornamental value in autumn and winter. The fruits are useful in other respects, too—small varieties attract robins, cedar waxwings, and other birds, while some larger varieties make excellent jelly. Most horticulturists recommend that fruits be given as much consideration as flowers when selecting a cultivar.

As a group, crab apples are subject to a great many diseases and insect pests. Rust, scab, powdery mildew, fireblight, borers, tent caterpillar, and scales can be especially troublesome. Cultivars differ greatly in their susceptibility to diseases, and only resistant ones should be planted. For information about the cultivars best suited to Iowa, see Olson's "Landscape Plants for Iowa."

These and other cultivars can be viewed at arboretums in Iowa and neighboring states. The Arie Den Boer Arboretum in Des Moines' Waterworks Park and the Morton Arboretum in Lisle, Illinois, have particularly fine collections.

Ornamental Pears

For years pears were grown almost exclusively for fruit. The common edible pear from Europe, *Pyrus communis* L., was the only one commonly seen in Iowa. More recently, the desirability of pears for landscaping has also become apparent.

Of special value are the cultivars of Callery pear, *P. calleryana* Dcne., a native of China. These trees offer showy displays of white flowers in spring; attractive, dark glossy leaves throughout the summer; and brilliant red and crimson foliage in late fall, after many other species have lost their leaves for the year. They are also resistant to fireblight, a serious disease of some other pears.

'Bradford' was the earliest and most widely planted cultivar. Growing 30 to 50 feet tall at maturity, it develops a broadly pyramidal to rounded crown. It has proved to be an adaptable and useful tree but is prone to weak crotches that may split in storms. Some newer cultivars have stronger, more horizontal branching.

Callery pear can be identified by its glabrous, ovate to roundish leaves 1½ to 3 inches long with shallow, rounded teeth; wooly buds ¼ to ½ inch long; and round, brown fruits about ⅜ inch in diameter.

The Ussury pear, *P. ussuriensis* Maxim., is another species that has shown promise in arboretum plantings, although it is not commonly available in nurseries. A native of northeastern Asia, it tolerates colder temperatures than other pears and is very resistant to fireblight. Ussury pear grows 30 to 50 feet tall with a broad, rounded crown.

Ussury pear is characterized by glabrous, ovate leaves 2 to 4 inches long with bristle-tipped teeth; brown, nearly glabrous buds ⅛ to ½ inch long; and roundish, greenish-yellow fruits about 1½ inches in diameter.

European Mountain-ash, *Pyrus aucuparia* (L.) Gaertn. (*Sorbus aucuparia L.*)

Distinguishing characteristics: *Leaves* once-pinnately compound, alternate; leaflets usually 13 or 15 in number (rarely 9, 11, or 17), 1 to 2¼ inches long, oblong with a blunt or acute tip, toothed, persistently hairy beneath. *Winter twigs* moderate in diameter, glabrous, gray or reddish-brown; leaf scars linear or crescent shaped, raised, each with 5 (rarely 3 or 7) bundle scars. *Buds* ovoid, with dark reddish-purple scales, the terminal ⅜ to ¾ inch long and more or less covered with pale hairs, much larger than the laterals. *Flowers* white, perfect, in showy corymblike cymes, appearing after the leaves in late spring. *Fruit* a pome about ⅜ inch in diameter, bright red or orange when ripe. *Bark* smooth and bronze-colored on young trees, becoming gray and slightly roughened on older trees.

Similar trees: Walnuts, hickories, and sumacs are the only other trees having alternate, pinnately compound leaves with toothed leaflets; and their leaflets are much larger than those of the mountain-ash. Winter: other trees having large hairy terminal buds with more than one scale have larger and more conspicuous leaf scars.

Distribution: Cultivated throughout the state and occasionally escaping to the wild.

THIS popular ornamental tree is not an ash at all but a close relative of the apple, crab apples, and pear. Its compound leaves resemble those of the ashes in shape, which probably explains the "ash" in its name, but they are arranged alternately on the twig instead of being attached opposite one another in the manner of true ashes. Its flowers and fruits are also quite different from those of the ashes, a further clue that it belongs in another family. The English avoid this confusing state of affairs by calling this species the *Rowan tree,* but the name *mountain-ash* has been used for so long in America that it is probably here to stay.

Mountain-ash develops an oval to rounded, rather open crown and attains a height of 20 to 40 feet. It is planted primarily for the large clusters of bright orange or reddish fruits that decorate its branches in late summer and early fall. A mountain-ash in full bloom is also an attractive sight; though less spectacular than the flowering crabs, redbud, and many other spring-blooming trees, it is a welcome addition to the late spring landscape. The dark green foliage contrasts vividly with both flowers and fruits, enhancing their appeal.

Unfortunately, this beautiful tree is not well adapted to our hot, dry summers and is susceptible to several diseases and insect pests. Apparently healthy trees may decline and die unexpectedly, just when they are reaching their prime as landscape specimens. Pest problems can be minimized by planting trees in fertile, well-drained soil and providing good care (see Chapter 2), but anyone planting a mountain-ash should be aware that this species is often short lived in cultivation.

The fruit of the mountain-ash is berrylike in size and general appearance but its development and internal structure is virtually identical to the pome of an apple, crab apple, or pear. Though unpalatable to people, these small pomes are eagerly devoured by robins, catbirds, cedar waxwings, grosbeaks, and other fruit-eating songbirds. This must have impressed botanists centuries ago, for the Latin name of the mountain-ash is *aucuparia,* which means "bird-catching."

The American mountain-ash [*P. americana* (Marsh.) DC] and showy mountain-ash [*P. decora* (Sarg.) Hyland] differ from the European mountain-ash in having sticky-scaled terminal buds that are nearly hairless (*P. americana*) to red-hairy on the inner scales (*P. decora*). These species range as far south as southwestern Wisconsin and may be native in northeastern Iowa as well, although there are no confirmed reports of their occurrence there.

Hawthorns, *Crataegus* L.

Distinguishing characteristics: *Leaves* simple, alternate, toothed, shallowly lobed in most species. *Winter twigs* slender to moderate; usually armed with slender, unbranched, sharp-pointed thorns at least 1 inch long (commonly smooth surfaced and often shiny); leaf scars small, half-round or crescent shaped, with 3 bundle scars. *Buds* globose to subglobose, with about 6 glabrous, fleshy and usually reddish scales; lateral buds often nearly equal to the terminal in size. *Flowers* perfect, in showy corymblike cymes, appearing with or shortly after the leaves in late spring; petals 5, white, nearly round; stamens 5 to 25; ovary inferior, with 1 to 5 styles. *Fruit* a small, usually reddish pome with 1 to 5 nutlike seeds. *Bark* gray to brown, scaly; branched thorns occasionally present on trunk.

Similar trees: Wild plum and wild crab apple are the only other trees with simple, toothed leaves and thorny twigs. Leaves and buds are commonly present along the surface of their thorns; hawthorns have no leaves on the thorns and buds are restricted to the base of the thorns. Winter: honey locust has stout, branched thorns and its buds are embedded in the leaf scars.

Distribution: Native and cultivated throughout the state (see following pages for ranges of individual species).

FEW tasks are more difficult than sorting out the numerous kinds of hawthorns that grow wild in North America; several hundred "species" have been described in the northeastern quarter of the United States alone. Although many of these are probably hybrids and varieties, even the valid species are so much alike that only specialists can recognize them with any degree of certainty. No wonder that most people are content to call these trees hawthorns and leave it at that!

Hawthorns are at most only small trees, and in poor soils they are often no more than shrubs. An individual 25 feet tall with a trunk 8 inches in diameter would be large for most species, although some (such as the downy hawthorn) reaches heights of 35 to 40 feet and diameters of 12 to 18 inches.

Hawthorns, being intolerant of shade, are usually found in open woods, clearings, woods edges, fencerows, and other well-lighted environments. They are very aggressive in invading pastures, prairies, and abandoned farmland near woods, although they grow more slowly than most pioneer trees. Most species will grow in a variety of soils, and some are found commonly in both bottomlands and uplands.

The small, applelike fruits of hawthorns are called "haws" or "thorn apples." They vary in size, color, and shape from one species to another but are commonly round, 1/4 to 1/2 inch in diameter, and red when ripe in late summer and early fall. They also vary considerably in texture and taste; the fruits of some species are dry, mealy, and insipid, while others are quite sweet and fleshy. Each haw contains from 1 to 5 bony seeds or nutlets that make up the bulk of the fruit. Haws are eaten by many small birds and mammals including pheasants, grouse, cedar waxwings, robins, fox sparrows, raccoons, skunks, and squirrels.

Some kinds of hawthorns make fine ornamental trees, but their limitations should be weighed against their assets before they are chosen. They tolerate poor soils; develop rugged, picturesque silhouettes; produce attractive flowers and fruits; and frequently color well in autumn. However, most species have very sharp thorns and as a group they are subject to many diseases and insects. Leaf rust, which spreads from eastern redcedar and other junipers to hawthorns, is especially troublesome for some species.

The wood of hawthorns is hard, heavy, and tough—the botanical name *Crataegus* is derived from the Greek word for strength. The wood is occasionally used for tool handles, canes, small turned articles, and fuel; but it is unimportant commercially because the trees are small and usually crooked.

The number of hawthorns native to Iowa is not certainly known, and much remains to be learned about the distributions of our native species. The most commonly encountered hawthorns are described and discussed below.

DOWNY HAWTHORN or RED HAW, *C. mollis* (T. & G.) Scheele.
Leaves broadly ovate, 8 to 10 lobed with rounded or slightly heart-shaped bases, 2½ to 4 inches long, often hairy beneath; petioles stout, usually hairy, ¾ to 2 inches long. *Thorns* slightly curved, 1 to 2½ inches long. *Flowers* with hairy, gland-toothed sepals and about 20 stamens. *Fruit* nearly round, ½ to ¾ inch in diameter, bright red when ripe, with 4 or 5 seeds and thick juicy flesh; deciduous in autumn.

DOWNY HAWTHORN is the largest and most common of our native hawthorns, ranging throughout all but the extreme northwestern corner of the state. It is also one of the easiest to identify, having large, prominently lobed leaves that are widest near the base. Its crown is broad and rounded, with wide-spreading, ashy gray branches that are sometimes nearly thornless.

Downy hawthorn is very attractive in landscape plantings, but unfortunately it is very susceptible to leaf rust. Its showy white flowers appear in early to mid-May, before those of most other hawthorns. Its large red fruits, which are unusual among hawthorns in being sweet and edible, are very attractive when they ripen in August and September. The leaves usually turn yellow or orange in autumn.

WASHINGTON HAWTHORN, *C. phaenopyrum* (L.f.) Med.
Leaves broadly ovate; 4 to 6 lobed; with truncate, rounded, or slightly heart-shaped bases; 1 to 2½ inches long; glabrous or nearly so; petioles slender, ¾ to 1½ inches long. *Thorns* nearly straight, 1 to 3 inches long. *Flowers* with glabrous, entire sepals and 20 stamens. *Fruit* nearly round; bright red when ripe; ³⁄₁₆ to ¼ inch in diameter; with 3 to 5 seeds and thin dry flesh, persisting in winter.

WASHINGTON HAWTHORN is native to the southeastern United States but is hardy throughout Iowa and frequently planted here as an ornamental. It is a small tree, 20 to 30 feet tall, and develops an oblong crown of upright branches. Its leaves, which are reddish-purple when they unfold in spring, are a dark glossy green throughout the summer and turn orange, red, or purple in autumn. The small berrylike haws persist on the trees all winter, providing food for birds. It flowers in late spring or early summer, later than our native hawthorns.

English hawthorn (*C. oxycantha* L.) and single-seed hawthorn (*C. monogyna* Jacq.) are two Eurasian species that are occasionally planted as ornamentals in Iowa. They have small, prominently lobed leaves similar to Washington hawthorn but differ from it in having fruits with one (*monogyna*) or two (*oxycantha*) seeds.

DOTTED HAWTHORN, *C. punctata* Jacq.
Leaves obovate to elliptic, unlobed or obscurely lobed on the upper half, with wedge-shaped bases, more or less hairy along the veins beneath, 1½ to 3 inches long; petioles stout, ¼ to ½ inch long. *Thorns* straight, 1 to 3 inches long. *Flowers* with entire, or nearly entire, hairy sepals and 20 stamens. *Fruit* nearly round, red or yellow with numerous white dots, ½ to ¾ inch in diameter, with 3 to 5 seeds and thick juicy flesh, deciduous in autumn.

DOTTED HAWTHORN is a flat-topped tree 20 to 25 feet tall with long, horizontal branches. It is native throughout most of the state but uncommon in the west and south.

COCKSPUR HAWTHORN, *C. crus-galli* L.
Leaves obovate to oblanceolate, unlobed, with wedge-shaped bases, 1 to 4 inches long, glabrous; petioles stout, ¼ to ⅜ inch long. *Thorns* slightly curved, 2 to 7 inches long. *Flowers* with entire, or nearly entire, glabrous sepals and 10 stamens. *Fruit* nearly round, red when ripe, about ⅜ inch in diameter, with 1 or 2 seeds and thin dry flesh, persisting in winter.

COCKSPUR HAWTHORN is native across the southern half of Iowa but uncommon in the western part of this range. It is a small tree up to 25 feet high and develops a low, rounded crown of wide-spreading branches. It is easily identified by its narrow, leathery, glossy leaves and unusually long thorns.

Cockspur is perhaps the most attractive of our native hawthorns and a desirable tree for landscape plantings. Its exceptionally long, sharp thorns can cause serious injury, so the thornless variety *inermis* is usually preferred. Trees normally flower in mid- to late May. The fruits persist on the branches in winter, providing food for birds.

MARGARET'S HAWTHORN, *C. margaretta* Ashe.
Leaves broadly diamond shaped, shallowly 4 to 8 lobed on the upper half, with wedge-shaped bases, 1 to 1¼ inches long, glabrous; petioles slender, ½ to 1 inch long. *Thorns* straight or slightly curved, ¾ to 1½ inches long. *Flowers* with hairy or glabrous, finely gland-toothed sepals and 20 stamens. *Fruit* nearly round, dark red or orange-red when ripe, ⅜ to ½ inch in diameter, with 2 or 3 seeds and thin dry flesh, deciduous in autumn.

MARGARET'S HAWTHORN is a small tree, 20 to 25 feet tall, with a narrow, open crown. It is native across most of the eastern half of Iowa. It was named for the wife-to-be of the botanist who described it.

FLESHY HAWTHORN, *C. succulenta* Shrad.
Leaves elliptic to diamond shaped, shallowly 8 to 10 lobed on the upper half, with wedge-shaped to nearly truncate bases, 1½ to 3 inches long, glabrous or hairy beneath; petioles ⅜ to 1¼ inches long. *Thorns* slightly curved, 1½ to 2½ inches long. *Flowers* with hairy, gland-toothed sepals and 10 or 20 stamens. *Fruit* nearly round, bright red when ripe, ¼ to ½ inch in diameter, with 2 or 3 seeds deeply indented on the inner face and thick juicy flesh, deciduous in autumn.

FLESHY HAWTHORN is native across most of Iowa but rare in most places. The variety *pertomentosa* (Ashe) Palmer, often called the prairie hawthorn, differs from the species in having the leaves persistently hairy beneath rather than glabrous and in having 10 instead of 20 stamens.

Fleshy hawthorn is one of our most attractive native hawthorns. A small tree about 20 feet high, it develops a broad, irregular crown. Its glossy, leathery leaves turn reddish-purple in autumn.

PEAR HAWTHORN, *C. calpodendron* (Ehrh.) Med. *Leaves* elliptic to diamond shaped, unlobed or shallowly 6 to 10 lobed on the upper half, with wedge-shaped bases, 1½ to 3 inches long, hairy beneath; petioles stout, about ⅜ inch long. *Thorns* straight, 1 to 1½ inches long. *Flowers* with hairy, gland-toothed sepals and 20 stamens. *Fruit* oblong or pear shaped, bright red to dull orange-red when ripe, about ⅜ inch long, with 2 or 3 seeds deeply indented on the inner face and thin juicy flesh, usually persisting in winter.

PEAR HAWTHORN is a flat-topped tree, 15 to 20 feet high, with nearly horizontal branches. It is native in southern, eastern, and central Iowa.

OTHER HAWTHORNS. The following species are rare and localized in distribution:

Fireberry hawthorn (*C. chrysocarpa* Ashe)—northwestern corner of the state

Scarlet hawthorn (*C. pedicellata* Sarg.) (*C. coccinea* of auth., in part)—northeastern and north central Iowa

Frosted hawthorn [*C. pruinosa* (Wendl.) K. Koch]—southeastern corner of state

Hannibal hawthorn (*C. hannibalensis* Palmer)—counties near Missouri border.

Downy Serviceberry, *Amelanchier arborea* (Michx.) Fern.

Distinguishing characteristics: *Leaves* simple, alternate, ovate to some-what oblong-obovate, 2 to 4 inches long with petioles ½ to 1½ inches long, toothed, slightly heart shaped at base; surfaces densely white-hairy when unfolding in spring but eventually glabrous or only slightly hairy beneath; veins branching freely and forming a network near the margin. *Winter twigs* slender, glabrous, red-brown to gray; leaf scars linear or crescent shaped, very small, with 3 bundle scars. *Buds* elongate, the terminal ¼ to ½ inch long and the laterals often nearly equal in size; scales commonly 4 to 6 in number, either red or yellow-green tinged with red. *Flowers* perfect, in showy racemes, appearing when the leaves are beginning to expand in early spring; petals 5, white, linear to narrowly oblong; stamens normally 20; ovary inferior, with 5 styles united at the base. *Fruit* a reddish-purple pome about ¼ inch in diameter. *Bark* light gray and very smooth, becoming darker and shallowly furrowed at the base of older stems.

Similar trees: Leaves of cherries have small glands on their petioles; leaves of ironwood and hornbeam have the veins running into the teeth. The distinctive elongate buds of the serviceberry further distinguish it from these and other species.

Distribution: Native throughout eastern, southern, and central Iowa; also known though uncommon in the natural lakes area and the Des Moines River valley in northwestern Iowa.

THE downy serviceberry is the earliest of our woodland trees to flower each spring, providing a welcome burst of color when the buds of other species are just beginning to open. Unfortunately, its delicate blooms are easily destroyed by April winds and showers, so the display is usually brief. In early summer the serviceberry again attracts considerable attention, as robins, catbirds, orioles, waxwings, and other wildlife arrive to feast on its small reddish-purple fruits. Then in autumn, its leaves turn a handsome yellow-orange or red.

The downy serviceberry, like the redbud, the flowering crabs, and most other spring-flowering trees, is natu-rally small. It is rarely more than 35 feet tall under ideal conditions, and on poor sites it may be no more than a tall shrub. When given plenty of room, its several upright stems give way to a round-topped crown of numerous slender branches; but on the wooded ridges and steep slopes where it normally grows it often takes on a crooked, picturesque appearance.

Downy serviceberry is often called *Juneberry* because its tiny berrylike fruits usually ripen in June. Though insipid to only slightly sweet in taste, they are a welcome snack after a long hike through the woods on a warm summer afternoon. The fruits also make good jams and jellies, but the birds like them so well that it is often hard to find enough to make the effort worthwhile.

Two other tree-sized serviceberries are native in extreme northeastern Iowa. Both are very similar to *Amelanchier arborea*. The Allegheny serviceberry (*A. laevis* Wieg.) can be distinguished at flowering time by its glabrous and usually bronze- or purple-tinted leaves. Inland serviceberry (*A. interior* Nielsen), differs in having the ovaries of its flowers pubescent on top. The latter is intermediate between *A. laevis* amd *A. sanguinea* (Pursh) DC, and some botanists believe it represents a hybrid swarm rather than a distinct species.

The serviceberries are desirable ornamental trees and are being increasingly planted. Like the hawthorns, flowering crabs, and other trees in the rose family, they are sometimes attacked by leaf rusts and other diseases. The apple serviceberry (*A. × grandiflora* Rehd.) is a hybrid between the downy and Allegheny serviceberries that is sometimes available in nurseries.

Black Cherry, *Prunus serotina* Ehrh.

Distinguishing characteristics: *Leaves* simple, alternate, oblong-lanceolate, 2 to 6 inches long with petioles ½ to ¾ inch long; margins finely toothed, the tips of the teeth curving inward; 1 or 2 glands normally present on the upper portion of the petiole near the base of the blade. *Winter twigs* slender, red-brown, glabrous; leaf scars small, half-round, with 3 bundle scars. *Buds* ovoid, ⅛ to ¼ inch long (occasionally larger), with about 6 glabrous, dark red-brown scales; the terminal bud equal to or only slightly larger than the laterals. *Flowers* perfect, in showy racemes, appearing shortly after the leaves in mid- to late spring; petals 5, white, broadly obovate; stamens commonly 15 to 20; ovary superior, with a single style. *Fruit* a drupe about ⅓ inch in diameter, purple-black when ripe, with a persistent calyx. *Bark* smooth with prominent lenticels, eventually separating into thin, light gray to black scales with upturned edges.

Similar trees: Leaves of chokecherry and bird cherry have sharp-pointed, outward-directed teeth and are frequently obovate in outline. American plum and pin cherry have flowers and fruits in small umbellike clusters of 2 to 5 rather than in racemes. Winter: bud scales of chokecherry are brown with tan margins; wild plums have false terminal buds.

Distribution: Native as far west as the natural lakes district in northwestern Iowa and the Missouri River in southwestern Iowa.

MOST trees in the rose family are valued primarily for their edible fruits—apples, pears, and plums, for example—but the principal asset of the black cherry is its wood. It has been admired since colonial times for its beautiful reddish or red-brown color and attractive luster. Yet beauty alone cannot account for its value in the marketplace. Cherry wood is moderately hard and heavy, works easily, takes a fine finish, resists shock, shrinks little when first dried, and seldom warps or checks during seasoning. Thus it is ideal for use in balances and other scientific instruments, where precision is a primary concern, and for printer's blocks, which must retain their shape and position when being used. Cherry is also an excellent choice for fine furniture and cabinetwork, paneling and interior trim, actions of pianos and organs, handles, and caskets.

Native black cherry occurs in upland woods, wood edges, and fencerows throughout all but the extreme northwestern corner of Iowa. Individuals growing in moist, fertile, well-drained soils may reach 60 feet in height and 2 feet in diameter, but many trees found on poorer sites are much smaller. Its common associates include several species of oaks, shagbark hickory, white ash, bigtooth and quaking aspens, ironwood, and chokecherry.

Black cherry is seldom used for landscaping in Iowa, but its flowers and glossy leaves do have considerable ornamental value. It grows fairly rapidly when given full sun, eventually forming an oval to spreading open crown of slightly drooping branches. Its tart, juicy fruits, which are sometimes used for jams and wines, attract robins, catbirds, grosbeaks, and other songbirds when they begin to ripen in late summer. The leaves usually turn light yellow in autumn.

Pin or fire cherry (*Prunus pensylvanica* L.f.) is a native shrub or small tree that is sometimes mistaken for the black cherry. The leaves and twigs of the two species are very similar; but the flowers and fruits of pin cherry are borne in small, umbellike clusters rather than in long racemes like the black cherry. Its buds are smaller than those of the black cherry and typically clustered at the tips of the twigs as in oaks. Pin cherry occurs in open woods and clearings across much of northeastern and north central Iowa but is common only in the far northeastern corner of the state.

Chokecherry, *Prunus virginiana* L.

Distinguishing characteristics: *Leaves* simple, alternate, 2 to 4 inches long with petioles ½ to 1 inch long, oval or obovate; margins finely toothed, the tips of the teeth sharp and pointing outward; two glands normally present on petiole near the base of the blade. *Winter twigs* slender, glabrous, gray or red-brown; leaf scars small, half-round, with 3 bundle scars. *Buds* long-ovoid, usually 3/16 to ¼ inch long (sometimes larger), terminal and laterals nearly equal in size; scales 6 or more, glabrous, brown with light-colored margins. *Flowers* similar to black cherry but commonly blooming earlier in spring; petals nearly round. *Fruit* a drupe ¼ to ⅓ inch in diameter, red or dark purplish-red when ripe, calyx deciduous. *Bark* gray, smooth.

Similar trees: Black and pin cherries have narrower leaves with incurved teeth. Flowers and fruits of wild plums are in small, umbellike clusters rather than racemes (see also discussion of May tree below). Winter: black cherry has dark red-brown bud scales and pin cherry has smaller, clustered end buds. Wild plums, ironwood, and elms have false terminal buds.

Distribution: Native throughout the state.

CHOKECHERRY is in many respects a miniature version of the black cherry; the two species have similar foliage, flowers, and fruits and occur in the same habitats. Their wood is also very similar, although chokecherry is too small to be of any commercial importance. It rarely exceeds a height of 30 feet or a diameter of 6 inches even under the best of conditions, and it is often no more than a shrub.

The fruits of chokecherry are tart and puckery like those of other wild cherries, but when ripe they are much more palatable than their name suggests. Chokecherries are a favorite food of ruffed grouse, pheasants, catbirds, robins, brown thrashers, cedar waxwings, several kinds of thrushes and woodpeckers, and many other birds. Their hard pits pass undamaged through the birds' digestive tracts; thus chokecherries are prevalent in woods, thickets, fencerows, and other places frequented by birds.

Like most other trees in the rose family, chokecherry is attacked by many diseases and insect pests. One of the most interesting is the black knot disease, which is a common cause of twig dieback throughout much of the state. The fungus that causes this disease produces hard, black, fruiting bodies (ascostroma) that resemble dried feces in shape and general appearance. They persist on infected twigs throughout the winter, providing a ready means of recognizing the chokecherry at that time of year.

Chokecherry is an excellent choice for wildlife plantings but wild-type trees are not especially desirable for landscaping. Their small white flowers are attractive in spring, but flowering crabs and several other kinds of small trees provide a much showier display. The chokecherry's short life span, habit of forming large thickets, and susceptibility to the unsightly growths of the black knot disease are additional reasons to consider another species when choosing a small ornamental tree.

Several other kinds of cherries are grown for fruit or used for landscaping in Iowa. Trees commonly planted for ornamental purposes include the European bird cherry or May tree (*Prunus padus* L.) and the Shubert or Canada red cherry (*P. virginiana* 'Shubert'), a cultivar of the chokecherry. The May tree closely resembles the chokecherry in most characteristics but has bigger flowers and grows larger in size (30 to 40 feet). Unfortunately, it is even more susceptible to black knot, sometimes to the point of being killed or seriously disfigured by this disease. 'Shubert' is a vigorously growing tree of pyramidal habit, maturing at a height of 20 to 30 feet. Its leaves are green at first but change to dark reddish-purple. It is subject to the same limitations as typical chokecherry.

American Plum, *Prunus americana* Marsh.

Distinguishing characteristics: *Leaves* simple, alternate, oval to oblong-oval, 2 to 4 inches long with petioles ½ to ¾ inch long, sharply toothed; petioles with or without glands; veins forming a network near the margins. *Winter twigs* slender to moderate, often thorny, otherwise similar to chokecherry. *Buds* ovoid, ⅟₁₆ to ¼ (usually about ⅛) inch long, the terminal absent; scales about 6, glabrous, red or reddish-brown. *Flowers* perfect, showy, in umbellike clusters of 2 to 5, appearing with or shortly before the leaves in spring; petals 5, white, nearly round; stamens 15 to 20; ovary superior with a single style. *Fruit* a drupe about 1 inch in diameter, red or light purple when ripe. *Bark* brown or dark gray, scaly.

Similar trees: Native cherries have nonthorny twigs with true terminal buds and smaller flowers and fruits that (except for pin cherry) are borne in long racemes. Leaves of goose and Canada plums have blunt or rounded teeth and their flowers have gland-toothed sepals.

Distribution: Native throughout the state.

IT would be difficult to find a wood edge, fencerow, or railroad right-of-way in Iowa that did not harbor at least one thicket of this thorny and often crooked little tree. It is an inconspicuous and rather nondescript member of our flora during most of the year, but in spring it livens the countryside with its showy white flowers. It is a display worthy of some carefully nurtured ornamental tree, not at all what one would expect from a clump of brush that grew up spontaneously.

The fruits of the American plum ripen in late August or early September. Their juicy yellow flesh has a mild, refreshing taste that varies considerably in sweetness from one tree to the next, but the reddish-purple skin contains an astringent that gives the fruit a sharp bite when eaten. Horticulturists have developed many varieties of edible plums from this species and have crossed it with several other species of wild plums in their efforts to obtain new and more flavorful varieties of fruit.

American plum is one of our most important native trees for wildlife but not for the reason one might expect. Its fruits, though high in food value, seem to be eaten by only a few species of animals. The plum's greatest value lies in the nesting and protective cover its dense, thorny branches provide to numerous species of birds and small animals. Its fast growth, resistance to drought, ability to grow well in a variety of soils, and tendency to form thickets make it useful for windbreaks and erosion control too.

American plum is also desirable for landscaping in natural settings, where its habit of forming thickets will not be a problem. It is less seriously harmed by diseases and insect pests than many other spring-flowering trees, an important point in its favor. When given plenty of room to grow, it usually branches freely near the ground and produces a broad, rounded crown 12 to 25 feet high.

American plum is closely related to several other species of fruit trees that either grow wild in Iowa or are planted here as ornamentals. These include the Canada plum (*Prunus nigra* Ait.), which is native on steep, wooded slopes in the extreme northeastern corner of the state; the goose plum (*P. hortulana* Bailey), which is native to Lee and Van Buren counties; the peach [*P. persica* (L.) Batsch.], which occasionally escapes from cultivation in southern Iowa; and the so-called purpleleaf plums, which are popular ornamentals because of their attractive purple leaves but unfortunately are short-lived in cultivation. Most of the latter are hybrids or cultivars of *P. cerasifera* Ehrh.

Redbud, *Cercis canadensis* L.

Distinguishing characteristics: *Leaves* simple, alternate, nearly round, 2 to 5 inches long with petioles 1 to 2 inches long; margins entire. *Winter twigs* slender, glabrous, dark brown, tinged with purple, dotted with numerous pale lenticels; leaf scars very small, raised, half-round, with 3 bundle scars. *Buds* dark purple, glabrous, the terminal absent and the laterals of two types—2-scaled leaf buds about ¹⁄₁₆ inch long and flower buds at least ⅛ inch long with 6 or more scales. *Flowers* small, dark pink (white in variety *alba*), perfect, irregular, in showy umbellike clusters of 4 to 8, appearing before the leaves in spring. *Fruit* a flattened pod (legume) 2 to 3½ inches long, tapered at ends, often persisting through winter. *Bark* scaly, gray or reddish-brown.

Similar trees: Poplars and lindens, the only other trees with leaves of this size and shape, have toothed leaf margins and much different fruits. Winter: cherries have terminal buds. Elms, hackberry, birches, and other trees with slender, nonthorny twigs and false terminal buds have small stipule scars. Their fruits, when present, are not pods.

Distribution: Native to southern third of the state, north along the Des Moines River to Boone County. Widely cultivated outside this range.

IT is the destiny of some trees to remain forever small, to never produce the valuable wood or abundant shade of their larger relatives. Nature is full of peculiar ironies, and it seems entirely appropriate that the most beautiful flowers are frequently found on the most modest trees. The redbud is perhaps the best example of this; though often no more than a shrub in size and usually crooked when it becomes a tree, it provides a floral display that few other trees can match.

The redbud is native across most of southern and parts of central Iowa but is much more commonly seen in cultivation than in the wild. Besides its attractive flowers and irregular, picturesque silhouette, several other useful features recommend it for landscaping. It is very adapt-able, tolerating a variety of soils and growing well in either full sun or partial shade. It is less frequently attacked by diseases and insect pests than many other ornamental trees. Its flowers, which have smaller, less exposed petals than those of most other spring-flowering trees, are not so easily destroyed by winds. Redbud is not reliably hardy in northern Iowa, so trees planted there should be obtained from locally proven sources rather than sources further south.

Native redbuds are found along rivers and streams, usually in the understory or edges of long-established woods. The trees sometimes attain a height of 30 feet and a trunk diameter of 1 foot but are usually much smaller.

Redbud is sometimes called "Judas-tree," a name more appropriately applied to a close relative in southern Europe and western Asia (*Cercis siliquastrum* L.). According to legend, Judas Iscariot hanged himself from a tree of this species after betraying Christ. The tree, as the story goes, was so embarrassed at the turn of events that it blushed, turning its normally white blossoms to pink!

The flowers of redbud differ from those of other spring-flowering trees in being irregular; that is, petals are of different sizes and shapes within the same flower. The fruit, which is a dry, flattened pod, is also quite unlike the fleshy, edible fruits of many other trees that bloom in spring. These characteristics place it in the legume family, a large and economically important group that includes locusts, the Kentucky coffee tree, beans, peas, alfalfa, and clovers. Most legumes can be recognized also by their pinnately compound leaves. However, the redbud defies convention at this point, producing simple rounded leaves resembling those of lindens and poplars.

Kentucky Coffee Tree, *Gymnocladus dioicus* (L.) K. Koch

Distinguishing characteristics: *Leaves* twice-pinnately compound, alternate, 1 to 3 feet long; leaflets 40 or more, 1½ to 4 inches long, ovate, entire, glabrous. *Winter twigs* very stout, dark reddish-brown mottled with gray, glabrous; pith very thick, orange; leaf scars large, heart shaped with 3 or 5 bundle scars. *Buds* greenish or brown, sunken within small craterlike depressions in the surface of the twig; the terminal bud absent. *Flowers* greenish-white, dioecious, slightly irregular, in racemes, appearing in early summer. *Fruit* a thick, woody pod 4 to 6 inches long with 3 to 9 seeds ⅝ to ¾ inch long; often persisting on the tree through winter. *Bark* on younger trees light gray and separating into thin, scaly ridges upturned on one edge; eventually somewhat darker and furrowed with short, scaly ridges or rows of small, scaly plates.

Similar trees: Honey locust is our only other tree with twice-pinnate leaves. It has smaller leaflets; relatively slender and often thorny twigs; and long, leathery, flattened, often twisted pods with smaller and more numerous seeds. Winter: tree-of-heaven is the only other species having stout twigs with large leaf scars and no terminal buds. It has 7 or more bundle scars and hairy buds exposed on the surface of the twig.

Distribution: Native throughout most of the state but only locally common. (See discussion following.)

THE common names of plants are often misleading, suggesting relationships that do not exist. The Kentucky coffee tree is a good example. It is not related to the coffee of commerce, but it is a legume like the honey locust, black locust, beans, and clovers. In fact, we might be calling it a locust today if the Kentucky settlers had not tried its hard, bitter, beanlike seeds as a substitute for coffee.

Coffee tree is one of several trees that are dioecious, with the male and female flowers occurring on seperate individuals. Only the female trees produce the characteristic pods, which persist on the branches during winter and help identify the trees at that time of year. Other common dioecious trees are the willows, cottonwood, poplars, osage orange, boxelder, ashes, and ginkgo.

Coffee tree has one of the most peculiar distributions of any native tree. Its geographical range includes the entire state, but it is rarely encountered outside our larger river systems, and even among them it is distributed sporadically. For example, it grows locally along the drainages of the Mississippi, Des Moines, Skunk, Cedar, and Big Sioux rivers but is apparently absent from the Wapsipinicon. The cause of this erratic distribution is unknown, but human hands may have been partly responsible. Native Americans are said to have eaten the pods and used the seeds in games and may have planted trees (or discarded seeds) at their encampments.

Native coffee trees are usually found on the rich, moist soils of floodplains, terraces, ravines, and lower slopes. Common associates on these sites include maples, ashes, hackberry, basswood, black walnut, butternut, honey locust, and bitternut hickory. Although seed is the primary means of reproduction, individual trees sometimes form colonies by root suckering.

Coffee tree is one of several native trees that has been needlessly neglected in home landscaping. It certainly has its limitations—its leaves come out late in spring and are not especially colorful in autumn, and some people object to the pods dropped by female trees. However, the trees produce a nice light, open shade and are attractive year round, especially in winter when their scaly bark and stout, crooked branches stand out in the landscape. Coffee tree is also adaptable as to soil and relatively free of insect and disease problems. Its growth rate is usually slow to moderate. Trees eventually grow 60 to 75 feet tall, with a spread of 40 to 50 feet.

The hard, heavy, durable wood of the coffee tree very closely resembles that of honey locust. It is occasionally used for fence posts, furniture, cabinetwork, and fuel; but it is unimportant commercially because of the relative scarcity of large trees.

Honey Locust, *Gleditsia triacanthos* L.

Distinguishing characteristics: *Leaves* once- or twice-pinnately compound (both types usually present on same tree), alternate, 6 to 12 inches long; leaflets oblong, ½ to 1½ inches long, with tiny, inconspicuous, widely spaced teeth. *Winter twigs* moderate in diameter, greenish or red-brown, glabrous and often glossy; those of wild trees commonly armed with smooth, stout, branched thorns; leaf scars small and irregularly shaped with 3 bundle scars. *Buds* brownish, embedded in the leaf scar and surface of the twig, with only their tips protruding; the terminal bud absent. *Flowers* small, greenish-white, regular, perfect or imperfect, in racemes, appearing in early summer. *Fruit* a flattened and often twisted leathery pod 6 to 18 inches long with 12 or more seeds about ⅓ inch long. *Bark* of younger trees gray and separating into long, thin, flattened ridges slightly upturned at the end; becoming deeply furrowed and nearly black.

Similar trees: Coffee tree has larger leaflets; much stouter twigs; and thick, woody pods. Black locust has small paired spines. Winter: hawthorns are the only other trees with large, smooth thorns. Their thorns are relatively slender and unbranched (rarely branched on trunks). They also have reddish buds clearly visible on the surface of the twig.

Distribution: Widely planted throughout the state and native across most of southern, eastern, and central Iowa.

FEW sights in nature are more formidable than the honey locust. Its thorns, which look as if they were specially designed for some cruel medieval weapon, are very sharp and often as long as 6 to 8 inches. They are such a conspicuous feature of wild trees that it seems the thornless locusts so widely planted in our towns and cities should be a different species altogether. However, a careful comparison of leaves, fruits, and other features reveals that wild and cultivated trees are in most respects identical.

The epidemic of Dutch elm disease initiated a search for shade trees that could replace the American elm, and the thornless variety of the common honey locust (*Gleditsia triacanthos* var. *inermis*) was one of the trees that re-

ceived a good deal of attention. Numerous cultivars were subsequently introduced, including the 'Moraine,' 'Shademaster,' 'Skyline,' and 'Sunburst' locusts. These trees have many qualities that recommend them for street and yard planting: ease in transplanting; fast growth; longevity; ability to thrive in a variety of soils and environments. They produce a light shade, allowing grass to grow well beneath them. Some have the further advantage of not producing the large, messy pods of wild locusts. Mature trees are usually 70 to 80 feet tall.

Unfortunately, many people have not learned the lesson of the Dutch elm disease and are replacing continuous plantings of American elm with continuous plantings of honey locust. This practice invites disease and pest problems. The honey locust was once considered remarkably free of diseases and insects, but pests are an increasing problem in many areas. Mimosa webworm, cankers, and borers have been especially troublesome.

Native honey locust was probably rather uncommon at the time of settlement, occurring as a minor associate of other trees along the largest rivers and streams. Then agriculture provided a new environment ideal for the spread of this species, and it has become a common weed of pastures and fence rows in many areas. Cattle feed eagerly on the pods, which contain a sweet, honeylike pulp, and subsequently disperse the seeds throughout the pasture. The animals' digestive juices do not damage the seeds but actually facilitate germination by softening the hard outer seed coat.

The attractive reddish wood of the honey locust is hard, heavy, strong, durable, and shock resistant. It is used for fence posts, railroad ties, furniture, interior finish, and fuel.

Black Locust, *Robinia pseudoacacia* L.

Distinguishing characteristics: *Leaves* once-pinnately compound, alternate, 8 to 14 inches long; leaflets 7 to 21 in number, 1½ to 2 inches long with stout stalks ⅛ to ¼ inch long, ovate-oblong in shape, with entire margins and glabrous surfaces. *Winter twigs* moderate in diameter, prominently angled and zigzagged, light reddish-brown, glabrous, with pairs of sharp stipular spines up to ½ inch long; leaf scars small, 3 lobed to broadly triangular, each with 3 bundle scars. *Buds* embedded in the leaf scars so apparently absent. *Flowers* white, perfect, irregular, in showy racemes, appearing in late spring or early summer. *Fruit* a flattened pod 2 to 4 inches long, abruptly tapered or rounded at ends, with 3 to 8 seeds about ³⁄₁₆ inch long. *Bark* deeply furrowed with thick, elongate ridges, reddish-brown to nearly black.

Similar trees: Prickly ash, the only other tree with paired spines, has sessile leaflets marked with tiny, translucent dots (seen against a strong light), straight rounded twigs, and reddish buds clearly visible in the axils of its leaves (above leaf scars in winter).

Distribution: Naturalized or escaped from cultivation throughout most of the state.

MOST of our introduced trees have "minded their manners" and stayed where planted, but a few species have escaped from cultivation and become established in the wild. One such tree is the black locust, which is native to forests in the Appalachian mountains, Ozark plateau, and southern Illinois. Today it grows naturally along the edges of woods and in other waste places across most of Iowa, usually forming thickets or small groves. It is especially common in the southern part of the state where its showy white blossoms are a conspicuous feature of the landscape in late spring and early summer.

Black locust has long been a popular ornamental tree in Europe, but it is seldom used for landscaping in the United States. Although relatively free of serious diseases and able to thrive in a variety of environments, it provides poor shade and is subject to attack by a number of insects in this country. The worst of these insects are the locust leaf miners, which may skeletonize the foliage of entire trees, and the locust borers, which deform or even kill the trees by burrowing into the trunks and larger branches. Susceptibility to these pests is apparently related to the condition of the tree; vigorously growing specimens are the most resistant.

Black locust is sometimes used in conservation plantings. It is especially desirable for reclaiming strip-mined or eroded land, as it tolerates dry, sterile, acid conditions and holds the soil from washing away with its wide-spreading root system. Black locust also improves the nutrient content of the soil through the decay of its leaf litter and the action of nitrogen-fixing bacteria in its root nodules. Its vigor is often reduced on poor sites so that it is more susceptible to insect attacks, but the trees sprout extensively from the roots when the tops are killed. The thickets thus provided are an excellent source of nesting and protective cover for wildlife. The seeds are eaten to a limited extent by quail and squirrels.

Black locust is also planted for its hard, strong, heavy wood, which is stiffer, is more resistant to decay, and possesses a higher fuel value than that of any other broadleaf tree native to temperate North America. It also shrinks and swells less than the wood of most other trees. These properties make it particularly useful for fence posts, railroad ties, mine timbers, treenails, insulator pins, and fuel. It is unfortunate that borers are such a serious threat to so valuable a tree.

Tree-of-Heaven, *Ailanthus altissima* (Mill.) Swingle

Distinguishing characteristics: *Leaves* once-pinnately compound, alternate, 1½ to 4 feet long; leaflets 9 to 41 in number, 3 to 6 inches long, ovate-lanceolate; margins entire except for 1 or 2 gland-tipped teeth near base; surfaces glabrous. *Winter twigs* stout, light brown, with thick light orange-brown pith; leaf scars large and shield shaped, with about 9 bundle scars. *Buds* dome shaped, ⅛ to 3⁄16 inch long, with 2 or 4 red-brown scales covered with pale hairs; the terminal bud absent. *Flowers* yellow-green, dioecious or less commonly perfect, in panicles, appearing in early summer. *Fruit* a twisted, oblong samara 1 to 1½ inches long with a single seed in the middle, persisting on the branches in winter. *Bark* smooth, gray with vertical white streaks; becoming slightly furrowed on large trees.

Similar trees: No other tree has entire leaflets with gland-tipped teeth at the base. Winter: coffee tree and sumacs are the only other trees having stout twigs with no terminal buds. Coffee tree has mottled twigs, 3 or 5 bundle scars, and buds embedded within the twig. Sumacs have narrow leaf scars that nearly encircle their cone-shaped buds.

Distribution: Widely cultivated in towns and cities, especially in the southern half of the state, often escaping to vacant lots and other waste places.

THE more one learns about trees, the more obvious it becomes that the ideal shade or ornamental tree does not exist. Some species are certainly better than others, but each has its advantages and disadvantages. There is perhaps no better example than the tree-of-heaven.

Many people judge a tree primarily on the rapidity of its growth. If this is one's only criterion, the tree-of-heaven is certainly the finest tree in existence. A rate of 3 to 5 feet per year is a maximum for all but our fastest growing native trees; yet the tree-of-heaven easily maintains this feverish pace and frequently grows even faster. Stump sprouts have been known to grow as much as 1 inch per day!

The tree-of-heaven also adapts to urban life better than any other tree, thriving in the poorest "soil" and the foulest air the city has to offer. It has no serious diseases or insect pests and has been known to survive submergence in seawater. Though less attractive than oaks, maples, and many other species, it is fairly handsome with its rounded crown of dark green, tropical-looking leaves. The large masses of reddish seeds produced by female trees add a touch of color in later summer.

Unfortunately, the tree-of-heaven also has many obnoxious features. Like most other fast-growing trees, it has weak, brittle wood that is easily broken by wind and ice. It leafs out late in spring and drops its foliage in autumn with little change in color. The flowers of male trees have an offensive odor and the propellerlike seeds of female trees are carried by the wind to vacant lots, neighboring yards, and cracks along buildings, producing a new generation of young trees in places where they are neither needed nor wanted. The tree-of-heaven also suckers readily from its roots, producing small jungles of rapidly growing sprouts that must be repeatedly cut back to the ground.

Tree-of-heaven, then, is anything but the angel its name suggests. In fact, the name probably originated in reference to this species' fast growth and large size in its native China, where it may reach a height of 90 to 100 feet. In the United States it is usually only 40 to 60 feet tall. Its botanical name means "tallest of the trees-of-heaven," indicating its large size in comparison to other trees in its genus.

Staghorn Sumac, *Rhus typhina* L.

Distinguishing characteristics: *Leaves* once-pinnately compound, alternate, 16 to 24 inches long; leaflets 11 to 31 in number, 2 to 5 inches long, oblong-lanceolate, sharply toothed (deeply lobed in some cultivars), nearly glabrous; petioles hairy. *Winter twigs* stout, brown, densely covered with velvety hairs; leaf scars ringlike, nearly encircling the buds, each with 3 to 9 bundle scars. *Buds* more or less cone shaped, ⅛ to 3⁄16 inch long, the scales obscured by a dense covering of golden-brown hairs; the terminal bud absent. *Flowers* very small, yellow-green, perfect or imperfect, in dense panicles, appearing in early summer. *Fruit* a red, hairy drupe about 3⁄16 inch in diameter borne in compact, upright clusters 3 to 5 inches long that persist through winter. *Bark* smooth, gray, with prominent orange lenticels, becoming scaly on larger stems.

Similar trees: Walnuts have chambered pith, true terminal buds, and large lobed leaf scars. Tree-of-heaven has entire leaflets and large shield-shaped leaf scars. (See also discussion of other sumacs.)

Distribution: Native from Allamakee and Winneshiek counties south to Clinton and Jones counties; also reported from Iowa County and from scattered locales in the north central part of the state west to Emmet County.

STAGHORN is an appropriate name for this little tree, for its stout, erect branches have a decided resemblance to the antlers of a stag, even to the soft hairs or velvet that covers them. Though rarely attaining a height of 40 feet under the best circumstances and usually no more than 15 to 25 feet tall, it is a veritable giant within the sumac clan, whose members are mostly shrubs and woody vines.

Staghorn sumac makes an interesting ornamental tree at all times of the year. Its large, compound leaves remain a handsome dark green from the time they appear in late spring until the first cool nights of autumn, whereupon they turn brilliant shades or orange, red, or crimson. The foliage is complemented by large showy clusters of tiny red fruits that remain on the tree from midsummer through the winter, enhancing the appeal of the tree's picturesque, flat-topped crown.

Staghorn sumac has several other advantages. It transplants easily; grows very fast; and is seldom bothered by diseases and insects. It is also a very adaptable species and will thrive in almost any well-drained soil. Its principal drawbacks are its tendency to form thickets, which precludes its use in small spaces, and the ease with which its weak brittle wood is broken by ice and wind.

Native staghorn sumacs are common along the edges of upland woods and in other dry, open waste places in extreme northeastern Iowa.

The smooth sumac (*R. glabra* L.) is a related species that is common in similar habitats throughout the state. It closely resembles staghorn sumac but can be distinguished from it by its reddish, hairless twigs and leafstalks. It is also smaller than the staghorn sumac, often remaining shrubby and rarely becoming more than 15 feet tall when a tree. Both species are often mistaken for the poison sumac (*R. vernix* L.), which does not occur in Iowa. It has white fruits and entire leaflets.

Smooth and staghorn sumacs are among the most important of our native plants for wildlife. Deer browse on the twigs and foliage, rabbits eat the bark, and many species of songbirds and gamebirds depend on the small seeds for food in winter when preferred fruits and seeds are scarce. Sumacs are also valuable for nesting and protective cover for wildlife and they are occasionally used for erosion control.

Silver Maple (Soft Maple), *Acer saccharinum* L.

Distinguishing characteristics: *Leaves* simple, opposite, palmately 5 lobed with deep narrow sinuses, 3 to 7 inches long; margins of lobes toothed; surfaces glabrous, the lower very pale or whitened; petioles 2 to 4 inches long, with watery sap. *Winter twigs* moderate to rather slender, dull red or light red-brown, glabrous; leaf scars V shaped, with 3 bundle scars, opposing leaf scars not touching but usually connected by a fine line. *Buds* ovoid (leaf buds) or globose (flower buds), bright red to dark reddish-purple, ⅛ to ¼ inch long, with 2 to 6 visible scales that are hairy along the edges; flower buds in conspicuous clumps. *Flowers* tiny, apetalous, red, hidden by bud scales; functional stamens and pistils on different flowers, both types commonly present on same tree. *Fruit* a pair of samaras joined at base, one of which is often aborted; wing 1½ to 2 inches long; samaras ripening and falling in late spring or early summer. *Bark* smooth, light gray on young trees; eventually separating into irregular rows of long, scaly, ashy-colored plates.

Similar trees: Norway, hard, and red maples have more shallowly lobed leaves. Winter: flower buds of other common maples are neither clumped nor bright red and their leaf scars touch at the tips.

Distribution: Native throughout the state.

SILVER MAPLE has long been one of our most popular shade trees. Its handsome appearance, fast growth, and adaptability were especially appreciated by settlers of prairie towns of western and central Iowa, who planted it side by side with American elm wherever there was room for trees of their size. Today most of the elms are gone, but many fine old maples remain to shade the descendants of those who planted them.

Silver maple owes its name to the pale undersurfaces of its leaves, which give the tree a silvery color when it is viewed from afar on windy summer days. It is one of our largest native trees, attaining a height of at least 60 and often 100 feet. It commonly develops a broad, rounded crown about two-thirds as wide as the tree is tall.

Silver maple grows much faster than either our native hard maple or the introduced Norway maple, often maintaining a rate of 2 to 3 feet per year when young. However, one should be prepared to accept the inevitable trade-offs when selecting a tree of this species over a slower growing relative. The wood of silver maple is weaker than that of the Norway and hard maples, so its limbs are more frequently broken by ice and windstorms. This detracts from the appearance of the tree and opens its trunk to invasion by decay fungi. Also, silver maple is less striking in autumn than many other maples, its leaves usually turning yellow instead of orange or red.

Native silver maples can be found on almost any stream bank and floodplain forest in Iowa, usually in the company of cottonwood, willows, boxelder, green ash, hackberry, and black walnut. Unlike most maples, their seeds mature by late spring or early summer and are able to germinate as soon as they fall from the tree. This permits them to take advantage of fresh deposits of silt and sand left by receding spring floodwaters.

Silver maple is the first of our native trees to bloom in spring, often as early as the end of March. Few people notice its tiny flowers, which lack petals and are hidden by bright red bud scales.

The wood of silver maple is usually sold as "soft maple" because it is softer than the wood of hard maple. It is used for furniture, veneer, boxes and crates, and many other products.

Hard Maple (Sugar and Black Maples), *Acer saccharum* Marsh. (*A. nigrum* Michx.)

Distinguishing characteristics: *Leaves* simple, opposite, palmately 3 to 5 lobed, 3 to 6 inches long; margins of lobes entire or with 1 or 2 pairs of teeth per lobe; lower surface glabrous or finely hairy; petioles 1½ to 4 inches long, with watery sap. *Winter twigs* moderate in diameter, light brown to orange-brown, often with a pale waxy coating; leaf scars V shaped, with 3 bundle scars. *Buds* ovoid, sharp pointed, dark brown to nearly black, glabrous or nearly so, the terminal ¼ to ⅜ inch long with 10 to 18 visible scales, the laterals smaller and fewer scaled. *Flowers* very small, greenish, perfect or imperfect, apetalous, long stalked, in umbellike clusters, appearing just before the leaves in spring. *Fruit* a pair of samaras joined at the base; wings ½ to 1 inch long, parallel or slightly divergent; samaras ripening and falling in summer or early autumn. *Bark* dark gray, irregularly furrowed with thick scaly ridges.

Similar trees: Norway maple has milky sap, fruits with widely divergent wings, and more shallowly furrowed bark with thin, interconnecting ridges. Winter: ashes and other maples have terminal buds with only 2 to 6 visible scales.

Distribution: Native west to the drainages of the Little Sioux (Clay and Cherokee counties), Raccoon (main fork), Middle, and Nishnabotna rivers, though rare and local along the edge of this range.

FEW sights in nature are more striking than a hard maple in autumn. The green color in its leaves begins to break down after the first cool nights of the season; and by the end of September or early October its entire crown is aglow with deep shades of orange, red, and golden yellow. It is no coincidence that the northeastern corner of Iowa, which has the largest concentration of hard maples in the state, has the reputation for the most spectacular autumn color!

Hard maple ranks with oaks and black walnut as one of our most important trees commercially. Its hard, heavy, strong, and shock-resistant wood is valued for a wide variety of products, including flooring, furniture, veneer, musical instruments, shoe lasts, bowling pins, billiard cues, croquet mallets and balls, handles, spools and bobbins,

and charcoal. Hard maple is also the source of most natural maple syrup sold in the United States.

Native hard maples occur primarily along river valleys. They can be found on a variety of well-drained sites but are especially common on moist, sheltered slopes facing to the north and east, where they often share dominance with basswood and red oak. Young maples are often abundant in the woodland understory as they are very tolerant of shade.

Hard maple in Iowa is represented by two varieties. Sugar maple (var. *saccharum*) has 5-lobed leaves with acute-angled sinuses, 1 or 2 pairs of sharp teeth per lobe, pale lower surfaces that are either glabrous or covered with appressed hairs, and petiole bases without stipules (see smaller photograph above). It occurs primarily in the eastern part of Iowa. Black maple (var. *nigrum*) is characterized by 3-lobed leaves with drooping sides, wide-angled sinuses, nearly entire margins, yellow-green lower surfaces with fine erect hairs, and petiole bases with small leaflike stipules that obscure the lateral buds. It predominates in central and western Iowa but can be found throughout the range of the species in Iowa. The two varieties often intergrade where their range overlap, producing trees with intermediate characteristics. Some botanists consider black maple to be a distinct species, *Acer nigrum* Michx. f.

The sugar and black maples make excellent large shade trees where the soil is well-drained and fertile. Both varieties develop dense, rounded to oval crowns and typically reach heights of 60 feet or more. Black maple tends to grow more slowly when young and its foliage shows less red in autumn, but as one might expect from a tree that ranges farther west, it is better adapted to Iowa's hot, dry summers. Similarly, sugar maples of midwestern origin usually grow better here than those from the eastern states.

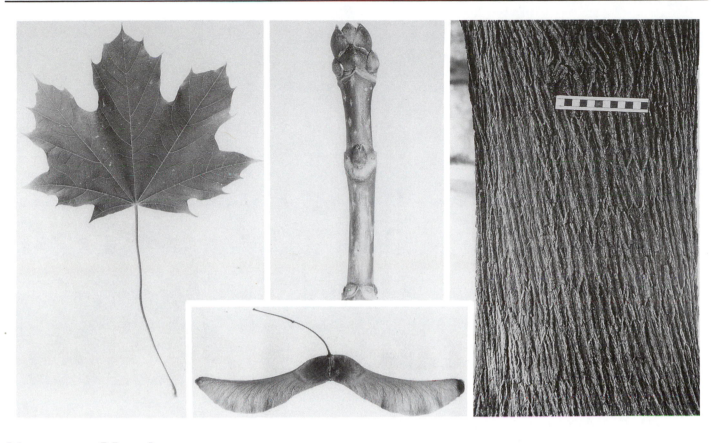

Norway Maple, *Acer platanoides* L.

Distinguishing characteristics: *Leaves* simple, opposite, palmately 5 (rarely 7) lobed, 2½ to 6 inches long; sinuses shallow; margins of lobes entire or with 1 or 2 pairs of sharp teeth per lobe; surfaces glabrous except for tufts of hairs beneath in the vein axils; petioles 3 to 4 inches long with milky sap. *Winter twigs* moderate in diameter, brown or olive-brown; leaf scars small, V shaped, with 3 bundle scars; opposing leaf scars touching at the ends, the pair thus encircling the twig. *Buds* subglobose, blunt tipped, the terminal ³/₁₆ to ⅓ inch long and the laterals smaller; bud scales 4 to 6, green turning to red or dark purple, glabrous or nearly so. *Flowers* yellow-green, perfect or imperfect, in corymbs, appearing just before the leaves in spring. *Fruit* a pair of samaras joined at the base; wings 1½ to 2 inches long, spreading apart at an angle of 180°; samaras ripening and falling from the tree in late summer. *Bark* gray, shallowly furrowed with narrow, slightly diagonal, interconnecting ridges enclosing diamond-shaped spaces.

Similar trees: Hard maples have clear sap, apetalous flowers, fruits with nearly parallel wings, sharp-pointed terminal buds with 10 to 18 scales, and more deeply and irregularly furrowed bark. Winter: the large, fat, blunt terminal buds easily distinguish this species from other maples.

Distribution: Cultivated throughout the state.

NORWAY MAPLE, as one would guess from its name, is a native of Europe. It has probably been more extensively planted in Iowa than any other introduced broadleaf tree. It would be difficult to find a town in the state that did not have at least one of these handsome trees planted next to a street or in someone's front yard.

This popularity is certainly understandable, for the Norway maple transplants easily, tolerates a variety of soil types, withstands city conditions, and casts excellent shade. It normally develops a broad, rounded crown and matures at a height of 40 to 60 feet, but can grow much larger. Its foliage turns bright yellow in late autumn, after many other trees have lost their leaves for the year.

Norway maples are usually rather trouble-free, but trees stressed by drought or injury are sometimes killed by verticillium wilt. Frost cracks also may be a problem, especially on young, thin-barked trees exposed to winter sun. Mulching, watering during drought, and wrapping the trunks of young trees in winter will help keep them healthy.

Lawn grasses sometimes grow poorly beneath the Norway maple because its dense crown and aggressive roots reduce light and moisture. Removing a tree's lower branches as it grows and creating a more open crown through pruning increase the light reaching the ground. Periodic pruning also helps to maintain the vigor and attractive shape of a tree.

More than 50 cultivars of Norway maple have been developed for landscaping. These differ in habit, vigor, leaf color, and other characteristics, and local nursery personnel can advise on which grow best in a particular area. Some selections, such as 'Schwedler' and 'Crimson King,' have dark reddish-purple leaves; these are frequently but erroneously called "red maple," a name more properly applied to another species of maple (see page 99).

Maples are interesting botanically because there is so much diversity in flower structure, color, arrangement, and blooming time among the various species. Though rather unspectacular when measured against the blossoms of redbud, crab apples, and other spring-flowering ornamentals, the flowers of the Norway maple are larger, showier, and more fragrant than those of our native maples. As in other maples, functional stamens and pistils are usually found in separate flowers, with rudimentary stamens occurring in pistillate flowers.

Boxelder, *Acer negundo* L.

Distinguishing characteristics: *Leaves* once-pinnately compound, opposite; leaflets 3 or 5 in number (rarely 7 or 9), ovate and sometimes shallowly 3 lobed, 2 to 4 inches long; margins entire or coarsely and shallowly toothed. *Winter twigs* moderate in diameter, green or purple, often coated with a white, waxy substance; leaf scars V shaped, with 3 bundle scars, opposing leaf scars joined at their ends and thus encircling the twigs, the junction prolonged upwards into a short point on each side of the twig. *Buds* ovoid, densely white-hairy, 1/8 to 1/4 inch long, with 2 or 4 visible scales, terminal and laterals often nearly equal in size. *Flowers* very small, greenish, dioecious, apetalous, appearing just before the leaves in spring; staminate long stalked, in umbellike clusters; pistillate in racemes. *Fruit* a pair of samaras joined at the base; wings 1 to 2 inches long, drooping; samaras ripening and falling in autumn or remaining on the tree through winter. *Bark* gray or brown, furrowed with scaly ridges.

Similar trees: Ashes, the only other common trees with opposite, pinnately compound leaves, have 7 to 11 leaflets and single, paddle-shaped samaras. Winter: easily distinguished from other maples and ashes by its greenish or purple twigs, white-hairy buds, and upward-pointing leaf scar junctions.

Distribution: Native throughout the state.

ONE would not guess the boxelder was a maple when first making its acquaintance. Its compound leaves resemble those of ashes more than maples, accounting for its other common name of "ash-leaved maple." Moreover, unlike our other native maples, it attains a height of only 30 to 50 feet, develops an open, irregular and often disheveled crown, and has little or no autumn color. Nevertheless, its flowers, fruits, and winter twigs are decidedly maplelike, betraying its kinship to some of our largest and most important shade and timber trees. Its sap can even be used to make a tasty maple syrup!

Today the boxelder has a bad reputation and is seldom planted as a shade tree. Better-looking, more tidy

trees are readily available, so we can afford to be selective about what we plant. A hundred years ago the situation was much different. The people who settled Iowa's open prairies needed trees for shade, shelter, and fuel and did not have access to the variety of plants we have today. The native boxelders that grew along the rivers and streams fitted their needs very well, for the boxelder grows extremely fast; is not fussy about soils; and withstands extremes of drought, heat, and cold. Most of the trees the settlers planted are gone today, as the boxelder reaches maturity at 50 to 75 years and begins to decline soon thereafter. However, a few misshapen old veterans still exist to remind us of their role in the settlement of our state.

Though shunned as a shade and ornamental tree today, the boxelder is occasionally planted as a temporary screen or windbreak and is a fine choice for difficult environments where better trees will not grow. It is also an excellent tree for wildlife plantings, as its seeds persist on the branches throughout winter and provide nourishment when other foods are scarce. The seeds are especially sought by evening grosbeaks, whose occasional invasions of Iowa and other midwestern states are usually correlated with a poor crop of boxelder seeds in their usual wintering range to the north.

When the name "boxelder" is mentioned, many people think of the familiar boxelder bugs that congregate outdoors in autumn and often invade houses in search of a place to hibernate. Though usually considered a nuisance, these insects do not eat clothing, infest food, or otherwise pose a threat to health or property. Adult bugs that winter outdoors lay their eggs on boxelder trees and other plants in spring. The resulting young bugs (nymphs) suck sap from the leaves, flowers, fruits, and tender young twigs.

Other Maples

IN addition to the maples discussed in the preceeding pages, the following three species are native or commonly planted in Iowa. Several other species are occasionally planted or are being tested in arboretums. All have opposite leaves and the familiar samara, or "key," fruit.

RED MAPLE, *Acer rubrum* L. *Leaves* shallowly 3 to 5 lobed, 2 to 6 inches long; margins of lobes toothed; lower surface very pale or whitened. *Winter twigs* and *buds* similar to silver maple. *Flowers* reddish, with petals, otherwise similar to silver maple. *Fruit* ripening in late spring or early summer; wings ½ to 1 inch long, slightly divergent.

RED maple is closely related to our native silver maple and hybrids between the two species are sometimes encountered in cultivation. It is an important forest tree throughout most of the eastern United States, ranging as far west as Minnesota, Wisconsin, Illinois, and Missouri. A population was recently discovered in Allamakee County in extreme northeastern Iowa, but it is not known whether these trees are native or naturalized.

Where environmental conditions favor its culture, red maple colors brilliantly in autumn and is a desirable ornamental tree. It usually grows best in moist, acid soils and often becomes chlorotic when planted in alkaline soils. (See discussion under *Pin Oak,* page 66). Plantings in Iowa have met with mixed success; some trees have grown well and shown excellent fall color while others have not. Nurseries can advise which cultivar has proved reliable in a local area.

MOUNTAIN MAPLE, *Acer spicatum* Lam. *Leaves* shallowly 3 lobed, 3 to 5 inches long; margins of lobes toothed. *Winter twigs* slender, red to brown. *Buds* red, 2-scaled, more or less hairy, the terminal ⅛ to ¼ inch long and the laterals smaller. *Flowers* yellow-green, in racemes, appearing after the leaves in late spring or early summer. *Fruit* ripening in late summer or early autumn; wings ½ to 1 inch long, slightly divergent.

MOUNTAIN MAPLE is a small understory tree, 25 to 30 feet tall, with a trunk diameter of 6 to 8 inches. It is native on steep, moist, usually north- and east-facing slopes in Allamakee, Clayton, Dubuque, and probably Winneshiek counties. This species is not recommended for general landscape use in Iowa as it is rather exacting in its requirements for a cool, shady environment and moist, acid, well-drained soil.

AMUR MAPLE, *Acer ginnala* Maxim. *Leaves* 3 lobed, the middle lobe much larger than the others; 1 to 3 inches long; margins toothed. *Winter twigs* slender, red or brown. *Buds* about ¹⁄₁₆ inch long, the terminal replaced by the stalks of the previous season's fruit clusters on some twigs; visible scales 4 or 6, light brown to red-brown, glabrous or hairy along the edges. *Flowers* yellowish-white, in panicles, appearing after the leaves in late spring or early summer. *Fruit* ripening in late summer; wings about 1 inch long, slightly divergent.

AMUR MAPLE is a small, usually multistemmed tree, 15 to 20 feet tall, introduced from eastern Asia for landscaping and conservation plantings. It has proved to be hardy, adaptable, easy to grow, and useful to wildlife, and has attractive dark, glossy leaves that turn bright yellow or red in autumn. Unfortunately, it sometimes escapes from cultivation and becomes a weed.

Ohio Buckeye, *Aesculus glabra* Willd.

Distinguishing characteristics: *Leaves* palmately compound, opposite; leaflets 5 to 7 in number (usually 5), 3 to 6 inches long, oblong-oval, gradually tapered to both the apex and the base; margins finely toothed. *Winter twigs* stout, red-brown to gray, glabrous; leaf scars rather large, half-round to shield shaped, bundle scars 3 or in 3 groups. *Buds* ovoid, light brown, with 5 or 6 pairs of dry brown scales, the terminal ½ to ⅔ inch long and the laterals smaller. *Flowers* yellow-green, perfect or imperfect, irregular, in panicles, appearing after the leaves in spring. *Fruit* a 1- or 2-seeded capsule 1 to 2 inches long; capsule wall thick and leathery, with deciduous prickles; seeds similar to horsechestnut. *Bark* ashy gray, separating into scaly plates divided by shallow furrows.

Similar trees: Horsechestnut, our only other tree with palmately compound leaves, has white flowers and obovate, coarsely toothed leaflets abruptly tapered to the apex. Winter: horsechestnut has dark, sticky buds.

Distribution: Native south of a line extending from Mills County northeast to Boone County east to Clinton County; planted or escaped elsewhere in the state.

SEVERAL midwestern states are nicknamed for well-known plants or animals that occur within their borders: Minnesota (the Gopher State), Wisconsin (the Badger State), Kansas (the Sunflower State). Ohio has long been called the Buckeye State, but many people are unaware that this name was taken from a small and rather unimportant forest tree that grows not only in Ohio but throughout most of the Midwest.

The name *buckeye* is derived from the tree's large, nutlike seed, which has a smooth, shiny, dark brown coat marked with a single large pale spot reminding one of the eye of a male deer (buck). These seeds have a thick, starchy meat that looks suitably edible but contains a bitter poisonous principle. The seeds are enclosed within dry, leathery husks that are yellow and prickly through most of the summer but become pale brown and relatively smooth in autumn, whereupon they split completely open and release the seeds. Though usually 1-seeded by abortion, the fruits occasionally contain 2 or even 3 seeds.

Native buckeyes occur in wooded river valleys across much of southern and central Iowa, usually on moist slopes or floodplains but occasionally in dry, level uplands. Though typically 25 to 40 feet tall with a trunk 6 to 12 inches in diameter, buckeye has been known to reach a height of 70 feet and a diameter of 2 feet.

Ohio buckeye is hardy throughout Iowa and is a desirable ornamental tree. Its attractive, unusually shaped leaves appear earlier in spring than those of most other trees and turn a brilliant yellow or orange in early autumn. It grows at a moderate rate, developing a low, rounded crown when planted in the open. Though seldom killed or seriously injured by diseases or insects, it is susceptible to leaf blotch and leaf scorch and may drop its leaves prematurely. (See following discussion under *Horsechestnut*.)

The wood of Ohio buckeye resembles that of cottonwood and aspens in being light, soft, straight grained, fine textured, and very pale. It is often used for artificial limbs because it resists splitting and is so light in weight. It is also used for shipping containers for food, as it does not impart a taste or odor to materials with which it comes into contact. Other uses include the hidden parts of furniture and pulpwood.

Horsechestnut, *Aesculus hippocastanum* L.

Distinguishing characteristics: *Leaves* palmately compound, opposite; leaflets 5 to 7 in number (usually 7), 4 to 8 inches long, obovate, abruptly tapered to the apex; margins coarsely toothed. *Winter twigs* stout, red-brown to gray-brown, glabrous; leaf scars large, triangular or shield shaped, with 3 to 9 bundle scars. *Buds* ovoid, sticky, with 4 to 6 pairs of large scales, the terminal ½ to 1 inch long and the laterals much smaller. *Flowers* white streaked with red or yellow, perfect or imperfect, irregular, in showy panicles, appearing after the leaves in spring. *Fruit* a 1- to 3-seeded, nutlike capsule about 2 inches in diameter; capsule wall thick, leathery, and prickly; seeds large, dark shiny brown, with a single large pale spot (hilum). *Bark* gray, scaly.

Similar trees: Ohio buckeye, the only tree even remotely resembling this species, has oblong-oval, finely toothed leaflets gradually tapered to the apex; yellow-green flowers; and light brown, nonsticky buds.

Distribution: Cultivated throughout the state.

THIS peculiar tree is not a chestnut at all but a close relative of our native Ohio buckeye. Though the origin of its name is uncertain, "chestnut" probably refers to the resemblance of its prickly, nutlike fruits to those of the chestnut. "Horse" may refer to the similarities between its seed and a horse's eye or to the reputed use of its fruits to treat diseases of horses. It is wise not to mistake it for a chestnut, for its seeds are poisonous!

Despite the similarity in names, chestnuts and horsechestnuts are easy to distinguish. True chestnuts have simple, alternate leaves, while horsechestnut leaves are palmately compound and opposite, with 5 to 7 separate leaflets. Another unique feature of the horsechestnut is its large sticky buds, which assure identification during winter.

Horsechestnut is native to the mountains of the Balkan Peninsula but has been widely planted outside this range. It has been cultivated in western Europe since the sixteenth century and was introduced to America in colonial times. It is one of our largest spring-flowering ornamental trees, commonly attaining a height of 50 to 75 feet with a nearly equal spread, and capable of reaching much larger sizes. Longfellow's famous poem about the village blacksmith, who worked beneath a "spreading chestnut tree," concerned a fine specimen of this species in Cambridge, Massachusetts.

Like most trees, horsechestnut has both advantages and disadvantages for landscaping. Desirable features include its showy white flowers, which occur in large, upright clusters up to one foot long; its interesting dark green leaves; its hardiness; and its ability to grow in a variety of soil. Disadvantages are its potentially large size, messy fruits, and poor autumn color. Also, it is susceptible to leaf blotch (a fungus disease) and leaf scorch (a physiological problem often related to hot, dry weather in late summer). Neither condition is fatal, but they reduce the ornamental value of the foliage and may cause premature defoliation. These and other problems can be minimized by planting the tree in a moist well-drained site sheltered from hot, dry winds and by mulching the area beneath its crown.

The wood of the horsechestnut is light, soft, brittle, and not naturally durable; but it is even textured and easy to work. In Europe it is used for food containers, kitchen utensils, artificial limbs, brush backs, toys, and small turned articles.

Basswood, *Tilia americana* L.

Distinguishing characteristics: *Leaves* simple, alternate, nearly round in outline, 3 to 6 inches long with petioles 1½ to 2 inches long; margins toothed; base heart shaped and often unequal; surfaces glabrous except for small tufts of hairs in the vein axils beneath. *Winter twigs* moderate in diameter, gray, glabrous; leaf scars small, half-round, with 3 or more bundle scars. *Buds* subglobose, 3/16 to ¼ inch long, lopsided, with 2 or 3 usually bright red scales; the terminal bud absent. *Flowers* white, perfect, fragrant, in open paniclelike clusters of 6 to 15, appearing in early summer; each inflorescence attached to an elongate, leaflike bract that persists in fruit. *Fruit* a dry, globe-shaped drupe ¼ to ⅓ inch in diameter, often persisting in winter. *Bark* smooth, light gray on young trees; becoming shallowly furrowed with long, narrow, parallel ridges.

Similar trees: Leaves of red mulberry are somewhat longer relative to their width with a rough upper surface, hairy lower surface, and only slightly heart-shaped base. The littleleaf linden has 1¼ to 2½ inch leaves that are pale bluish-green or whitened beneath. Winter: the bright red, 2- to 3-scaled buds of the basswood are distinctive.

Distribution: Native throughout the state.

THIS handsome tree is Iowa's only native member of the linden family, although several European relatives are frequently planted here as ornamentals. Native Americans used its tough, fibrous inner bark, or "bast," for making cords, thongs, and ropes, so the pioneers dubbed it "bastwood." Eventually the letter "t" was dropped, giving rise to the name we use today. Basswood is also called "American linden," the English equivalent of its botanical name.

Basswood is a common and often dominant tree in moist, upland woods throughout Iowa, especially on sheltered, north- and east-facing slopes in stream valleys. Frequent associates on such sites include hard maple, red oak, and bitternut hickory. Basswoods sprout readily from the base and in this manner renew themselves as their older trunks die, forming characteristic clumps of several stems.

Basswood is the favorite tree of both honeybees and their keepers. Its plain but fragrant June flowers attract bees and the strong-flavored nectar gives a distinctive taste to the resulting honey. The trees' heartwood is not naturally resistant to decay, so old trees in the woods are apt to be hollow, thus providing homes for colonies of wild bees and other animals. The wood is light, soft, and easily worked, imparting no taste or odor to foods it contacts, making it ideally suited for the frames of honeycombs and other apiary supplies. Other uses include boxes, crates, barrels, venetian blind slats, and veneer for the hidden parts of cabinets and furniture. Basswood is also a favorite for wood carving.

Basswood grows quickly and provides good shade, but its usefulness for landscaping is limited by its potentially large size—70 to 80 feet. Trees are usually pyramidal when young but tend to develop oval to oblong crowns as they age. The cultivar 'Redmond' can be purchased at many nurseries.

Of the European lindens planted in Iowa, the littleleaf linden, *Tilia cordata* Mill., has proved especially useful for street and yard plantings and is the most commonly planted. It grows more slowly than the basswood and is somewhat smaller in size, developing a dense, pyramidal crown that becomes broader with age. Like the basswood, its leaves turn yellow in autumn. Several cultivars are available.

Lindens are usually rather trouble-free, but the smooth, thin bark of younger trees is sometimes damaged by sunscald or cracking during winter. Borers and various leaf-feeding insects also may become a problem.

Russian-Olive, *Elaeagnus angustifolia* L.

Distinguishing characteristics: *Leaves* simple, alternate, linear to oblong-lanceolate, 1½ to 5 inches long with petioles ³⁄₁₆ to ⅜ inch long; margins entire; upper surface dark green and dotted with minute silver-gray scales, lower surface shiny silver-gray. *Winter twigs* slender, dark brown, covered by minute silver-gray scales, often bearing short thorns; leaf scars very small, half-round, with 1 bundle scar. *Buds* globose to short-ovoid, ¹⁄₁₆ to ⅛ inch long, gray-brown to silver-gray, with 4 visible scales. *Flowers* small, perfect or imperfect, yellow on inside, apetalous, solitary or in clusters of 2 to 4 from the axils of the leaves, appearing in early summer. *Fruit* oblong-ovoid, about ⅜ inch long, drupelike with a sweet mealy flesh, yellow with a covering of minute silver-gray scales, ripening in early autumn and persisting on the tree in winter. *Bark* light gray; separating into long, vertically oriented, often shreddy strips; eventually furrowed with flattened ridges.

Similar trees: No other tree has the minute silvery scales that cover the leaves, twigs, and fruits of this species.

Distribution: Cultivated throughout the state, occasionally escaping to woods and open areas.

MOST small ornamental trees are planted primarily for showy flowers or fruits, but the greatest asset of the Russian-olive is its attractive foliage. The minute silvery scales covering the dark green surfaces of its leaves and young twigs give the crown of the tree a handsome gray-green cast when viewed from a distance. These scales, which appear as tiny dots on the upper surface of the leaves and as a thin coat of silver plating on their lower surface, resemble silvery stars through a microscope.

Russian-olive is a small, fast-growing tree with a short trunk and an open, rounded crown. It usually matures at a height of 12 to 20 feet but occasionally grows to 40 feet or more. At one time, the largest specimen in the United States was located on a residential property in Ames. This tree was 63 feet tall with a 45-foot spread and a trunk over 3 feet in diameter.

Because of its hardiness, adaptability, and handsome foliage, Russian-olive has been widely planted in Iowa for landscaping, conservation, and highway beautification. It will grow in most soils, including alkaline ones, and tolerates drought, salt, and dirty air. It is a soil-improving species like many legumes, harboring nitrogen-fixing bacteria in nodules on its roots. Wild birds and mammals relish its small, berrylike fruits, which persist on the trees in winter.

Unfortunately, Russian-olive is usually short-lived in cultivation and tends to develop a straggly, disheveled appearance as it ages. It is susceptible to both verticilium wilt and phomopsis canker, especially when stressed by injury or poor drainage. Sixty years is considered a ripe old age for a tree of this species and most lose their ornamental value long before then.

Russian-olive is native from Central Asia to southeastern Europe, growing in a wide variety of habitats. In the Soviet Union its fruits are used to make a strong alcoholic beverage; its bark and foliage are employed in tanning; and its wood is used for posts, beams, fuel, and musical instruments.

Russian-olive is a member of the small but widely distributed Oleaster family and not related to the olive of commerce. Other members of this family that can be seen in Iowa are the autumn-olive (*Elaeagnus umbellata* Thunb.), which was introduced from the Orient for wildlife plantings, and the buffalo berry (*Shepherdia argentea* Nutt.), which is native in the loess hills of extreme western Iowa. Like other members of the family, both have silver scales on their leaves. Autumn-olive can be distinguished by its juicy red fruits and in having brownish scales as well as silver ones; buffalo berry has opposite leaves. Both species are shrubs.

Dogwoods, *Cornus* L.

MOST upright woody plants can be easily placed in one of two clearly defined categories, trees or shrubs, but this distinction blurs when dogwoods are considered. Though usually no taller than 15 feet (the size range of shrubs), dogwoods are often single stemmed like trees. If one encounters an unfamiliar plant of this size in the woods, nothing indicates whether it is a tree sapling or merely a tall shrub that has abandoned its typical clumped habit.

Dogwoods as a group are fairly easy to recognize. Relatively few trees have simple, unlobed leaves with entire (untoothed) margins; among those that do, dogwoods are unique in having strongly curved leaf veins that follow the margins. Dogwood leaves are also arranged opposite one another on the twig (except in one species), another distinctive feature among entire-leaved trees. When the leaves fall in autumn, the bases of their petioles (stalks) remain on the twig, so the resulting scars are conspicuously raised, easily distinguishing dogwoods from maples and the handful of other trees having twigs with opposite leaf scars.

Despite the distinctiveness of dogwoods as a group, the many species are similar to one another and often hard to identify. Characteristics used to separate species include the shape of the leaves; the type and relative abundance of hairs on the surfaces of the leaves; the color of the twigs, pith, stems, and ripe fruits; and the arrangement of the flowers. Winter identification is especially difficult.

Dogwoods are among the most important of our native plants to wildlife. Their small, berrylike drupes are eagerly devoured by many songbirds (including the cardinal, robin, bluebird, wood thrush, cedar waxwing, catbird, brown thrasher, purple finch, and evening grosbeak) as well as by important gamebirds (such as the pheasant, quail, turkey, and ruffled grouse). Dogwood thickets provide shelter and nesting cover for many small birds and mammals and their twigs and foliage are eaten by deer and rabbits.

Six dogwoods are native to Iowa and several introduced species are planted here as ornamentals. They are included in the key at the end of this book. Further information on their botanical characteristics can be obtained from Fernald (1950) and Rehder (1940).

ALTERNATE-LEAF DOGWOOD, *Cornus alternifolia* L. Native in moist upland woods as far west as the Des Moines River. It is our only dogwood with alternate leaves. It is also our largest native dogwood, frequently becoming treelike in stature and 10 to 25 feet tall. Many people call it the "pagoda dogwood" because its numerous horizontal branches are arranged in distinct tiers like the stories of an oriental pagoda. Alternate-leaf dogwood is a handsome ornamental tree. Its tiny white flowers, which appear after the leaves are grown in late spring, are packed together in showy, flat-topped clusters 1½ to 2½ inches in diameter. It requires a moist, fertile, well-drained soil and seems to prefer partial shade.

ROUGH-LEAF DOGWOOD, *C. drummondii* Meyer. Native in thickets, open woods, and wood edges across most of Iowa, though more common in the south than the north. It is the largest of our opposite-leaved dogwoods, often becoming single-stemmed and 10 to 15 feet tall. Its leaves are about twice as long as wide, with rough upper surfaces and 3 to 5 pairs of veins. Its lower leaf surfaces are densely covered with tiny, curled hairs that are quite conspicuous through a magnifying glass, though obscure to the naked eye. The tiny white flowers occur in dense, slightly round-topped clusters and the ripe fruits are white.

RED-OSIER DOGWOOD, *C. stolonifera* Michx. (*C. sericea* L.). Easily identified at all times of the year by its bright red stems, which typically form large clumps. It is native in moist, low-lying places in northern Iowa, but it is seen more frequently in cultivation than in the wild. It closely resembles several introduced species that are also sold as "red-stemmed dogwoods."

GRAY DOGWOOD, *C. racemosa* Lam. Our most common native dogwood, occurring in dry open woods and edges throughout all but extreme northwestern Iowa. Its leaves are at least twice as long as wide, with 3 to 5 pairs of veins and tiny, straight, closely appressed hairs scattered over the smooth surfaces. Its open, paniclelike flower clusters are about as tall as wide, with bright red branches. The ripe fruits are white.

ROUNDLEAF DOGWOOD, *C. rugosa* Lam. Native on moist, wooded slopes in the eastern one-half to two-thirds of Iowa, though common only in the northeastern part of the state. It is one of the easiest dogwoods to identify, having nearly round leaves with 6 to 8 pairs of veins and greenish stems usually blotched with purple.

SILKY DOGWOOD, *C. obliqua* Raf. (*C. purpussii* Koehne). Native along stream banks, shorelines, and edges of bottomland woods throughout all but extreme northwestern Iowa. It is very similar to gray dogwood, but it has flat-topped flower clusters with greenish branches and blue fruits.

CORNELIAN-CHERRY, *C. mas* L. Small cultivated tree 20 to 25 feet high with a low, rounded crown. Its tiny yellow flowers, which appear before its leaves in spring, are borne in small, umbellike clusters. Its pear-shaped fruits are bright red when ripe in summer and about ⅝ inch long. Cornelian-cherry is recommended for landscaping where hardy in southern, central, and eastern Iowa. It transplants easily, will grow in a variety of soils, and has no serious diseases or insect pests.

FLOWERING DOGWOOD, *C. florida* L. Small, flat-topped tree 10 to 30 feet tall that is native throughout most of the eastern and southern United States, where it is highly prized as an ornamental. It grows satisfactorily in southern, eastern, and central Iowa when planted in good soils; but its flower buds usually do not survive the winters in most parts of Iowa.

Green Ash, *Fraxinus pennsylvanica* Marsh.

Distinguishing characteristics: *Leaves* once-pinnately compound, oppo-site (rarely subopposite), 10 to 12 inches long; leaflets 5 to 9 in number (usually 7), oblong-lanceolate or less commonly elliptic, 2 to 6 inches long, tapering at the base and extending along the upper side of their 1/16 to 3/16 inch stalks; margins conspicuously toothed; upper surface dark green and often glossy, lower surface light green and either glabrous or hairy. *Winter twigs* moderate in diameter, gray, glabrous or finely hairy; leaf scars small, half-round to nearly round, bundle scars numerous and very close together, forming a fine curved line. *Buds* globose to subglobose, brown, with 1 or 2 pairs of visible scales, the terminal 1/8 to 1/4 inch long and the laterals varying from much smaller to nearly equal in size. *Flowers* dioe-cious, apetalous, very small, appearing with or before leaves; stami-nate in short compact panicles, pistillate in open panicles. *Fruit* a narrow, paddle-shaped samara 1 to 2 inches long that often persists in winter; wing extending along upper half of seed cavity. *Bark* ashy gray or gray-brown, furrowed, with narrow interconnecting ridges enclosing diamond-shaped spaces.

Similar trees: Black ash has 9 to 11 unstalked leaflets and fruits with indistinct, flattened seed cavities. (See also discussion under *White Ash.*)

Distribution: Native throughout the state.

THE green ash is one of our most adaptable native trees and has long been popular for street and yard plantings in Iowa. It grows rather quickly, provides good shade, thrives in a variety of soils and environments, and has attractive leaves that turn bright yellow in autumn. When grown in the open it reaches a height of 50 to 70 feet and develops an irregular or rounded crown. The branches tend to bend downward, then curve up at the tips.

Like other ashes, the green ash is dioecious. This means that the staminate (male) and pistillate (female) flowers occur on separate trees, so some trees never fruit.

The female trees produce prodigious numbers of small, winged seeds that are dispersed by the wind, producing new generations of trees in hedges, shrubbery, fencerows, wood edges, and other uncultivated areas.

The oldest green ash in our towns and cities were seedling trees, probably collected locally. Because of natu-ral variation within wild populations, these trees differ in habit of growth and other characteristics. Most of the trees sold in nurseries today are cultivars, which are propa-gated vegetatively to insure uniformity. These trees were selected for desirable horticultural features such as sym-metry in form, glossy foliage, and in some cases, lack of seeds.

When green ash are growing vigorously, they are sel-dom troubled by diseases or insects. If a tree is weakened by drought or injury, however, it may be attacked by bor-ers, cankers, or verticillium wilt. Wet spring weather may foster the development of foliage diseases such as anthrac-nose, leaf spot, or rust, which can cause defoliation but usually do not seriously harm the tree. Other common but usually minor problems include powdery mildew, aphids, plant bugs, sawflies, and flower gall mites. The latter cause the staminate flowers to develop aberrantly, produc-ing unsightly brown galls that persist on the trees in winter.

Some botanists distinguish two varieties of green ash. The form most commonly seen in Iowa is variety *subinte-gerrima,* which has glabrous twigs and leaves. Variety *pennsylvanica,* often called red ash, has densely pubescent twigs and thinner leaflets, usually pubescent beneath.

Native green ash usually grows in moist, low-lying areas such as floodplains and lakeshores. It is a desirable tree for reforestation where the soil is not too dry.

White Ash, *Fraxinus americana* L.

Distinguishing characteristics: *Leaves* pinnately compound, opposite, 8 to 12 inches long; leaflets 5 to 9 in number (usually 7), ovate-lanceolate to oval, 2 to 6 inches long with stalks ³⁄₁₆ to ½ inch long; margins entire or obscurely toothed (rarely with conspicuous teeth); upper surface dark green and sometimes glossy, lower surface light green or very pale, glabrous. *Winter twigs* moderate in diameter, gray or brown, glabrous; leaf scars small, half-round to nearly round, with a conspicuous V-shaped notch in the top, bundle scars numerous and very close together, forming a fine curved line. *Buds* and *flowers* similar to green ash. *Fruit* a paddle-shaped samara 1 to 2 inches long, often persisting into winter; wing not extending along seed cavity. *Bark* similar to green ash.

Similar trees: See discussion below.

Distribution: Native west to the Cedar River in northern Iowa, to the Des Moines River and its principal tributaries in the central part of the state, and to the Missouri River in southern Iowa.

WHITE ASH is the largest of our native ashes and one of the most important broadleaf timber trees in the United States. Its hard, heavy, tough, straight-grained, and shock-resistant wood is the principal source of handles for rakes, hoes, shovels, and other long-handled tools. Ash wood is also the preferred material for a variety of sporting goods, including baseball bats, tennis rackets, skis, snowshoes, oars, paddles, and polo and hockey sticks. Other important uses include chair bottoms and the bent parts of furniture, veneer, agricultural implements, dairy and apiary supplies, woodenware, firewood, boxes and crates, barrels, and pallets. Few trees are so useful for such a variety of products.

White ash usually grows in upland woods with oaks, hickories, and black cherry but also occurs on moist, sheltered slopes with hard maple and basswood. Although it is seldom a dominant tree in Iowa, its seedlings are often abundant in the forest understory as they are tolerant of shade. Small white ash are also common in the edges of upland woods and neighboring uncultivated areas. In autumn it is one of the earliest native trees to turn color, with leaves varying from bright yellow to dark purple.

White ash makes an excellent shade tree, but it is planted less often than the faster-growing and more adaptable green ash. It may grow 70 to 80 feet tall with a trunk diameter of 2 to 3 feet, and usually develops an open, rounded crown. Nurseries offer several cultivars that were selected for attractive habit of growth, dark green summer foliage, and purple fall color. Disease and insect problems are similar to those of green ash.

White ash closely resembles the green ash in most respects and the two species are often confused, but one can learn to distinguish them with practice. White ash has relatively broad leaflets with entire or obscurely toothed margins and stalks about ¼ inch long; its leaf scars are usually notched at the top; and the wing of its samara (seed) does not extend along the edge of the seed cavity. Green ash tends to have narrow, conspicuously toothed leaflets with stalks about ⅛ inch long; the upper edge of its leaf scars are straight or curved; and the wing of its samara extends along the upper half of the seed cavity. Both species are quite variable, so it is wise to examine several features and not rely on just one.

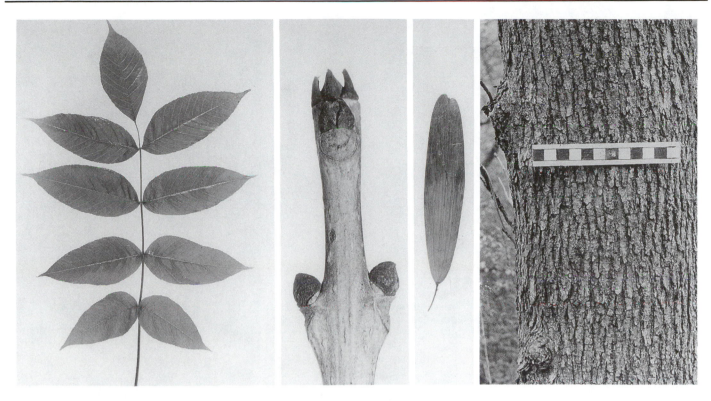

Black Ash, *Fraxinus nigra* Marsh.

Distinguishing characteristics: *Leaves* pinnately compound, opposite, 12 to 16 inches long; leaflets 7 to 13 in number (usually 9 to 11), oblong-lanceolate, 3 to 6 inches long, sessile, conspicuously toothed, glabrous except for tufts of orange-brown hairs where they join leaf stem. *Winter twigs* moderate to stout, gray, glabrous; leaf scars half-round to nearly round; bundle scars numerous and close together, forming a fine curved line. *Buds* similar to green ash, but usually black. *Flowers* polygamous or dioecious, apetalous, very small, appearing with or before the leaves in spring; staminate in short compact panicles, pistillate in open panicles. *Fruit* a paddle-shaped samara 1 to 1½ inches long, often persisting in winter; wing notched at apex, surrounding the flat indistinct seed cavity. *Bark* gray, scaly, becoming shallowly and rather indistinctly furrowed on large trees.

Similar trees: Green ash has 7 short-stalked leaflets per leaf, brown buds, and narrow samaras with distinct seed cavities that are rounded in cross section. Hickories and walnuts have alternate leaves and leaf scars.

Distribution: Native west to the Des Moines River valley.

BLACK ASH is less familiar to most Iowans than the green and white ashes, because it is much less common in forests here and is rarely used in landscaping. It is easy to identify once encountered, having longer leaves, stouter twigs, darker buds, and much different seeds and bark than its well-known relatives.

Black ash grows in moist habitats throughout most of southeastern Canada and the northeastern United States. In Iowa it occurs on floodplains, terraces, ravines, and the bases of steep sheltered slopes in stream valleys, usually as a minor associate of better known and more important species. These include silver maple, cottonwood, black walnut, hackberry, and elms in bottomlands and hard maple, red oak, and basswood on higher ground. Its saplings, being intolerant of shade, are uncommon in the woodland understory except where the canopy is fairly open.

The wood of black ash is somewhat lighter, softer, and weaker than that of the white and green ashes and is usually marketed separately from those species. The best logs are used for the same purposes as white ash; and black ash is often preferred for cabinetwork and interior trim because of its more attractive figure. "Curly ash," a handsome grain highly esteemed for veneer, comes from tumorlike growths called burls from the trunks of this species. Native Americans and pioneers used black ash for making baskets, as its tough, flexible wood splits easily along the narrow annual growth rings.

Another native ash that is not very well known is the blue ash (*Fraxinus quadrangulata* Michx.). It grows only in Lee and Des Moines counties in the southeastern corner of the state, inhabiting dry bluffs overlooking the Des Moines and Mississippi rivers. From Iowa its range extends south to Arkansas and east to Tennessee, Kentucky, and Ohio.

Blue ash is characterized by 5 to 11 (usually 7) short-stalked, ovate to lanceolate leaflets; square twigs with 4 corky wings; perfect flowers; scaly bark; and samaras with indistinct, flattened seed cavities. It is named for its mucilaginous inner bark, which turns blue when exposed to the air and was once used to dye fabrics.

Little is known about the value of the black and blue ashes for landscaping, but both are being grown and evaluated at several midwestern arboretums, so more information about their potential use should be available in the future. In nature they grow to be medium-sized trees, 40 to 70 feet tall, with rather narrow, open crowns.

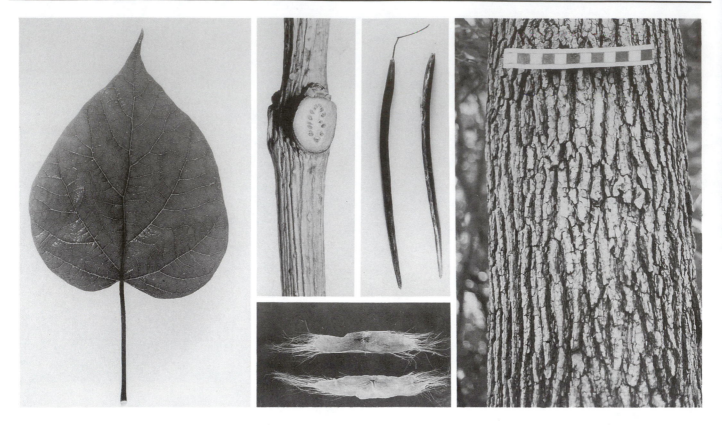

Northern Catalpa, *Catalpa speciosa* Warder

Distinguishing characteristics: *Leaves* simple, opposite or in whorls of 3, broadly ovate, 6 to 12 inches long with petioles 5 to 6 inches long; margins entire; base heart shaped or truncate. *Winter twigs* moderate to stout, brown, glabrous; leaf scars large, round with numerous bundle scars arranged in an elliptic or circular pattern. *Buds* globose, with about a half dozen loosely attached scales, partially embedded in the bark of the twigs and often inconspicuous; the terminal bud absent. *Flowers* white, indistinctly dotted with yellow and/or purple, perfect, irregular, 1½ to 2 inches long and about 1½ inches across, in panicles, appearing in early summer. *Fruit* a pencil-shaped pod (capsule) 6 to 20 inches long and about ½ inch in diameter, persisting on the tree in winter; seeds winged, with long white hairs at the tips of the wings. *Bark* brown or gray, separating into small scaly plates; eventually shallowly furrowed with short, scaly ridges.

Similar trees: Red mulberry is the only other common tree having leaves of this size and shape, but its leaves have toothed margins and are alternately arranged. Winter: the large, round, opposite or whorled leaf scars and persistent pods are distinctive.

Distribution: Cultivated throughout the state; persisting in abandoned farmsteads and occasionally escaping to stream banks, roadsides, and waste places.

THIS tropical-looking tree seems strangely out of place in the prairie towns and farms of Iowa. When European settlers first ventured west of the Appalachians, it was restricted to a small range centered in the boot-heel region of southeastern Missouri. However, the settlers soon found it to be a useful, adaptable, and hardy species that would grow well throughout the Midwest. Today it is seldom planted, but many fine old specimens remain in farm groves and along city streets to remind us of the popularity it once enjoyed.

The most interesting feature of the catalpa is the long, pencil-shaped seed pods or "Indian beans" that appear on its branches in midsummer. They change from green to brown when they ripen in autumn, whereupon they split open along two seams and release the seeds within. At least some of the pods remain on the branches throughout the winter, making the catalpa easy to recognize then. The seeds, which have a papery wing suggestive of a propellor in shape, are easily blown about by the wind and may germinate if they land in a suitable seedbed. In this manner the catalpa sometimes escapes to stream banks, roadsides, open woods, and other uncultivated places.

Catalpa is one of our largest ornamental flowering trees, attaining a height of 30 to 60 feet and developing an open, irregularly pyramidal or oval crown. Its attractive blossoms, fast growth, and tolerance of many soil types are points in its favor, although its large size should be considered before planting it in a small yard. Other disadvantages are its poor autumn color and the debris created by the large leaves and pods when they fall.

The wood of the catalpa is light, soft, and weak but naturally durable when properly seasoned. Many groves of this species were planted during the 1930s; as it thrives in a variety of soils, tolerates droughty conditions, and was reputed to produce good quality fence posts in a shorter period of time than any other tree. Though unimportant as a timber tree today, catalpa is occasionally used for posts, rails, interior finish, cabinetwork, picture frames, and firewood.

The southern catalpa (*C. bignonioides* Walt.) is occasionally planted in southern Iowa. It closely resembles northern catalpa but has flowers only 1 to 1½ inches long and 1 inch across that are conspicuously spotted with yellow or purple, leaves with a fetid odor when bruised, and pods ¼ to ⅓ inch in diameter. It is native to the Gulf Coast states.

Other Trees

THE preceding pages describe and illustrate Iowa's native and common introduced trees. Included here are several less common, non-native species that are of interest ornamentally or commercially. All are included in the Key to Trees of Iowa (Chapter 5). For further information about these and other trees occasionally planted in Iowa, consult the reference books cited in the bibliography.

BALDCYPRESS, *Taxodium distichum* (L.) Rich. *Leaves* linear, flat, ¼ to ¾ inch long, green on both surfaces, spirally arranged but appearing two ranked, deciduous in autumn. *Cones* ball shaped, ¾ to 1 inch in diameter, with thick woody scales. *Bark* gray or red-brown, dividing into flat ridges separated by shallow furrows.

BALDCYPRESS is native to swamps in the southeastern United States and might seem to be an unsuitable tree for planting in Iowa. It is hardy far to the north of its natural range, however, and has proved to be an adaptable species that will grow in both upland and bottomland sites. In cultivation it is narrowly to broadly pyramidal in habit, eventually reaching a height of 60 feet or more. Unlike most conifers, its leaves are completely deciduous in autumn.

The moderately hard and heavy wood of this species is exceptionally durable when exposed to the elements. It is widely used for posts, beams, dock and bridge timbers, siding, millwork, tanks, vats, and caskets.

Eastern hemlock

EASTERN HEMLOCK, *Tsuga canadensis* (L.) Carr. *Leaves* linear, evergreen, flat, ⅓ to ½ inch long, dark green above and marked with 2 white bands below, spirally arranged but appearing two ranked, with those on the upper surface of the twig shorter and frequently upside down. *Cones* ½ to ¾ inch long, with thin papery scales. *Bark* gray, and scaly, often with a reddish cast, eventually becoming deeply furrowed.

HEMLOCK is one of the most handsome of our ornamental conifers but unfortunately it is sensitive to heat and dryness. Individual hemlocks often do very well in cool,

moist, sheltered locations, especially in eastern and central Iowa, but trees of this species should not be planted on dry or exposed sites. The trees develop a pyramidal crown and eventually attain heights of 60 to 70 feet.

Hemlock is native to the northeastern United States and southeastern Canada. It is not poisonous; the beverage that killed Socrates was made from an herb of the parsley family, not the tree. Native Americans made a poultice from the inner bark of the hemlock and brewed a medicinal tea from its leaves and twigs. Its wood is used for pulp and construction lumber.

EUROPEAN ALDER, *Alnus glutinosa* (L.) Gaertn. *Leaves* simple, alternate, nearly round, 2 to 5 inches long, coarsely toothed with veins running to the tips of the teeth. *Winter twigs* slender, brown, with exposed catkins. *Buds* stalked, ovoid, ¼ to ½ inch long, with 2 dark purple scales that meet along their edges without overlapping. *Fruit* a nutlet borne with others of its kind in a woody "cone" ⅜ to ¾ inch long, the cones persisting on the twigs in winter. *Bark* smooth, gray, with prominent white lenticels on small trees, eventually dark and scaly.

THIS wide-ranging European tree was introduced to America during colonial times for the production of timber for charcoal. In recent years it has attracted the interest of foresters at research institutions who believe it shows promise as a commercial source of pulp and furniture wood, a "nurse" tree for more valuable timber species, and a reclaimer of strip-mined land. It is a soil-improving species like the legumes, harboring nitrogen-fixing microorganisms in nodules on its roots.

European alder makes an attractive ornamental and is occasionally used for landscaping in Iowa. Its tolerance of wet soils makes it especially useful for the borders of ponds, streams, and areas that are frequently flooded. Trees grow quickly when young, eventually reaching a height of 40 to 60 feet and developing an irregularly ovoid or oblong crown. The leaves are a handsome dark, glossy green throughout the summer and fall, with little color change in autumn.

American beech

AMERICAN BEECH, *Fagus grandifolia* Ehrh. *Leaves* simple, alternate, elliptic to oblong-ovate, 2½ to 6 inches long, distantly toothed, with the veins running to the tips of the teeth. *Winter twigs* slender, brown, with long narrow stipule scars. *Buds* elongate, ½ to 1 inch long, with numerous brown scales. *Flowers* tiny, monoecious, apetalous, the staminate in ball-shaped clusters and the pistillate in pairs or short spikes, appearing shortly after the leaves in spring. *Fruit* an edible, pyramid-shaped nut ½ to ¾ inch long, 2 or 3 within a small bur covered with short weak spines. *Bark* light gray and very smooth throughout the life of the tree.

AMERICAN BEECH is a common forest tree throughout most of the eastern United States, ranging as far west as eastern Wisconsin, extreme eastern Illinois, and southeastern Missouri. It makes a beautiful ornamental but is not well suited for general landscape use in Iowa, being very sensitive to heat and dryness. Nevertheless, individual trees may do very well in eastern and central Iowa if planted in a cool, sheltered location where the soil is moist but well-drained. Beech trees eventually attain a height of 70 to 80 feet.

The wood of the American beech is hard, heavy, and strong but not naturally durable. It is used for clothespins, the bent parts of furniture, food barrels, charcoal, railroad ties (when treated with preservative), pulp, and many other products.

AMERICAN CHESTNUT, *Castanea dentata* (Marsh.) Borkh. *Leaves* simple, alternate, oblong-lanceolate, 5½ to 8 inches long, sharply toothed, with the veins running to the tips of the teeth. *Winter twigs* moderate, red-brown. *Buds* ovoid, about ¼ inch long, red-brown, with 2 or 3 visible scales. *Flowers* monoecious, in catkins, appearing after the leaves. *Fruit* an edible nut ½ to 1 inch long, 2 or 3 within a large bur covered with long sharp spines. *Bark* brown, furrowed.

AMERICAN CHESTNUT was once a common forest tree in the eastern United States, but most large trees have been killed by the chestnut blight. Although there is no cure for this disease, small trees are still common in many areas because chestnut sprouts readily from the stumps. The resulting stems remain uninfected for several years, often becoming large enough to bear flowers and a few nuts before succumbing to the blight.

Chestnut is not native to Iowa but once was widely planted here for its valuable lumber and nuts. Unfortunately, chestnut blight has now reached the Hawkeye State. The Chinese chestnut (*C. mollissima* Bl.) is resistant to the disease and should be planted instead of the American species if a chestnut is desired.

Chestnut was once an important source of tannin and its durable wood was widely used for poles, posts, railroad ties, furniture, and caskets. Wood salvaged from large blight-killed trees is still highly valued for paneling.

TULIP TREE, *Liriodendron tulipifera* L. *Leaves* simple, alternate, 4 lobed with shallowly notched apices, 4 to 6 inches long, entire. *Winter twigs* moderate, dark red-brown, aromatic when cut, with conspicuous round leaf scars; stipule scars encircling the twig at each node. *Buds* duckbill shaped, with 2 green or dark red scales that meet along the edges without overlapping, the terminal about ½ inch long. *Flowers* large, perfect, yellow-green marked with orange on the inside, solitary at the twig tips, blooming in early summer. *Fruit* a conelike aggregate of samaras, persisting on the twigs in winter. *Bark* gray, shallowly furrowed.

Tulip tree

THIS tree is occasionally planted as an ornamental in southern, eastern, and central Iowa. The species is not reliably hardy in the northern part of the state, but individual trees sometimes do very well in a sheltered location with proper care. Tulip trees should not be planted in a small yard; they commonly reach heights of 80 to 100 feet and sometimes become much larger.

Tulip tree is native to the eastern United States. It is often called "yellow poplar" or "tulip poplar," but it is actually a member of the magnolia family and not related to the poplars. Its light, soft, greenish wood is used for veneer, paper pulp, doors, window sash and blinds, core stock for plywood, and many other products.

SASSAFRAS, *Sassafras albidum* (Nutt.) Nees. *Leaves* simple, alternate, entire, 3 to 6 inches long, of three shapes on the same tree: unlobed, mitten shaped (1 lobed), and 3 lobed. *Winter twigs* moderate, green, with a spicy taste. *Buds* subglobose, green, with 3 or 4 scales, the terminal about ⅓ inch long. *Flowers* small, yellow-green, dioecious, in racemes, appearing with the leaves in spring. *Fruit* a dark blue drupe about ⅓ inch in diameter, supported by a bright red clublike stalk. *Bark* red-brown, furrowed.

SASSAFRAS is common throughout the eastern United States, ranging as far west as Michigan, Illinois, Missouri, Oklahoma, and Texas. It is often reported as being native in southeastern Iowa, but the only wild-growing specimens so far discovered are in and near an abandoned farmstead in Lee County. These trees were probably introduced many years ago, although there is no way to determine their origin.

Sassafras is usually a small tree but sometimes attains a height of 60 feet or more when grown on moist, fertile soils. Its picturesque branching, unusual leaves, and beautiful autumn color make it an interesting ornamental and it is occasionally cultivated in the southern part of Iowa. Oil of sassafras, an aromatic substance distilled from the root bark of the tree, has been used for flavoring root beer, candy, medicine, tea, and spring tonics. The durable wood is used for fence posts and occasionally for small boats.

SWEETGUM, *Liquidambar styraciflua* L. *Leaves* simple, alternate, star shaped (palmately 5 to 7 lobed), 4 to 7 inches long, toothed. *Winter twigs* moderate, green or red-brown, often developing corky outgrowths their second year. *Buds* ovoid, reddish-brown, with 6 or more scales, the terminal ¼ to ½ inch long. *Flowers* small, green, monoecious, the staminate in racemes and the pistillate in ball-shaped heads, appearing with the leaves in spring. *Fruit* ball shaped, woody, prickly, 1 to 1½ inches in diameter, composed of many small capsules. *Bark* gray-brown, furrowed.

SWEETGUM is common in the river bottom forests of the southeastern United States and frequently is grown as a shade tree where native. It is not dependably hardy in most parts of Iowa, often suffering twig dieback during severe winters, and only trees from the northern part of its range should be planted here. The species is well known for beautiful autumn color, but this varies from one individual to the next. Mature trees are often 80 or more feet tall.

Sweetgum is one of the most important broadleaf timber trees in the United States. Its moderately hard and heavy wood is used for veneer, furniture, cabinets, interior trim, and many other goods.

YELLOWWOOD, *Cladrastis lutea* (Michx.) K. Koch. *Leaves* once-pinnately compound, alternate; leaflets 5 to 11 in number, oval, 2 to 4 inches long, entire. *Winter twigs* moderate, brown. *Buds* cone shaped, ⅛ to ¼ inch long, hairy, hidden within the bases of the petioles. *Flowers* perfect, white, irregular, in showy racemes, blooming in late spring or early summer. *Fruit* a flattened pod (legume) 3 to 4 inches long with thin papery walls and 4 to 6 small seeds. *Bark* smooth, gray.

THIS attractive ornamental tree is native to a limited area in the south central United States but is hardy in Iowa and other states far north of its natural range. Its trunk usually ends a few feet above the ground, giving way to a broad, rounded crown of handsome, bright green leaves. Trees grow well in most well-drained soils and are seldom bothered by diseases and insects, but they have an unfortunate tendency to produce weak crotches that split easily in storms. They are usually 30 to 50 feet tall at maturity.

The yellow heartwood of this species is hard and strong, but it is of little importance commercially because the trees are scarce and have unusually short trunks. The settlers obtained a yellow dye from the roots by chopping them up and boiling the resulting chips.

AMUR CORKTREE, *Phellodendron amurense* Rupr. *Leaves* once-pinnately compound, opposite; leaflets 5 to 13 in number, ovate, 2 to 4 inches long, distantly and obscurely toothed, dotted with tiny glands (hold up to light). *Winter twigs* moderate to rather stout, orange-brown. *Buds* cone shaped, small, hairy, hidden within the bases of the petioles. *Flowers* dioecious, small, yellow-green, in panicles, blooming in late spring or early summer. *Fruit* a black drupe about ⅜ inch in diameter. *Bark* smooth and gray on saplings, becoming dark and deeply furrowed.

THIS small- to medium-sized tree is hardy throughout Iowa and is occasionally used for landscaping. It develops a broad, open crown and is picturesque in winter with its thick, corky bark and wide-spreading branches. It is also easy to transplant, very adaptable to soil, and remarkably free of diseases and insect pests. Its leaves turn yellow in autumn and fall quickly.

Although the corktree has many desirable features, it sometimes "escapes" from cultivation and becomes a weed. The small, berrylike fruits produced by pistillate trees are eaten by birds, which then spread the seeds to woods and other uncultivated areas. This problem can be avoided by planting grafted staminate trees, which do not bear fruit.

The corktree is native to Manchuria and northern China. It is closely related to orange, lemon, lime, and other citrus trees as well as to our native prickly-ash and hoptree.

PERSIMMON, *Diospyros virginiana* L. *Leaves* simple, alternate, oval to oblong-ovate, 2 to 6 inches long, entire. *Winter twigs* rather slender, gray-brown. *Buds* subglobose, about ⅛ inch long, with 2 scales that commonly persist at the bases of new shoots and 1-year-old twigs. *Flowers* dioecious, bell shaped, yellow-green, solitary or in small clusters from the leaf axils in spring. *Fruit* edible, yellow or pale orange berry ¾ to 1½ inches in diameter, often persisting on the twig in winter. *Bark* dark brown or gray, separating into characteristic thick, blocky plates.

PERSIMMON, a small- to medium-sized tree, 25 to 50 feet tall, grows naturally throughout the southeastern United States as far north as Missouri, Illinois, Indiana, Ohio, Pennsylvania, and Connecticut. It has long been cultivated in southern Iowa and persists around abandoned farmsteads, forming large thickets as if native. Wild-growing persimmons have also been reported in woods along the Des Moines River in Van Buren County, but the origin of the trees there is unknown.

Persimmon is best known for its fruits, which remain puckery and inedible until their skin becomes wrinkled and their flesh soft in late autumn. They are greatly appreciated by opossums, raccoons, skunks, foxes, and many birds as well as by people. The larger persimmons sold in stores are from an Asian relative of this species (*Diospyros kaki* L.).

Persimmon is also valued for its wood, which is hard, heavy, strong, and wears very smooth. It is used largely for shuttles, spools, bobbins, and golf club heads.

JAPANESE TREE LILAC, *Syringa reticulata* (Blume) Hara. *Leaves* simple, opposite, broadly ovate, 2 to 5½ inches long, entire. *Winter twigs* rather slender, greenish-brown or brown. *Buds* subglobose, about ⅛ inch long, with 4 to 6 pairs of light brown scales. *Flowers*, perfect, white, in large terminal panicles, blooming in early summer. *Fruit* a 2-celled, thin-walled, cigar-shaped pod (capsule) about ¾ inch long, splitting open at maturity and remaining on the twig all winter. *Bark* rather smooth, dark gray, with prominent white lenticels, eventually separating into small plates.

MOST of the many species of lilacs planted in Iowa are shrubs, but this species becomes a small tree, 20 to 30 feet tall, with an oval to rounded crown. Though perhaps best known for its showy, fragrant flowers, which bloom later than those of shrub lilacs, it is also very attractive in winter with its cherrylike bark and picturesque branching pattern. It is hardy throughout Iowa.

Large Native and Naturalized Shrubs

THE DIFFERENCE between trees and shrubs is usually obvious but some woody plants do not fit well into either category. The wahoo and prickly-ash, which grow naturally in all parts of Iowa, are two examples. Both are usually no more than 6 to 12 feet high and thus are in the size range of shrubs; but they commonly develop a single main stem and are decidedly treelike in appearance. Other species, such as the bladdernut, are usually multistemmed and 10 to 15 feet tall but occasionally develop a single stem up to 25 feet tall.

In the absence of any reliable natural distinctions between trees and shrubs, it becomes necessary to construct artificial ones. The United States Forest Service defines a tree as a woody plant having a single erect stem (trunk) at least 3 inches in diameter at breast height, a minimum height of 12 feet, and a definitely formed crown of leaves. Species that typically or at least frequently conform to this definition are described in the preceding pages; those that only occasionally do so are described below. All are included in the key at the end of this book (Chapter 5).

Several other native shrubs, though not known to reach tree size in Iowa, are apt to be mistaken for tree saplings in the woods because their leaves and twigs are so similar to those of common trees. These shrubs are also described below and included in the key.

CANADA YEW, *Taxus canadensis* Marsh. *Leaves* linear, evergreen, alternate, ⅜ to 1 inch long, dark green above and light green below, abruptly tapered to short-pointed tips. *Seeds* black; about 3⁄16 inch long; seated in bright red, fleshy, cup-shaped structures; solitary in the leaf axils. Plants dioecious.

CANADA YEW is native on rocky bluffs and moist wooded slopes in eastern Iowa. A prostrate shrub only 2 or 3 feet high, it sometimes forms large colonies that are very difficult to walk through.

Yews have beautiful, dark green foliage and several introduced species have long been popular in landscaping, especially the Japanese yew (*T. cuspidata* Sieb and Zucc.). This species resembles our native yew in foliage and seed but has upright stems. Its slow growth and ability to withstand frequent pruning recommend it for foundation and hedge plantings. It requires a moist but well-drained soil.

The seeds of yews, which are found only on female plants, are seated in bright red cups that greatly enhance the ornamental value of the foliage. Unfortunately, the seeds, bark, and foliage are poisonous.

COMMON JUNIPER, *Juniperus communis* L. *Leaves* needle like, evergreen, in whorls of 3, ¼ to ⅝ inch long, the upper surface concave and marked with a vertical white band. *Cones* blue or black, berrylike, about ¼ inch in diameter. Plants dioecious.

COMMON JUNIPER has the broadest range of any conifer; it is native across much of Europe, Asia, and North America. Some of its numerous varieties grow upright and become small trees, but the junipers native to the midwestern United States (var. *depressa* Pursh) grow horizontally and remain shrubby. Individual plants can be several yards across and only a few feet high.

In Iowa, native junipers are confined to a few counties in the northeastern corner of the state and to the Iowa River valley in Hardin County. Forest competition limits them to limestone cliffs, sparsely wooded ridges, and other open sites with thin, calcareous soils. They are especially common on the dry, stony "goat prairies" that occur on exposed bluffs overlooking the Mississippi and Upper Iowa rivers.

Common juniper and several related species are planted as ornamentals in Iowa. Many of the cultivated junipers are varieties of our native redcedar (*Juniperus virginiana* L.). Another common species is the Chinese juniper (*J. chinensis* L.).

AMERICAN HAZELNUT, *Corylus americana* Walt. *Leaves* simple, alternate, broadly ovate, 2 to 5 inches long, coarsely toothed, with the veins running to the tips of the teeth; petioles and young twigs covered with stiff, erect, gland-tipped hairs. *Winter twigs* slender, brown, with ashy gray exposed catkins. *Buds* globose to subglobose, about ⅛ inch long, with 4 to 6 brown scales. *Fruit* an edible nut about ½ inch in diameter, enclosed by a pair of leathery bracts.

THIS shrub is common in wood edges and dry open woods throughout Iowa. Its slender stems are 3 to 8 feet tall and typically form large clumps or thickets. A close relative of the filbert, it produces small nuts that are relished by squirrels, chipmunks, and people. Deer and rabbits browse the twigs and foliage.

The beaked hazelnut (*C. cornuta* Marsh.) is a similar species that is native on moist wooded slopes and bluffs in the far northeastern corner of Iowa. It differs from the American hazelnut in that its nut-bracts are prolonged into a beak and its petioles and young twigs have scattered long hairs.

SPECKLED ALDER, *Alnus rugosa* (Du Roi) Spreng. *Leaves* simple, alternate, oval to nearly round, 2 to 5 inches long, toothed, with the veins running to the tips of the teeth. *Winter twigs* slender, dark brown, with dark brown exposed catkins. *Buds* stalked, ovoid, ¼ to ⅜ inch long, with 2 scales that meet along the edges without overlapping. *Fruit* a nutlet borne with others of its kind in a woody "cone" about ½ inch long, the cones commonly persisting on the twigs in winter. *Bark* of stems smooth, dark gray, marked with numerous white, warty lenticels.

SPECKLED ALDER is a shrub 6 to 12 feet high. It is native in low-lying, sandy places in northeastern Iowa.

WITCH-HAZEL, *Hamamelis virginiana* L. *Leaves* simple, alternate, broadly oval to nearly round, 2 to 6 inches long, wavy margined, with unequal bases. *Winter twigs* slender, brown. *Buds* stalked, ovoid-elongate, naked, brown, ⅛ to ⅜ inch long, often with 2 scalelike stipules at the base. *Flowers* perfect, yellow, in small clusters from the leaf axils, blooming in late autumn. *Fruit* a 2-celled woody capsule ⅜ to ½ inch long, forcibly ejecting the shiny black seeds in autumn.

WITCH-HAZEL is a shrub or small tree that may grow up to 25 feet tall. It is native on moist wooded slopes in northeastern and extreme east central Iowa, becoming a dominant component of the understory in some locales. It is occasionally cultivated as an ornamental elsewhere in the state.

Witch-hazel is peculiar in blooming in late autumn after most trees have lost their leaves. An aromatic extract from its bark, twigs, and dried leaves was once widely used in after-shave lotions, tonics, and patent medicines. Forked branches of this species were once favored for "water-witching."

INDIGO BUSH, *Amorpha fruticosa* L. *Leaves* once-pinnately compound, alternate, with 11 to 27 pairs of entire, oblong leaflets ¾ to 1½ inch long that are marked with tiny, translucent dots. *Winter twigs* slender, gray or brown. *Buds* subglobose, 1/16 to 3/16 inch long, dark brown, with 2 to 4 visible scales. *Flowers* tiny, perfect, with a single purple petal and 10 orange stamens, in dense upright racemes, blooming in early summer. *Fruit* a legume about ¼ inch long, persisting on twigs in winter.

INDIGO BUSH is a shrub with slender stems up to 10 feet tall. It is native on low ground along streams, lakes, and ponds throughout most of Iowa.

PRICKLY-ASH, *Xanthoxylum americanum* Mill. *Leaves* once-pinnately compound, alternate, the leaf stems (rachises) often prickly; leaflets 7 to 11, ovate, unstalked, ¾ to 2½ inches long, dotted with tiny glands (seen against strong light), the margins minutely and distantly toothed. *Winter twigs* moderate in diameter, brown, armed with small paired spines. *Buds* globose, ⅛ to 3/16 inch in diameter, red, with indistinct scales. *Flowers* tiny, greenish, dioecious, in small cymes, blooming in spring. *Fruit* a tiny red follicle with 1 or 2 shiny black seeds about ⅛ inch long that are suspended by slender stalks.

PRICKLY-ASH is a single-stemmed shrub or small tree 4 to 12 feet tall that often forms large thickets. It is common throughout the state in clearings, open woods, and wood edges in both wet and dry soils. It is often mistaken for the black locust but differs in having unstalked leaflets and conspicuous red buds.

Prickly-ash is sometimes called "toothache tree" because its tiny fruits numb the mouth and lips when chewed and thus provides relief from toothaches. The leaves and the leathery rinds of the fruits contain tiny oil glands and are very aromatic, indicating the relationship of this species to the lemon, orange, and other citrus trees. The bark is also aromatic and was once used as a stimulant and as a home remedy for flatulence and diarrhea.

HOPTREE OR WAFER-ASH, *Ptelea trifoliata* L. *Leaves* once-pinnately compound, alternate; leaflets 3, elliptic-ovate, essentially unstalked, 2½ to 5 inches long, with minutely and distantly toothed margins. *Winter twigs* slender to moderate, reddish-brown, with numerous warty lenticels. *Buds* hidden within the bases of the petioles. *Flowers* greenish-white, perfect or imperfect, in paniclelike cymes, appearing after the leaves in spring. *Fruit* a round, 2-seeded samara ⅔ to 1 inch in diameter.

HOPTREE is a shrub or small tree 10 to 20 feet tall. It is native in wood edges, wooded stream banks, rocky bluffs, and low sandy places in southeastern and extreme east central Iowa. Plants are occasionally found growing wild in the central part of the state as well, but it is not known if these are native or escaped from cultivation.

The leaves of hoptree are very similar to those of poison ivy, but the terminal (middle) leaflet is unstalked rather than long-stalked. The elmlike samaras of hoptree are also quite unlike the white berrylike fruits of poison ivy. The samaras contain a bitter principle and were once used as a substitute for hops.

POISON IVY, *Rhus radicans* L. *Leaves* once-pinnately compound, alternate; leaflets 3, ovate, 2 to 5 inches long, entire or coarsely toothed, the terminal (middle) one on a stalk much longer than those of the other two. *Winter twigs* slender to moderately stout, light brown; leaf scars V shaped with 5 to 9 bundle scars. *Buds* stalked, ovoid, naked, yellow-brown, the terminal about ¼ inch long and the laterals smaller. *Flowers* tiny, greenish-yellow, dioecious or polygamous, in small panicles from the leaf axils, blooming in early summer. *Fruit* a yellowish-white drupe about 3/16 inch in diameter, persisting on the twig in winter.

POISON IVY is usually a woody vine but occasionally becomes a thicket-forming shrub 5 or 6 feet tall. As a vine it often climbs high on the trunks of trees, producing long straight branches that can be easily mistaken for those of the tree. Poison ivy occurs throughout Iowa in a variety of habitats but is especially common in disturbed woods, fencerows, wood edges, and waste places near woods.

The skin-irritating principle of poison ivy is carried in a nonvolatile resin found in all parts of the plant. The resin usually reaches a person's skin through direct contact with the leaves; but it can also be spread by smoke from burning plants or by touching tools, clothing, pets, or other contaminated objects. Some people are able to handle the plants with impunity but this "immunity" can vanish at any time.

Though universally condemned by humans, poison ivy is one of the most important woody plants for wildlife. Its small berrylike fruits are eaten by many birds including flickers and other woodpeckers, catbirds, chickadees, hermit thrushes, quail, pheasants, and turkeys. Deer and rabbits occasionally browse the twigs and stems.

Forms of poison ivy with deeply incised leaf margins are sometimes called "poison oak," but this name is more appropriately applied to two other species, *R. toxicodendron* L. of the southeastern United States and *R. diversiloba* Torr. and Gray of the Pacific Coast states. Poison sumac (*R. vernix* L.) occurs throughout much of the eastern United States, including southeastern Minnesota and southwestern Wisconsin, but there are no authenticated reports of it from Iowa.

Fragrant sumac (*R. aromatica* Ait.) is a harmless shrub that resembles poison ivy but has red fruits and unstalked terminal leaflets. It is native in dry open woods and thickets in southwestern and south central Iowa. It is also cultivated.

WAHOO, *Euonymus atropurpureus* Jacq. *Leaves* simple, opposite, elliptic, 2 to 5 inches long, finely toothed. *Winter twigs* slender to moderate, green or purple, usually marked with 4 longitudinal lines. *Buds* ovoid, ⅛ to 3/16 inch long, colored like twigs, with 3 or 4 pairs of scales. *Flowers* very small, perfect, purplish, in small cymes from the leaf axils, blooming in early summer. *Fruit* a small pinkish 3- or 4-lobed capsule that opens in early autumn and persists on the twig all winter; seeds with red fleshy coverings, suspended by slender stalks.

WAHOO is a single-stemmed, treelike shrub 6 to 10 (rarely 25) feet tall. It is native throughout Iowa in moist open woods and low-lying areas near woods, often forming thickets. Its peculiar fruits are similar to those of its close relative, the bittersweet, but differ in being deeply lobed. The colorful seeds are reputedly poisonous.

The Sioux used the hard, close-grained wood of this species for arrows, and it is believed that the name wahoo was derived from an Indian word meaning "wood of the arrow." The settlers pulverized the bitter root bark and employed it in home remedies.

BLADDERNUT, *Staphylea trifolia* L. *Leaves* once-pinnately compound, opposite, with 3 toothed, broadly elliptic leaflets 1½ to 4 inches long. *Winter twigs* slender to moderate, purple or green. *Buds* subglobose, 1/16 to 3/16 inch long, with 4 purple scales. *Flowers* perfect, white, bell shaped, in racemes, appearing with or shortly after the leaves in spring. *Fruit* a green, inflated, 3-chambered capsule 1 to 2 inches long, with thin papery walls, turning brown in autumn and remaining on the twigs through winter. *Bark* of stems smooth, light gray, with vertical white stripes.

BLADDERNUT is a shrub or small tree 5 to 15 (rarely 25) feet tall. It is native on moist wooded slopes as far west as the Missouri and Little Sioux rivers. It makes a handsome ornamental but is seldom cultivated in Iowa.

COMMON BUCKTHORN, *Rhamnus cathartica* L. *Leaves* simple, subopposite (i.e., arranged in pairs at the nodes but not exactly opposite), broadly elliptic, 1½ to 2 inches long, toothed, with 3 pairs of strongly curved veins. *Winter twigs* slender, gray, usually tipped by a short thorn. *Buds* ovoid, 1/8 to 3/8 inch long, with about 6 dark brown scales. *Flowers* polygamous or dioecious, small, yellowish-green, in small umbellike clusters of 2 to 5 from the leaf axils. *Fruit* black, berrylike, 3- or 4-seeded, about ¼ inch in diameter, persisting on the twig in winter.

THIS Eurasian species is a shrub or small tree 6 to 25 feet tall. Originally introduced for hedge plantings, it has now become naturalized across much of Iowa and is a bad weed in many natural woodlands. It serves as the alternate host of an organism causing oat leaf rust and is considered a primary noxious weed in Iowa.

BUTTONBUSH, *Cephalanthus occidentalis* L. *Leaves* simple, opposite or whorled, elliptic to oblong-ovate, 3 to 6 inches long, entire, with 6 to 9 pairs of curved veins. *Winter twigs* slender, reddish-brown; leaf scars round with a single U-shaped bundle scar. *Buds* embedded in the twig. *Flowers* tiny, white, perfect, in dense ball-shaped heads about 1 inch in diameter, blooming in late summer. *Fruit* a long stalked, ball-shaped aggregation of nutlets, persisting on the twig in winter.

BUTTONBUSH is a shrub 3 to 6 (rarely 15) feet tall. It is native along stream banks and the shores of lakes and ponds across southern, eastern, and central Iowa.

HONEYSUCKLES, *Lonicera* spp. *Leaves* simple, opposite, entire, rather small, short petioled, with straight or slightly curved veins. *Winter twigs* slender with persisting bud scales at the base. *Buds* variously shaped, small, their scales arranged in 4 vertical rows. *Flowers* perfect; either white, pink, or light yellow; paired at the ends of short stalks from the leaf axils; blooming in spring. *Fruit* a small red or orange berry, often persisting on the twig in winter.

THE honeysuckles are a group of woody vines and tall shrubs that have long been important in landscaping and conservation. Most of the species grown in Iowa are not native but have been introduced from east and central Asia. Several kinds of songbirds eat their small berries and subsequently disperse the seeds to fencerows and woods. In this manner honeysuckles frequently escape from cultivation and become weeds.

COMMON ELDERBERRY, *Sambucus canadensis* L. *Leaves* once-pinnately compound, opposite, with 5 to 11 (usually 7) toothed, elliptic leaflets 2 to 6 inches long. *Winter twigs* moderate in diameter, light gray, weak and pithy, with conspicuous leaf scars and warty lenticels. *Buds* subglobose, 1/16 to 3/16 inch long, brown or gray, with 3 to 5 pairs of scales. *Flowers* very small, white, perfect, in large flat-topped cymes, blooming in early summer. *Fruit* dark purple, berrylike, 3 seeded, about 3/16 inch in diameter.

ELDERBERRY is a shrub 3 to 12 feet tall. It is common throughout Iowa on stream banks, roadside ditches, and moist open woods, often forming thickets. Its juicy fruits are eaten by many birds and often used to make pies, jellies, and wines. The rest of the plant is mildly poisonous.

Red elderberry (*S. pubens* Michx.) is similar but has brown instead of white pith, spring-blooming flowers in tall paniclelike clusters, and red fruits. It is native on moist wooded slopes in the northeastern corner of Iowa.

NANNYBERRY, *Viburnum lentago* L. *Leaves* simple, opposite, oval, or elliptic, 2 to 5 inches long, finely toothed, with slightly winged petioles. *Winter* twigs rather slender, gray or red-brown. *Buds* ovoid or elongate, with 2 brown scales that meet along the edges without overlapping, the terminal 3/8 to 1 inch long. *Flowers* small, white, perfect, in terminal cymes, blooming in late spring or early summer. *Fruit* an edible, dark purple drupe about 3/8 inch long, often persisting in winter.

NANNYBERRY, also called "sheepberry" and "wild raisin," is a shrub or small tree 10 to 20 (rarely 30) feet tall. It is native in moist upland woods and thickets across most of Iowa, though common only in the northeastern and north central parts of the state. Hardy, adaptable, and easily propagated, it is an excellent species for wildlife plantings and the borders of windbreaks.

5: KEY TO TREES OF IOWA

THE FOLLOWING KEY includes all native trees except a few rare species of hawthorns and those introduced trees important in landscaping and conservation. Large shrubs that may be easily mistaken for tree saplings have also been included. Species belonging to small genera (i.e., those having only one or two species in Iowa) are included in the main body of the key and those belonging to large genera are keyed in separate sections at the end. Crab apples, pears, and junipers are keyed to genus only because identification of the many cultivated types is very difficult for nonspecialists.

The key is based primarily on characteristics of fully developed leaves, but it includes fruit, twig, flower, and bark characteristics where necessary for accurate identification. Technical terms used in the key are defined in Chapter 3. Instructions on how to use the key are also found in that chapter.

GENERAL KEY

1. Leaves needlelike or scalelike (Fig. 5.1a, b), usually evergreen 2
1. Leaves broad and flat, with branching veins (Fig. 5.1c), deciduous in autumn 13
    2. Some or all leaves scalelike and less than ⅛ inch long, overlapping in pairs, and closely appressed to twigs (Fig. 5.1b) 3
    2. Leaves all needlelike (Fig. 5.1a), 3/16 inch or more long, pointing away from twigs 4

FIG. 5.2

5. At least some leaves in dense tufts of 20 to 30 at the ends of short spur shoots (Fig. 5.3) . . . . . EUROPEAN LARCH, *Larix decidua*
5. Spur shoots absent; leaves all alternate or whorled 6

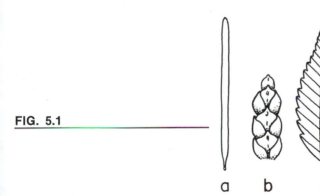

FIG. 5.1

a   b   c

FIG. 5.3

3. Leafy twigs flattened, with only scalelike leaves; cones woody . . . . . ARBORVITAE (NORTHERN WHITE CEDAR), *Thuja occidentalis*
3. Leafy twigs angled or round in cross section, usually with both scalelike and needlelike leaves conspicuous; cones fleshy and berrylike . . . . . JUNIPERS, *Juniperus* spp.
    4. Leaves in fascicles (bundles) of 2, 3, or 5 (Fig. 5.2) . . . . . PINES, *Pinus* spp. (key to species on p. 120)
    4. Leaves not in fascicles of 2 to 5 5

6. Leaves in whorls of 3, conspicuously whitened on their upper surfaces; seeds in bluish, berrylike cones; plant shrubby, rarely becoming a small tree . . . . . COMMON JUNIPER, *Juniperus communis*
6. Leaves alternate, either green or blue-green above; seeds in woody or papery cones or solitary in red, fleshy cups 7

7. Leaves 4-sided and easily rolled between thumb and forefinger; with woody, peglike bases that remain on the twigs when the green portions fall (seen on dead twigs) (Fig. 5.4) . . . . . SPRUCES, *Picea* spp. (key to species on p. 121)

(key to species on p. 121)

FIG. 5.4

7. Leaves flat, not easily rolled between thumb and forefinger 8
   8. Buds ovoid, sharp pointed; cones with protruding 3-pointed bracts between scales . . . . . DOUGLAS-FIR, *Pseudotsuga menziesii*
   8. Buds subglobose to short-ovoid, with rounded or blunt-pointed tips; bracts of cones small and inconspicuous, not protruding between the scales 9
9. Leaves abruptly tapered to sharp-pointed tips; seeds, when present, in red fleshy cups; plant shrubby, rarely becoming a small tree . . . . . YEWS, *Taxus* spp.
9. Leaves with blunt or rounded tips; seed in cones; a tree 10
   10. Many if not all leaves 1½ to 2 inches long, blue-green on both surfaces . . . . . WHITE FIR, *Abies concolor*
   10. Leaves all ³⁄₁₆ to 1¼ inches long, dark green above and either green or whitened below 11
11. Leaves green on both surfaces; deciduous in autumn . . . . . BALDCYPRESS, *Taxodium distichum*
11. Leaves dark green above and whitened below, evergreen 12
   12. Leaves with short but distinct petioles (Fig. 5.5); cones ½ to ¾ inch long . . . . . EASTERN HEMLOCK, *Tsuga canadensis*

FIG. 5.5

   12. Leaves without petioles; cones at least 2 inches long, disintegrating when mature . . . . . BALSAM FIR, *Abies balsamea*
13. Leaves compound 14
13. Leaves simple 38
   14. Leaves opposite 15
   14. Leaves alternate 16
15. Many if not all leaves with 3 leaflets 34
15. Leaves all with 5 to 13 leaflets 17
   16. Leaflets 5 or more 23
   16. Leaflets 3 35
17. Leaflets palmately arranged 18
17. Leaflets pinnately arranged 19
   18. Leaflets abruptly tapered at apex (Fig. 5.6a), usually 7 in number; buds dark brown, sticky . . . . . HORSE-CHESTNUT, *Aesculus hippocastanum*
   18. Leaflets gradually tapered to apex (Fig. 5.6b), usually 5 in number but sometimes 6 or 7; buds light brown, dry . . . . . OHIO BUCKEYE, *Aesculus glabra*

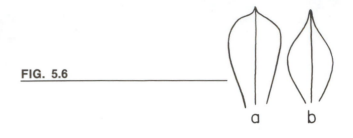

FIG. 5.6

19. Most if not all leaves with 5 leaflets; buds white-hairy . . . . . BOXELDER, *Acer negundo*
19. Leaflets mostly 7, 9, or 11; buds glabrous 20
   20. Leaflets closely and conspicuously toothed (Fig. 5.7a) 22
   20. Leaflets either entire or with a few inconspicuous and widely spaced teeth (Fig. 5.7b) 21

FIG. 5.7

21. Buds hidden within bases of petioles; fruit a drupe; rare cultivated tree . . . . . AMUR CORKTREE, *Phellodendron amurense*
21. Buds visible in leaf axils and at twig tips; fruit a paddle-shaped samara . . . . . WHITE ASH, *Fraxinus americana*
   22. Terminal bud lacking on most if not all twigs; fruit a purple berry; tall shrub with weak, pithy stems . . . . . COMMON ELDERBERRY, *Sambucus canadensis*
   22. Terminal bud present; fruit a paddle-shaped samara; a tree . . . . . ASHES, *Fraxinus* spp. (key to species on p. 125)
23. Leaflets closely and conspicuously toothed (Fig. 5.7a) 24
23. Leaflets either entire or with a few inconspicuous and widely spaced teeth (Fig. 5.7b) 29
   24. Leaflets 1 to 2¼ inches long and ½ to ¾ inch wide; fruit a small, berrylike, orange or orange-red pome . . . . . MOUNTAIN-ASH, *Pyrus* (*Sorbus*) *aucuparia*
   24. Largest leaflets more than 2¼ inches long and ¾ inch wide; fruit a nut or drupe 25
25. Terminal bud absent, lateral buds hidden by bases of petioles; fruit a small red drupe . . . . . SUMACS, *Rhus* spp. (key to species on p. 124)
25. Terminal bud present, lateral buds normally visible in leaf axils; fruit a nut 26
   26. Leaflets 5, 7, or 9 . . . . . HICKORIES, *Carya* spp. (key to species on p. 122)
   26. Leaflets 11 to 23 27
27. Leaflets conspicuously curved in shape; pith of twigs continuous; husk of nut with 4 ridges . . . . . PECAN, *Carya illinoensis*
27. Leaflets not curved; pith chambered; husk lacking ridges 28
   28. Terminal bud subglobose, gray, ³⁄₁₆ to ⅓ inch long; nut round; trunk bark dark gray or black . . . . . BLACK WALNUT, *Juglans nigra*
   28. Terminal bud ovoid-elongate, yellow-brown, ⅜ to ¾ inch long; nut football shaped; trunk bark light gray . . . . . BUTTERNUT, *Juglans cinerea*
29. Twigs bearing thorns or spines 30

29. Twigs not thorny or spiny 32
  30. Twigs bearing branched thorns at least ¾ inch long
    . . . . HONEY LOCUST, *Gleditsia triacanthos*
  30. Twigs bearing unbranched spines ½ inch or less long
    in pairs at bases of petioles 31
31. Leaflets stalkless or nearly so, marked with tiny translucent
  dots (seen against strong light); buds red, visible in leaf
  axils and at twig tips . . . . . PRICKLY-ASH, *Xanthoxylum americanum*
31. Leaflets with thick stalks ⅛ to ¼ inch long, not marked
  with dots; buds hidden by bases of petioles, so apparently
  absent . . . . . BLACK LOCUST, *Robinia pseudoacacia*
  32. Leaflets less than ¾ inch wide 33
  32. Largest leaflets ¾ to 3 inches wide 36
33. Leaflets entire, often marked with tiny dots (seen against
  strong light); leaves strictly once-pinnate; tall shrub with
  slender stems . . . . . INDIGO BUSH, *Amorpha fruticosa*
33. Leaflets distantly and obscurely toothed, not marked with
  dots; leaves once- or twice-pinnate, with both types often
  present on the same tree . . . . . HONEY LOCUST, *Gleditsia triacanthos* var. *inermis*
  34. Leaflets entire or with no more than 5 teeth per inch
    of margin . . . . . BOXELDER, *Acer negundo*
  34. Leaflets with 10 to 20 teeth per inch of
    margin . . . . . BLADDERNUT, *Staphylea trifolia*
35. Buds hidden by bases of petioles, so apparently absent;
  fruit a 2-seeded, elmlike samara . . . . . HOPTREE, *Ptelea
  trifoliata*
35. Buds visible in leaf axils or at twig tips; fruit a drupe
  . . . . . SUMACS, *Rhus* spp. (key to species on p. 124)
  36. Leaves twice-pinnately compound . . . . . KEN-
    TUCKY COFFEE TREE, *Gymnocladus dioicus*
  36. Leaves once-pinnately compound 37
37. Base of each leaflet with 1 or 2 gland-tipped teeth (Fig. 5.8);
  twigs very stout . . . . . TREE-OF-HEAVEN, *Ailanthus
  altissima*

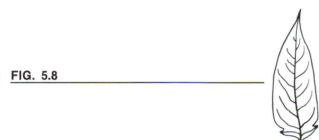

FIG. 5.8

37. Bases of leaflets lacking gland-tipped teeth; twigs slender
  . . . . . YELLOWWOOD, *Cladrastis lutea*
  38. Leaves lobed 39
  38. Leaves not lobed 51
39. Leaves opposite . . . . . MAPLES, *Acer* spp. (key to species on p. 124)
39. Leaves alternate 40
  40. Leaves half-round or fan shaped; with 2 or more lobes
    and numerous crowded, nearly parallel veins (Fig.
    5.9), GINKGO, *Ginkgo biloba*

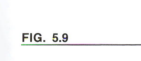

FIG. 5.9

  40. Leaves neither half-round nor fan shaped, veins freely
    branching 41

41. Leaves palmately veined (i.e., having 3 or 5 equally prominent veins originating from point where petiole joins blade,
  with numerous smaller veins branching from these) (Fig.
  5.10a) 42
41. Leaves pinnately veined (i.e., having single prominent midvein and numerous smaller veins branching from it at more
  or less regular intervals) (Fig. 5.10b) 46

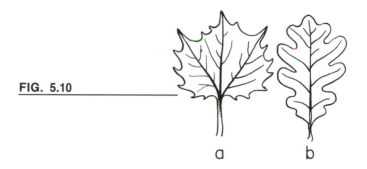

FIG. 5.10

  42. Buds hidden within swollen bases of petioles; stipules
    or their scars forming ring around twig at base of each
    petiole . . . . . SYCAMORE, *Platanus occidentalis*
  42. Bud visible in leaf axils; stipules not encircling
    twigs 43
43. Leaves white beneath; bark on upper trunk and larger
  branches white with black markings . . . . . WHITE POP-
  LAR, *Populus alba*
43. Leaves green beneath; bark gray, brown, or light orange 44
  44. Leaves star shaped; fruit a woody, prickly
    ball . . . . . SWEETGUM, *Liquidambar styraciflua*
  44. Leaves not star shaped; fruit blackberrylike
    45
45. Leaves glabrous or with hairs restricted to largest veins beneath, their lobes gradually tapered to blunt or short-
  pointed tips (Fig. 5.11a); leaves usually 2 to 4 inches
  long . . . . . WHITE MULBERRY, *Morus alba*
45. Leaves hairy along small veins beneath, their lobes abruptly
  tapered to long-pointed tips (Fig. 5.11b); largest leaves 4 to
  9 inches long . . . . . RED MULBERRY, *Morus rubra*

FIG. 5.11

  46. Leaf lobes entire or with a few bristle-tipped teeth at
    tips (Fig. 5.12a, b); twigs never thorny 47
  46. Leaf lobes closely toothed (Fig. 5.12c); twigs often
    thorny 50

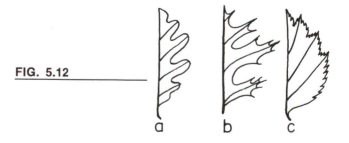

FIG. 5.12

47. Leaves with 5 to 11 lobes . . . . . OAKS, *Quercus* spp. (key
  to species on p. 122)
47. Leaves with 2, 3, or 4 lobes 48

48. Lobed and unlobed leaves present on same tree and often on same twig . . . . . SASSAFRAS, *Sassafras albidum*
48. Leaves all lobed 49
49. Leaves 4-lobed, with notched apex (Fig. 5.13) . . . . . TU-LIP TREE, *Liriodendron tulipifera*

FIG. 5.13

49. Leaves 3-lobed, with rounded apex . . . . . BLACKJACK OAK, *Quercus marilandica*
   50. Buds pubescent; thorns, when present, with leaves or leaf scars along their surfaces . . . . . CRAB AP-PLES, *Pyrus* spp.
   50. Buds glabrous; surfaces of thorns smooth, without leaves or leaf scars . . . . . HAWTHORNS, *Crataegus* spp. (key to species on p. 123)
51. Leaves entire 52
51. Leaves toothed 67
   52. Leaves opposite or in whorls of 3 53
   52. Leaves alternate 57
53. Leaves in whorls of 3 at some or all nodes 54
53. Leaves opposite at all nodes 55
   54. Leaves broadest near base, 6 to 12 inches long; fruit a pencil-shaped pod 6 or more inches long; a tree . . . . . NORTHERN CATALPA, *Catalpa speciosa*
   54. Leaves broadest near middle, 3 to 6 inches long; fruit a ball-shaped head of achenelike units; a large shrub . . . . . BUTTONBUSH, *Cephalanthus occidentalis*
55. Leaf veins strongly curved, following margins (Fig. 5.14a); each bud enclosed by a single pair of scales . . . . . DOG-WOODS, *Cornus* spp. (key to species on p. 124)
55. Leaf veins straight or only slightly curved, branching freely near margins (Fig. 5.14b, c); each bud enclosed by several pairs of overlapping scales 56

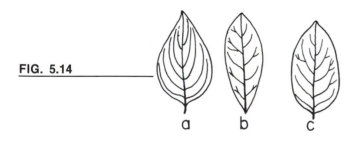

FIG. 5.14

a   b   c

   56. Leaves broadly ovate with petioles ⅜ to ¾ inch long; flowers and fruits (capsules) in large panicles at tips of twigs . . . . . JAPANESE TREE LILAC, *Syringa reticulata*
   56. Leaves not broadly ovate, with petioles no more than ¼ inch long; flowers and fruits (berries) in pairs from axils of leaves . . . . . HONEYSUCKLES, *Lonicera* spp.
57. Leaves half-round or fan shaped, with numerous crowded, nearly parallel veins (Fig. 5.9) . . . . . GINKGO, *Ginkgo biloba*
57. Leaves neither fan shaped nor half-round, their veins freely branching 58

58. Leaves nearly round, each with several large veins meeting at base of blade . . . . . REDBUD, *Cercis canadensis*
58. Leaves distinctly longer than wide, each with single large vein in middle and several smaller veins branching from it at more or less regular intervals 59
59. Lower surfaces of leaves a shiny silver color 60
59. Lower surfaces of leaves green or white 61
   60. Leaves linear or linear-lanceolate (4 to 7 times longer than wide), uniformly silver below; ripe fruits yellow with a silver coating . . . . . RUSSIAN-OLIVE, *Elaeagnus angustifolia*
   60. Leaves elliptic or ovate-oblong (2 or 3 times longer than wide) silvery with brown specks below; ripe fruits red . . . . . AUTUMN-OLIVE, *Elaeagnus umbellata*
61. Three or 4 buds clustered at tips of twig, each with many tiny scales arranged in vertical rows; midvein of leaf usually extending beyond apex, forming a short bristle . . . . . SHINGLE OAK, *Quercus imbricaria*
61. Buds naked or with 1 to 5 visible scales, solitary at twig tips; leaves not bristle tipped 62
   62. Terminal bud ⅓ to ¾ inch long, with dense covering of soft, greenish hairs; stipules or their scars forming ring around twig at base of each petiole or leaf scar . . . . . MAGNOLIAS, *Magnolia* spp. (key to species on p. 123)
   62. Terminal bud absent or lacking a covering of soft greenish hairs if present; stipules or their scars not encircling twigs 63
63. Leaves 6 to 12 inches long . . . . . PAWPAW, *Asimina triloba*
63. Leaves less than 6 inches long 64
   64. Each bud enclosed by single scale . . . . . WILLOWS, *Salix* spp. (key to species on p. 121)
   64. Each bud enclosed by 2 to 5 scales 65
65. Leaf veins strongly curved, following margin; fruit ¼ to ⅓ inch in diameter . . . . . ALTERNATE-LEAF DOG-WOOD, *Cornus alternifolia*
65. Leaf veins straight or slightly curved, forming network near margin; fruit ¾ inch or more in diameter 66
   66. Two dark-colored scales from last year's bud persisting at base of each shoot (twig) of current growing season (Fig. 5.15); fruit a berry ¾ to 1½ inches in diameter; twigs not thorny . . . . . PERSIMMON, *Diospyros virginiana*

FIG. 5.15

   66. Scales from last year's bud not persisting at twig base; fruit a green, warty ball 3 to 5 inches in diameter; twigs often thorny . . . . . OSAGE ORANGE, *Maclura pomifera*
67. Leaves opposite or subopposite (i.e., associated in pairs at nodes but not exactly opposite) 68
67. Leaves alternate 72
   68. Leaf veins strongly curved, following margins; twigs usually tipped by short thorns . . . . . COMMON BUCKTHORN, *Rhamnus cathartica*
   68. Leaf veins straight or slightly curved, not following margins; twigs tipped by buds 69

69. Largest veins ending near the margin, forming network of many smaller veins (Fig. 5.16a) 71
69. Largest veins running straight to tips of teeth, branched or not (Fig. 5.16b) 70

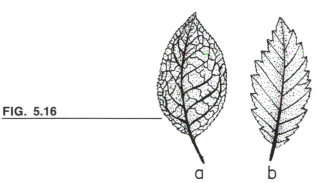

FIG. 5.16

70. Leaves apparently opposite, actually paired at ends of short spur shoots that are alternately arranged on twigs and branchlets . . . . BIRCHES, *Betula* spp. (key to species on p. 122)
70. Leaves opposite; spur shoots absent . . . . MAPLES, *Acer* spp.
71. Terminal bud ⅜ to 1 inch long, enclosed by single pair of scales; petioles slightly winged (Fig. 5.17); fruit a purple-black drupe . . . . NANNYBERRY, *Viburnum lentago*

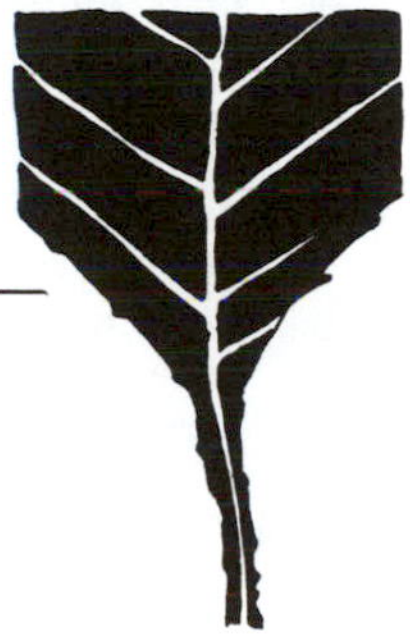

FIG. 5.17

71. Terminal bud less than ⅜ inch long, enclosed by 3 or 4 pairs of scales; petioles not winged; fruit a capsule with red, drupe-like seeds . . . . WAHOO, *Euonymus atropurpureus*
    72. Upper portion of petioles vertically flattened . . . . . POPLARS, *Populus* spp. (key to species on p. 121)
    72. Upper portion of petioles round 73
73. Each leaf with 3 or more large veins originating from point where blade joins petiole, with smaller veins branching from these at more or less regular intervals (Fig. 5.10a) 74
73. Each leaf with single large vein in middle and several smaller veins branching from it at regular intervals (Fig. 5.10b) 78
    74. Leaves about twice as long as wide, broadest at base; pith of twigs intermittently chambered . . . . . HACKBERRY, *Celtis occidentalis*
    74. Leaves round or only slightly longer than wide, usually broadest near middle; pith continuous 75
75. Largest leaves 4 to 9 inches long 76
75. Largest leaves 2 to 4 inches long 77
    76. Leaves hairy along smaller veins beneath; bud scales 3 to 7 . . . . . RED MULBERRY, *Morus rubra*
    76. Leaves glabrous except for tufts of hair in angles of largest veins beneath, bud scales usually 2 . . . . . BASSWOOD, *Tilia americana*
77. Leaves longer than wide, gradually tapered to blunt or short-pointed tips (Fig. 5.11a); bud scales 3 to 7 . . . . . WHITE MULBERRY, *Morus alba*

77. Leaves nearly round, abruptly tapered to long-pointed tips (Fig. 5.11b); bud scales usually 2 . . . . LITTLELEAF LINDEN, *Tilia cordata*
    78. Leaves 5 to 12 times longer than wide . . . . WILLOWS, *Salix* spp. (key to species on p. 121)
    78. Leaves 1 to 4 times longer than wide 79
79. Small, lumplike glands present on upper portion of petiole near its junction with blade (Fig. 5.18) 80

FIG. 5.18

79. Petioles lacking glands 81
    80. Each bud enclosed by single scale; flowers lacking petals, in catkins; fruit a small, flask-shaped capsule present only in spring and early summer . . . . . WILLOWS, *Salix* spp. (key to species on p. 121)
    80. Each bud enclosed by several scales; flowers with showy white petals, in racemes or umbellike clusters; fruit a drupe ripening in summer or fall . . . . . CHERRIES, PLUMS, *Prunus* spp. (key to species on p. 124)
81. Leaves conspicuously uneven at base (Fig. 5.19a) 82
81. Leaves equal or nearly so at base (Fig. 5.19b) 85

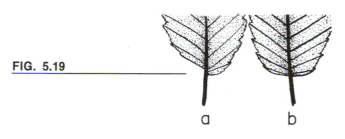

FIG. 5.19

    82. Leaves wavy margined with tiny, widely spaced teeth; buds naked . . . . . WITCH-HAZEL, *Hamamelis virginiana*
    82. Leaves with conspicuous, closely spaced teeth; buds enclosed by scales 83
83. Leaves alternate on twigs but paired at tips of short spur shoots on branchlets; twigs with faint taste of wintergreen . . . . . YELLOW BIRCH, *Betula alleghaniensis*
83. Leaves strictly alternate; twigs lacking wintergreen 84
    84. Each half of leaf blade with 4 to 7 large veins ending near margin, forming network of numerous tiny veins (Fig. 5.20a); buds enclosed by 3 or 4 scales . . . . . HACKBERRY, *Celtis occidentalis*
    84. Each half of leaf blade with 7 or more large veins that run straight to tips of teeth (Fig. 5.20b); buds enclosed by 6 or more scales. . . . . ELMS, *Ulmus* spp. (key to species on p. 123)

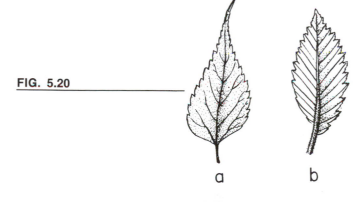

FIG. 5.20

85. Largest leaf veins either ending near margin or curving upward and following margin, then branching into several tiny veins that run into teeth (Fig. 5.16a) 98
85. Largest leaf veins running straight to tips of teeth, branched or not (Fig. 5.16b) 86
    86. Leaves with 2 to 5 teeth per inch of margin at midleaf 87
    86. Leaves with more than 5 teeth per inch of margin at midleaf 89
87. Leaf teeth tiny and rather inconspicuous; buds elongate, ⅜ to 1 inch long; trunk bark very smooth . . . . . AMERICAN BEECH, *Fagus grandifolia*
87. Leaf teeth large and prominent; buds ovoid, about ¼ inch long; trunk bark scaly or furrowed 88
    88. Buds clustered at twig tips, each with numerous tiny scales arranged in vertical rows; bases of nuts enclosed in cuplike structures . . . . . OAKS, *Quercus* spp. (key to species on p. 122)
    88. Buds solitary at twig tips, each with 2 or 3 visible scales; nuts enclosed in large spiny burs . . . . . AMERICAN CHESTNUT, *Castanea dentata*
89. Twigs thorny 90
89. Twigs not thorny 91
    90. Thorns bearing leaves or leaf scars . . . . . WILD CRAB APPLE, *Pyrus ioensis*
    90. Thorns smooth, without leaves or leaf scars . . . . HAWTHORNS, *Crataegus* spp. (key to species on p. 123)
91. Leaves alternate on twigs but paired at ends of spur shoots on branchlets . . . . BIRCHES, *Betula* spp. (key to species on p. 122)
91. Leaves strictly alternate; spur shoots absent 92
    92. Lateral buds stalked, each with 2 scales that meet along edges without overlapping; fruit conelike, ⅜ to ¾ inch long 93
    92. Lateral buds not stalked, each with several overlapping scales; fruit not conelike 94
93. Each half of leaf blade with 5 or 6 large veins; cultivated tree . . . . . EUROPEAN ALDER, *Alnus glutinosa*
93. Each half of leaf blade with 8 or more large veins; native shrub, northeastern Iowa . . . . . SPECKLED ALDER, *Alnus rugosa*
    94. Leaves with blunt or rounded tips; fruit a small, berrylike pome . . . . . SERVICEBERRIES, *Amelanchier* spp. (key to species on p. 123)
    94. Leaves with pointed tips; fruit a small nut or samara 95

95. Petioles and twigs covered with stiff, erect, gland-tipped hairs; tall native shrub, often forming thickets in upland woods and wood edges . . . . . HAZELNUT, *Corylus americana*
95. Petioles and twigs glabrous or with tiny appressed hairs; a tree 96
    96. Bud scales marked with fine parallel lines (seen with magnifying glass); leaves very soft to touch; fruits (nuts) in small papery sacs that hang from twigs in hoplike clusters . . . . . IRONWOOD, *Ostrya virginiana*
    96. Bud scales not marked with parallel lines; leaves either smooth or very rough to the touch; fruits not in papery sacs 97
97. Bud scales arranged in 2 rows; fruit a samara; trunk bark scaly or furrowed . . . . . ELMS, *Ulmus* spp. (key to species on p. 123)
97. Bud scales arranged in 4 rows; fruit a small nut subtended by 3-pointed, leaflike bract; trunk bark very smooth . . . . . HORNBEAM, *Carpinus caroliniana*
    98. Each bud enclosed by a single scale . . . . . WILLOWS, *Salix* spp. (key to species on p. 121)
    98. Each bud enclosed by several scales 99
99. Terminal bud fragrant when crushed, sticky, over ⅝ inch long; flowers without petals, in catkins; fruit a small flask-shaped capsule present only in late spring and early summer . . . . . BALSAM POPLAR, *Populus balsamifera*
99. Terminal bud lacking the above combination of characteristics, or terminal bud absent; flowers with showy white or pink petals; fruit a drupe or pome 100
    100. Terminal bud elongate; flower petals mostly 3 to 4 times longer than wide; fruit a small, berrylike pome ripening in early summer . . . . . SERVICEBERRIES, *Amelanchier* spp. (key to species on p. 123)
    100. Terminal bud, if present, either ovoid or subglobose; petals round or only slightly longer than wide; fruit ripening in mid- to late summer or autumn 101
101. Each flower with 2 to 5 styles; fruit (pome) with more than 1 seed . . . . . APPLES, CRAB APPLES, PEARS, *Pyrus* spp.
101. Each flower with 1 style; fruit (drupe) 1-seeded . . . . . CHERRIES, PLUMS, *Prunus* spp. (key to species on p. 124)

Key to Pines *(Pinus)*

1. Leaves in fascicles of 5 . . . . . WHITE PINE, *P. strobus* (see also limber pine, p. 26)
1. Leaves in fascicles of 2 or 3 2
    2. Leaves ¾ to 3 inches long 3
    2. Leaves over 3 inches long 6
3. Cone scales tipped by sharp prickles 1/16 to 1/8 inch long; tree common on coal spoils in southern Iowa, rarely seen elsewhere . . . . . VIRGINIA PINE, *P. virginiana*
3. Cone scales lacking prickles or with inconspicuous prickles less than 1/16 inch long; widely planted 4
    4. Small ornamental tree branching freely near the ground, producing several arching trunks of equal size instead of one central trunk . . . . MUGO PINE, *P. mugo*
    4. Tree with single erect trunk and numerous more or less

horizontal branches 5
5. Leaves 1 to 3 inches long, the 2 leaves in each fascicle parallel or only slightly spread apart (Fig. 5.21a, b); bark orange on upper trunk and larger branches . . . . . SCOTS PINE, *P. sylvestris*
5. Leaves ¾ to 1½ inches long, the 2 leaves in each fascicle spread widely apart (Fig. 5.21c); bark gray . . . . . JACK PINE, *P. banksiana*

FIG. 5.21

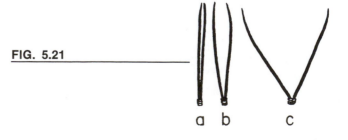

a   b   c

6. Leaves all 3 to 4 inches long . . . . . SCOTS PINE, *P. sylvestris*

6. Many if not all leaves over 4 inches long 7

7. Leaves in fascicles of 2 and 3 on same tree . . . . . PONDEROSA PINE, *P. ponderosa*

7. Leaves all in fascicles of 2 8

   8. Leaves less than 1/16 inch thick, breaking readily when bent double; buds brown; cones mostly under 2 inches long, fallen ones with pronounced basal cavity because lower scales are missing . . . . . RED PINE, *P. resinosa*

   8. Leaves 1/16 to 1/8 inch thick, not breaking readily when bent double; buds more or less covered with white, waxy material; cones 2 to 3 inches long, fallen ones lacking a basal cavity . . . . . AUSTRIAN PINE, *P. nigra*

Key to Spruces (*Picea*)

1. Cones 4 to 6 inches long; twigs and smaller branches usually drooping . . . . . NORWAY SPRUCE, *P. abies*

1. Cones less than 4 inches long; twigs and smaller branches more or less horizontal 2

   2. Cones more than 2 inches long, their scales with irregularly toothed margins; young twigs orange; leaves 3/4 to 1 1/4 inches long, often (but not always) strongly blue-green in color . . . . . BLUE SPRUCE, *P. pungens*

   2. Cones less than 2 inches long, their scales with entire (unbroken) margins; young twigs gray; leaves dark green to light blue-green, often less than 3/4 inch long . . . . . WHITE SPRUCE, *P. glauca*

Key to Willows (*Salix*)

THE following key identifies native, naturalized, and commonly planted willows that reach tree size, using characteristics of fully grown leaves and twigs. It is impossible to devise a workable key that considers all variations in the foliage of willows, so only typical representatives are considered here. Flowers are often necessary to confirm identification of willows.

1. Margins of fully developed leaves entire or distantly toothed (teeth mostly 3 to 10 per inch at midleaf) 2

1. Margins closely toothed (teeth mostly 11 to 25 per inch) 6

   2. Leaves linear (8 to 30 times longer than wide); tree often forming large thickets . . . . . SANDBAR WILLOW, *S. interior*

   2. Leaves lanceolate or broader (2 to 4 times longer than wide); stems solitary or clumped, but not forming thickets 3

3. Leaves glabrous or nearly so when full grown . . . . . NATIVE PUSSY WILLOW, *S. discolor*

3. Leaves persistently hairy on one or both surfaces 4

   4. Leaves mostly 1 1/3 to 2 times longer than wide, becoming glabrous and shiny above; twigs glabrous to sparsely hairy . . . . . GOAT (EUROPEAN PUSSY) WILLOW, *S. caprea*

   4. Leaves 2 to 3 times longer than wide, often persistently hairy above; twigs densely gray-hairy 5

5. Native . . . . . BEBB WILLOW, *S. bebbiana*

5. Cultivated . . . . . GRAY WILLOW, *S. cinerea*

   6. Branches long and drooping, often reaching or nearly

reaching the ground . . . . . WEEPING WILLOWS, *S. × blanda* and *S. × sepulcralis*

   6. Branches not long and drooping 7

7. Lower surfaces of leaves light green 8

7. Lower surfaces of leaves coated with a thin, waxy material making them pale bluish-green or white 11

   8. Leaves linear-lanceolate to lanceolate (4 to 10 times longer than wide), with or without tiny dotlike glands on the upper part of the petiole 9

   8. Leaves broadly lanceolate to ovate (2 to 4 times longer than wide), very glossy above, with prominent glands on the upper part of the petiole 10

9. Bud scale with freely overlapping edges on back (twig) side of bud (seen with magnifying glass); leaves narrowly lanceolate (6 to 10 times longer than wide), finely and closely toothed, often slightly curved . . . . . BLACK WILLOW, *S. nigra*

9. Bud scale caplike with no visible edges; leaves lanceolate (4 to 7 times longer than wide), coarsely and somewhat distantly toothed . . . . . CRACK WILLOW, *S. fragilis*

   10. Leaves tapered to long, slender, taillike tips; rare native tree of northern Iowa . . . . . SHINING WILLOW, *S. lucida*

   10. Leaves short-pointed; cultivated tree, rarely escaping to stream banks and other moist places . . . . . BAYLEAF WILLOW, *S. pentandra*

11. Twigs persistently hairy 12

11. Twigs glabrous 13

   12. Stipules of vegetative shoots conspicuous, persisting in summer; buds 1/2 to 3/4 inch long, densely hairy . . . . . MISSOURI RIVER WILLOW, *S. eriocephala* (*S. missouriensis*)

   12. Stipules early deciduous; buds less than 1/2 inch long . . . . . WHITE WILLOW, *S. alba*

13. Cultivated tree with spirally twisted twigs resembling corkscrews . . . . . CORKSCREW WILLOW, *S. matsudana* 'Tortuosa'

13. Twigs not spirally twisted 14

   14. Bud scales with freely overlapping margins on the back (twig) side of bud (seen with magnifying glass); petioles long and often twisted, 1/4 to 1/2 as long as the blades . . . . . PEACHLEAF WILLOW, *S. amygdaloides*

   14. Bud scale fused into caplike structure with no visible edges; petioles shorter relative to length of blades 15

15. Twigs greenish or brown . . . . . CRACK WILLOW, *S. fragilis*

15. Twigs yellow . . . . . GOLDEN WILLOW (a common name for several clones of ornamental willows, which are probably hybrids between *S. alba* and other species)

Key to Poplars (*Populus*)

1. Leaves triangular or diamond shaped 2

1. Leaves round or broadly ovate 3

   2. Leaves with 5 to 9 teeth per inch of margin, tiny glands at junction of petiole and blade; terminal bud 3/8 to 3/4 inch long . . . . . COTTONWOOD, *P. deltoides*

   2. Leaves with 12 or more teeth per inch of margin, lacking glands at junctions of petioles and blades; terminal bud 3/16 to 1/4 inch long . . . . . LOMBARDY POPLAR, *P. nigra* var. *italica*

3. Each half of leaf blade with 20 to 40 small, rounded teeth 4

3. Each half of leaf blade with 3 to 15 large, blunt teeth or shallow lobes 5

4. Leaves round; upper portion of petiole distinctly flattened
. . . . QUAKING ASPEN, *P. tremuloides*

4. Leaves ovate with round petioles . . . . BALSAM POP-
LAR, *P. balsamifera*

5. Leaves green beneath when mature; petiole strongly flattened
. . . . BIGTOOTH ASPEN, *P. grandidentata*

5. Leaves white beneath; petiole slightly flattened
. . . . WHITE POPLAR, *P. alba*

Key to Hickories (*Carya*)

1. Many if not all leaves with 5 leaflets . . . . SHAGBARK
HICKORY, *C. ovata*

1. Leaves with 7 or more leaflets 2

2. Leaflets conspicuously curved, usually 11 to 17 in number
. . . . . PECAN, *C. illinoensis*

2. Leaflets not noticeably curved, usually 7 to 9 in number
. 3

3. Terminal bud slender, covered with 2 bright yellow scales that
meet along edges without overlapping; husk of nut less than
⅛ inch thick . . . . . BITTERNUT HICKORY, *C. cordiformis*

3. Terminal bud plump, covered with several brown or tan, overlapping scales; husk ⅛ to ½ inch thick 4

4. Leaves 15 to 22 inches long, petioles glabrous or nearly so;
bark of larger trees separating into large, flat, loosely attached pieces that give the trunk a shaggy appearance; tree
of floodplain woods . . . . . SHELLBARK HICKORY, *C.
laciniosa*

4. Leaves with hairy petioles, usually less than 15 inches long;
trunk bark shallowly furrowed; tree of dry upland woods
. . . . MOCKERNUT HICKORY, *C. tomentosa*

Key to Birches (*Betula*)

1. Trunk bark gray, brown, gold, orange, or mixed orange and
white 4

1. Trunk bark uniformly white or white with black markings.
These species are variable and not easily distinguished from
one another, but typical specimens differ as follows:

2. Leaves as broad or broader at middle than at base, tapered
only on upper third of margin; native tree, sometimes cultivated . . . . . PAPER BIRCH, *B. papyrifera*

2. Leaves broadest below middle, gradually tapered to
pointed tips; introduced ornamental tree 3

3. Leaf bases wedge-shaped (Fig. 5.22a); leaves glabrous beneath . . . . . EUROPEAN WHITE BIRCH, *B. pendula*

3. Leaf bases truncate (Fig. 5.22c) to slightly heart-shaped;
leaves usually with tufts of hairs in the vein axils beneath
. . . . JAPANESE WHITE BIRCH, *B. platyphylla* var. *japonica*

4. Leaves with wedge-shaped bases (Fig. 5.22a) and 7 to 9
veins on each side; bark separating into papery flakes or
scales, at first orange or mixed orange and white, later
orange-brown to gray . . . . RIVER BIRCH, *B. nigra*

4. Leaves with rounded bases (Fig. 22b) and 9 to 12 veins on
each side; bark smooth at first but becoming scaly, gray to
gold in color . . . . YELLOW BIRCH, *B. alleghaniensis*

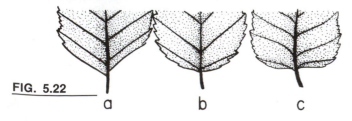

FIG. 5.22   a   b   c

Key to Oaks (*Quercus*)

1. Largest veins extending beyond tips of lobes or teeth (or
beyond apex of the leaf if it is neither toothed nor lobed),
forming short bristles (red oaks) 2

1. Lobes or teeth not bristle tipped (white oaks) 8

2. Leaves unlobed or shallowly 3 lobed 3

2. Leaves 5 to 9 lobed 4

3. Leaves elliptic or oblong in shape, not lobed. . . . . SHIN-
GLE OAK, *Q. imbricaria*

3. Leaves obovate, shallowly 3 lobed on upper half
. . . . BLACKJACK OAK, *Q. marilandica*

4. Length of leaf lobes less than, equal to, or slightly
greater than width of central, undivided portion of blade
. . . . . RED OAK, *Q. rubra*

4. Length of largest leaf lobes 2 to 6 times greater than
width of central, undivided portion of blade 5

5. Fully grown buds ¼ to ½ inch long, densely covered with
white or brown hairs; scales around rim of acorn-cup loosely
attached, forming fringe . . . . . BLACK OAK, *Q. velutina*

5. Fully grown buds ¹⁄₁₆ to ¼ to inch long, either glabrous or
only partially hairy; scales of acorn-cup all tightly attached
. . . . 6

6. Buds hairy on upper half, largest ones ³⁄₁₆ to ¼ inch
long; acorn with concentric grooves around its apex; tree
cultivated in Iowa but not native . . . . . SCARLET
OAK, *Q. coccinea*

6. Buds glabrous or sparsely hairy over entire surfaces,
largest ones ⅛ to ³⁄₁₆ inch long; acorn lacking concentric
grooves around apex; tree cultivated or native 7

7. Acorn hemisphere-shaped, ⅜ to ½ inch long, with saucer-
shaped cup covering only the base; tree cultivated throughout state but native only in southeastern corner, usually in
low-lying woods near streams . . . . . PIN OAK, *Q. palustris*

7. Acorn football shaped, ½ to 1 inch long, with cone-shaped
cup covering about ½ of the nut; tree native in upland woods
in northeastern and north central Iowa . . . . . HILL'S
OAK, *Q. ellipsoidalis*

8. Leaves glabrous on both surfaces 9

8. Leaves sparsely to densely hairy beneath (seen with magnifying glass) 10

9. Leaf blades 2½ to 5 inches long, with 2 small earlike projections at base; acorns with stalks longer than leaf petioles;
cultivated tree . . . . ENGLISH OAK, *Q. robur*

9. Leaf blades 5 to 9 inches long, without earlike projections at
base; acorns not stalked or with stalks shorter than leaf petioles; native tree, occasionally cultivated . . . . WHITE
OAK, *Q. alba*

10. Leaves toothed or shallowly lobed (i.e., spaces between
lobes or teeth extending less than half the distance between margin and midvein) 11

10. Leaves deeply lobed (i.e., at least some of spaces between lobes extending more than half the distance between margin and midvein) 13

11. Petioles ⅛ to ⅜ inch long; small, shrubby tree bearing
acorns when only a few feet tall . . . . . DWARF OAK, *Q.
prinoides*

11. Petioles ½ to 1½ inches long; a tree 12

12. Each half of leaf with 8 to 13 usually sharp-pointed
teeth; acorns unstalked or with very short stalks; tree
native in dry upland woods, rarely cultivated
. . . . CHINKAPIN OAK, *Q. muhlenbergii*

12. Each half of leaf with 4 to 6 blunt teeth or lobes; acorns
with stalks 1 to 4 inches long; tree native in moist low-
lying woods, frequently cultivated . . . . SWAMP
WHITE OAK, *Q. bicolor*

13. Leaves crosslike in outline with 3 squarish lobes on upper
half and 2 to 4 much smaller lobes on lower half; acorn-cup

lacking fringe of bristles; rare native tree, extreme southeastern Iowa . . . . . POST OAK, *Q. stellata*

13. Leaves irregularly shaped, with none or few crosslike in outline; acorn-cup with conspicuous fringe of soft bristles around rim; tree common throughout Iowa . . . . . BUR OAK, *Q. macrocarpa*

Key to Elms (*Ulmus*)

1. Leaves mostly 1 to 2½ inches long; buds less than ³⁄₁₆ inch long . . . . . SIBERIAN ("CHINESE") ELM, *U. pumila*
1. Leaves 2½ to 6 inches long; largest buds ³⁄₁₆ to ¼ inch long 2
    2. Leaves very rough above 3
    2. Leaves smooth above 4
3. Bud scales dark purple, those toward tip of bud more or less covered with shiny, copper-colored hairs; edges of samaras glabrous . . . . . SLIPPERY ELM, *U. rubra*
3. Bud scales reddish-brown with dark margins, usually glabrous; edges of samaras hairy . . . . . AMERICAN ELM, *U. americana*
    4. Samaras in racemes; branchlets covered with thick, corky outgrowths . . . . ROCK ELM, *U. thomasii*
    4. Samaras in umbellike clusters; branchlets lacking corky outgrowths . . . . . AMERICAN ELM, *U. americana*

Key to Magnolias (*Magnolia*)

1. Flowers green, appearing after leaves in late spring; large tree with brown, scaly, or furrowed bark . . . . . CUCUMBER TREE, *M. acuminata*
1. Flowers white or pink, appearing before leaves in early spring; small tree with smooth, gray bark 2
    2. Flowers white tinged with pink, with 9 petallike parts (3 sepals and 6 petals); terminal buds ½ to ¾ inch long . . . . SAUCER MAGNOLIA, *M. ×soulangeana*
    2. Flowers white, with 12 to 18 petallike parts (3 sepals and 9 to 15 petals); terminal buds ⅓ to ½ inch long . . . . STAR MAGNOLIA, *M. stellata*

Key to Serviceberries (*Amelanchier*)

SERVICEBERRIES are difficult to distinguish from one another and much remains to be learned about this genus in Iowa. The following key will identify typical individuals of the three native trees discussed in Chapter 4, plus two wide-ranging shrubby species. Pending further study of *Amelanchier* in Iowa, specimens of *A. humilis* Wieg. are referred here to *A. sanguinea* (Pursh) DC or *A. spicata* (Lam.). K. Koch.

A. ×grandiflora, a hybrid between the downy and Allegheny serviceberries that is sometimes seen in cultivation, has young leaves pubescent and purple-tinged, mature leaves glabrous.

1. Leaf veins either unforked or once forked, running straight into the tips of the teeth; shrub or small tree with clumped stems, rarely colonial . . . . ROUNDLEAF SERVICEBERRY, *A. sanguinea*
1. Leaf veins branching freely near the margin, forming a network of many tiny veins 2

2. Low shrub forming a colony of many stems; petals of flowers less than ⁷⁄₁₆ inch long . . . . LOW SERVICEBERRY, *A. spicata*
2. Tall shrub or tree with stems solitary or in a clump; petals ⁷⁄₁₆ to ¾ inch long 3
3. Top of ovary densely pubescent, with some of this pubescence persisting in fruit; native in northeastern Iowa only . . . . . INLAND SERVICEBERRY, *A. interior*
3. Top of ovary glabrous 4
    4. Leaves densely white-hairy beneath when young, becoming nearly glabrous when full grown; native tree of eastern, southern, and central Iowa . . . . . DOWNY SERVICEBERRY, *A. arborea*
    4. Leaves glabrous at all stages of development; tree native in northeastern Iowa . . . . . ALLEGHENY SERVICEBERRY, *A. laevis*

Key to Hawthorns (*Crataegus*)

THE hawthorns make up a large, taxonomically difficult genus and the distributions of several native species in Iowa are poorly known. The following key identifies the most common and widely distributed species.

1. Leaves prominently lobed, widest near base 2
1. Leaves unlobed or shallowly and rather obscurely lobed on upper half, widest near middle or above 5
    2. Leaves 2½ to 4 inches long with stout, usually hairy petioles, veins running to lobe tips but not to sinuses; native tree, often cultivated . . . . . DOWNY HAWTHORN, *C. mollis*
    2. Leaves 1 to 2½ inches long with slender, glabrous petioles, veins running to lobe tips and to sinuses; cultivated tree 3
3. Leaf lobes gradually tapered to sharp-pointed tips; fruits 3 to 5 seeded . . . . . WASHINGTON HAWTHORN, *C. phaenopyrum*
3. Leaf lobes rounded or blunt pointed; fruits 1 or 2 seeded 4
    4. Leaf lobes finely toothed; fruits 2 seeded . . . . . ENGLISH HAWTHORN, *C. oxycantha*
    4. Leaf lobes entire or with a few teeth at tips; fruits 1 seeded . . . . . SINGLESEED HAWTHORN, *C. monogyna*
5. Leaves obovate or oblanceolate (widest above middle) 6
5. Leaves elliptic or diamond shaped (widest near middle) 7
    6. Leaves glossy above, glabrous; fruits about ⅜ inch in diameter, 1 to 2 seeded . . . . . COCKSPUR HAWTHORN, *C. crus-galli*
    6. Leaves dark green but not glossy above, hairy at least along veins beneath; fruits ½ to ¾ inch in diameter, 3 to 5 seeded . . . . . DOTTED HAWTHORN, *C. punctata*
7. Seeds (nutlets) conspicuously indented on surface facing middle of fruit; sepals coarsely toothed 8
7. Seeds (nutlets) not indented; sepals entire or finely toothed 9
    8. Leaves dark glossy green above; fruits nearly round . . . . . FLESHY HAWTHORN, *C. succulenta*
    8. Leaves dull yellow-green above; fruits oblong or pear shaped . . . . . PEAR HAWTHORN, *C. calpodendron*
9. Leaves glabrous; fruits ⅜ to ½ inch in diameter, 2 or 3 seeded . . . . MARGARET'S HAWTHORN, *C. margaretta*
9. Leaves hairy at least along veins beneath; fruits ½ to ¾ inch in diameter, 3 to 5 seeded . . . . . DOTTED HAWTHORN, *C. punctata*

Key to Cherries and Plums

(Prunus)

1. Leaves reddish-purple 2
1. Leaves green 3
   2. Leaves green at first but changing to reddish-purple with small glands on upper portions of petioles; flowers and fruits in racemes at ends of leafy shoots . . . . . CHOKECHERRY, *P. virginiana* 'Shubert'
   2. Leaves reddish-purple throughout growing season, usually without glands on petioles; flowers and fruits solitary or paired on twigs of previous growing season. . . . . . PURPLELEAF PLUMS (Several small trees key out here, including the so-called Newport and Pissard plums. Most are hybrids or cultivars of *P. cerasifera*.)
3. Leaves with sharp, outward-pointing teeth (Fig. 5.23a) 4
3. Leaves with blunt or incurved teeth (Fig. 5.23b) 6

FIG. 5.23

a   b

   4. Bud scales red; flowers and fruits in umbellike clusters of 2 to 5 on twigs of previous growing season; trunk bark scaly . . . . . AMERICAN PLUM, *P. americana*
   4. Bud scales brown with grayish margins; flowers and fruits in racemes on leafy shoots (twigs) of current growing season; bark remaining smooth 5
5. Petals of flowers about twice as long as stamens; pit of fruit with corrugated surface; introduced ornamental tree . . . . . BIRD CHERRY (MAY TREE), *P. padus*
5. Petals and stamens nearly equal in length; pit of fruit with smooth surface; small native tree, occasionally cultivated . . . . . CHOKECHERRY, *P. virginiana*
   6. Flowers and fruits in racemes on leafy shoots (twigs) of current growing season; leaves frequently with orange hairs along lower portion of midvein beneath; common native tree with scaly bark . . . . . BLACK CHERRY, *P. serotina*
   6. Flowers and fruits in small, umbellike clusters on twigs of previous growing season; leaves lacking orange hairs beneath; uncommon shrub or small tree of northern or extreme southeastern Iowa 7
7. Terminal bud and 2 or 3 lateral buds clustered at tip of each twig; fruit about ¼ inch in diameter . . . . . PIN CHERRY, *P. pensylvanica*
7. Twigs tipped by solitary false terminal buds; fruit about 1 inch in diameter 8
   8. Leaves abruptly tapered at tip; tree native in northern Iowa . . . . . CANADA PLUM, *P. nigra*
   8. Leaves gradually tapered at tip; tree native in southeastern Iowa . . . . . GOOSE PLUM, *P. hortulana*

Key to Sumacs *(Rhus)*

1. Leaves with 3 leaflets 2
1. Leaves with 11 or more leaflets 3
   2. Terminal leaflet of each leaf on stalk much longer than stalks of other 2 leaflets; terminal bud present; fruit white . . . . POISON IVY, *R. radicans*
   2. Terminal leaflet of each leaf unstalked or nearly so; terminal bud absent, twigs often tipped by catkinlike cluster of flower buds; fruit red . . . . . FRAGRANT SUMAC, *R. aromatica*
3. Twigs glabrous . . . . . SMOOTH SUMAC, *R. glabra*
3. Twigs hairy . . . . . STAGHORN SUMAC, *R. typhina*

Key to Maples *(Acer)*

1. Leaves compound . . . . . BOXELDER, *A. negundo*
1. Leaves simple 2
   2. Leaf margins entire or with 1 or 2 pairs of teeth per lobe; trunk bark of larger trees dark and furrowed (hard maples) 3
   2. Leaf margins conspicuously toothed, with 3 to 15 pairs of teeth per lobe; trunk bark light gray, either smooth or scaly (soft maples). 5
3. Terminal bud plump, blunt pointed, green changing to reddish-purple, with 2 or 3 pairs of visible scales; petioles usually exuding a drop of milky sap when broken, especially in spring and early summer . . . . . NORWAY MAPLE, *A. platanoides*
3. Terminal bud slender, sharp pointed, brown, with 5 to 9 pairs of visible scales; petioles with clear, watery sap (native hard maple). This tree can be divided into two more or less distinct forms, which botanists have variously interpreted as two species or varieties of a single species. Typical representatives of each form key out as follows:
   4. Leaves entire or nearly so, finely hairy beneath, with 3 drooping lobes and right-angled sinuses; petiole bases of most leaves with small leaflike stipules . . . . . BLACK MAPLE, *A. saccharum* var. *nigrum* (*A. nigrum*)
   4. Leaves toothed, glabrous beneath, with 5 nondrooping lobes and acute-angled sinuses; petiole bases without stipules . . . . . SUGAR MAPLE, *A. saccharum*
5. Leaves about as wide as long (measure width as distance between tips of 2 largest lateral lobes) 6
5. Leaves 1½ to 2 times longer than wide . . . . . AMUR MAPLE, *A. ginnala*
   6. Leaves deeply lobed, with central (largest) pair of sinuses extending about ¾ the distance from apex to base of leaf; central lobe widest near middle, tapering to both apex and base . . . . . SILVER MAPLE, *A. saccharinum*
   6. Leaves shallowly lobed, with central pair of sinuses extending only ⅓ to ½ of the distance to base of leaf; central lobe widest at base, gradually tapered to apex 7
7. Terminal bud with 2 or 3 pairs of visible scales; introduced ornamental tree . . . . . RED MAPLE, *A. rubrum*
7. Terminal bud with single pair of visible scales; small native tree of steep wooded slopes; extreme northeastern Iowa . . . . . MOUNTAIN MAPLE, *A. spicatum*

Key to Dogwoods *(Cornus)*

1. Flowers appearing with or before leaves in spring; small cultivated tree with red fruits and large bulb-shaped flower buds 2
1. Flowers appearing shortly after leaves in spring; native tree or shrub with white or blue fruits and small ovoid buds 3
   2. Flowers with large white "petals" and greenish centers; leaves with 5 to 7 pairs of veins, glabrous except for hairs

along veins beneath . . . . . FLOWERING DOGWOOD, *C. florida*

2. Flowers bright yellow; leaves with 3 to 5 pairs of veins, hairy on both surfaces (seen with magnifying glass) . . . . . CORNELIAN-CHERRY DOGWOOD, *C. mas*

3. Leaves alternate . . . . . ALTERNATE-LEAF DOGWOOD, *C. alternifolia*

3. Leaves opposite 4

    4. Twigs and small branches bright red . . . . . RED-OSIER DOGWOOD, *C. stolonifera*

    4. Twigs red or not; small branches a color other than red 5

5. Leaves round or nearly so, with 6 to 8 pairs of veins; branches of shrub green blotched with purple . . . . . ROUNDLEAF DOGWOOD, *C. rugosa*

5. Leaves much longer than wide, with 3 to 5 pairs of veins; branches of shrub gray, brown, or dark reddish-brown 6

    6. Lower surfaces of leaves covered with short curved hairs that are quite conspicuous through a magnifying glass; upper surfaces of leaves usually rough . . . . . ROUGH-LEAF DOGWOOD, *C. drummondii*

    6. Lower surfaces of leaves glabrous or with scattered short, straight hairs; upper leaf surfaces usually smooth 7

7. Twigs of current growing season glabrous or nearly so; inflorescence open and paniclelike, about as tall as wide, with bright red stems; fruits white when ripe in late summer . . . . GRAY DOGWOOD, *C. racemosa*

7. Twigs hairy; inflorescence compact and flat topped, with greenish stems; fruits blue when ripe . . . . . SILKY DOGWOOD, *C. obliqua* (*C. purpussii*)

Key to Ashes (*Fraxinus*)

1. Twigs square in cross section with 4 corky wings along angles; flowers perfect; rare native tree of dry bluffs, Lee and Des Moines counties . . . . . BLUE ASH, *F. quadrangulata*

1. Twigs round, not winged; flowers imperfect; widely distributed tree 2

    2. Leaflets on stalks 3/16 to 1/2 inch long, margins either entire or distantly and rather obscurely toothed; wing of samara not extending along edge of seed cavity . . . . . WHITE ASH, *F. americana*

    2. Leaflets unstalked or on short stalks up to 3/16 inch long, margins conspicuously toothed; wing of samara extending along edge of seed cavity 3

3. Leaflets short stalked, usually 7 per leaf, glabrous or with white hairs; wing of samara extending along upper half of seed cavity, which is round in cross section . . . . . GREEN ASH, *F. pennsylvanica*

3. Leaflets unstalked, 9 or 11 per leaf, usually with tufts of orange-brown hairs at junctions with rachis (leaf stem); wing of samara extending to base of flattened and rather indistinct seed cavity . . . . . BLACK ASH, *F. nigra*

6: WINTER KEY TO COMMON DECIDUOUS TREES

THE FOLLOWING KEY identifies deciduous trees from the time they lose their leaves in autumn until their overwintering buds open the following spring. Most genera are keyed to species in the main body of the key; but the willows, oaks, poplars, elms, maples, and ashes are keyed in separate sections at the end. Crab apples, hawthorns, dogwoods, and a few smaller genera are not keyed to species because accurate identification requires leaves; fruits; and in some cases, flowers. Several large native shrubs that are common in the woodland understory and apt to be mistaken for tree saplings have been included.

The key is based on characteristics of the twigs and persistent fruits, supplemented with bark and distribution where appropriate. When collecting twigs for identification, select healthy looking specimens with intact tips and clearly defined leaf scars. The size, shape, bark type and color, and specific location of each tree should also be noted for future reference.

Become thoroughly familiar with the characteristics of poison ivy before collecting twigs or attempting to identify trees outdoors. This species is a shrub or vine rather than a tree, but it often climbs high on the trunks of forest trees and produces long, straight branches that can be easily mistaken for the branches of the trees. Fortunately, poison ivy is an easy species to recognize—it is our only woody plant with the combination of naked, yellow-brown buds and alternate, V-shaped leaf scars with more than 3 bundle scars.

A tree that does not key out after repeated attempts may be a rare species not covered in this key. In such cases a more complete key such as Harlow (1959) should be consulted. Rare species have been omitted from this key to make the identification of common trees quicker and easier.

GENERAL KEY

1. Fruits from previous growing season either persisting on twigs or lying on ground beneath tree 2
1. Fruits absent 37
    2. Fruits 1 seeded 3
    2. Fruits with 2 or more seeds 22
3. Individual fruits with thin papery wings (Fig. 6.1) 4

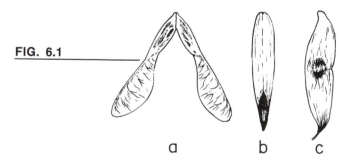

FIG. 6.1

a   b   c

3. Fruits not winged (stalk of fruit cluster winged in some species) 6
    4. Fruit paddle shaped or key shaped, with seed at base (Fig. 6.1a, b) 5
    4. Fruit propellor shaped, with seed in center (Fig. 6.1c) . . . . . TREE-OF-HEAVEN, *Ailanthus altissima*
5. Fruits key shaped, attached to twig in pairs (Fig. 6.1a)

. . . . . MAPLES, *Acer spp.* (key to species on p. 132)
5. Fruits paddle shaped, not in pairs (Fig. 6.1b) . . . . . ASHES, *Fraxinus* spp (key to species on p. 132)
    6. Fruit a nut, usually enclosed by husk, sac, or similar structure 7
    6. Fruit a small, berrylike drupe, never enclosed by sac or husk 13
7. Nut seated in bowl-, cone-, or saucer-shaped structure covered with tiny overlapping scales . . . . . OAKS, *Quercus* spp. (key to species on p. 131)
7. Nut enclosed by husk or saclike structure 8
    8. Nut about ⅓ inch long, enclosed by thin papery sac . . . . . IRONWOOD, *Ostrya virginiana*
    8. Nut 1 inch or more long; enclosed by leathery, woody, or semifleshy husk 9
9. Nut with corrugated shell, enclosed by husk that does not split open 10
9. Nut with smooth shell, enclosed by husk that splits completely or partially 11
    10. Nut round . . . . BLACK WALNUT, *Juglans nigra*
    10. Nut football shaped . . . . BUTTERNUT, *Juglans cinerea*
11. Shell of nut (actually large, nutlike seed) dark brown and glossy, with single large, pale spot . . . . . HORSECHEST-NUTS (BUCKEYES), *Aesculus* spp. (see couplet 56 for key to species)

11. Shell of nut uniformly white or light brown 12
    12. Husk less than ⅛ inch thick, splitting about halfway open . . . . . BITTERNUT HICKORY, *Carya cordiformis*
    12. Husk more than ⅛ inch thick, splitting completely open . . . . . SHAGBARK HICKORY, *Cary ovata*
13. Fruits red, in compact, upright clusters 14
13. Fruits a color other than red, either attached individually to twigs or in small open clusters 15
    14. Twigs hairy . . . . STAGHORN SUMAC, *Rhus typhina*
    14. Twigs glabrous . . . . . SMOOTH SUMAC, *Rhus glabra*
15. Fruit ¾ to 1 inch long 16
15. Fruit less than ½ inch long 17
    16. Fruit with strong rank odor when fresh in early winter; each leaf scar with 2 bundle scars; large tree . . . . . GINKGO, *Ginkgo biloba*
    16. Fruit not especially foul smelling; each leaf scar with 3 bundle scars; shrub or small tree . . . . . AMERICAN PLUM, *Prunus americana*
17. Twigs with opposite leaf scars 18
17. Twigs with alternate leaf scars 19
    18. Terminal bud ⅜ to 1 inch long . . . . . NANNYBERRY, *Viburnum lentago*
    18. Terminal bud less than ⅜ inch long . . . . . DOGWOODS, *Cornus* spp.
19. Fruits 1 to several on branched stalk attached to thin, papery wing (Fig. 6.2) . . . . . LINDENS (BASSWOODS), *Tilia* spp.

FIG. 6.2

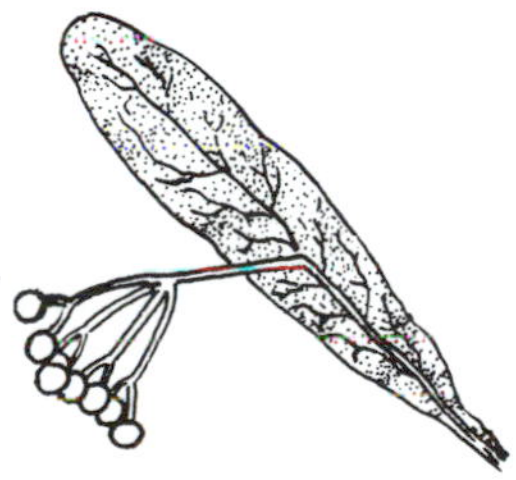

19. Fruits otherwise 20
    20. Fruits in racemes . . . . . CHERRIES, *Prunus* spp. (see couplet 109 for key to species)
    20. Fruits attached individually to twigs, either solitary or in groups of 2 or 3 21
21. Fruits dark purple or black . . . . . HACKBERRY, *Celtis occidentalis*
21. Fruits pale colored . . . . RUSSIAN-OLIVE, *Elaeagnus angustifolia*
    22. Fruit a ball composed of numerous tiny achenes or drupelike units 23
    22. Fruit a cone, pod, berry, or pome 24
23. Fruit light brown, about 1 inch in diameter . . . . . SYCAMORE, *Platanus occidentalis*
23. Fruit green, 3 to 5 inches in diameter . . . . . OSAGE ORANGE, *Maclura pomifera*
    24. Fruit a pod or cone 25
    24. Fruit a berry or small, berrylike pome 33
25. Fruit a cone . . . . EUROPEAN LARCH, *Larix decidua*
25. Fruit a pod 26
    26. Twigs with alternate leaf scars; pod (legume) distinctly flattened 27
    26. Twigs with opposite or whorled leaf scars; pod (capsule) rounded or triangular in cross section 30
27. Pod ⅝ to 1½ inches wide with seeds ⅓ to ½ inch long 28

27. Pod ⅜ to ½ inch wide with seeds 3/16 inch long 29
    28. Pod 6 to 18 inches long, leathery and usually twisted, with at least 12 seeds; trees often bearing large thorns . . . . HONEY LOCUST, *Gleditisa triacanthos*
    28. Pod thick and woody, usually less than 6 inches long, with 3 to 9 seeds; thorns never present . . . . KENTUCKY COFFEE TREE, *Gymnocladus dioicus*
29. Pod with rounded or abruptly tapered apex (Fig. 6.3a, b); twigs usually bearing small paired spines . . . . BLACK LOCUST, *Robinia pseudoacacia*
29. Pod gradually tapered to apex (Fig. 6.3c); twigs never spiny . . . . REDBUD, *Cercis canadensis*

FIG. 6.3

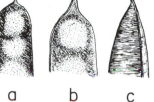

a   b   c

    30. Pod pencil shaped, 6 to 20 inches long . . . . NORTHERN CATALPA, *Catalpa speciosa*
    30. Pod no more than 2 inches long 31
31. Seeds with red fleshy coverings, suspended from small open pods by slender stalks . . . . . WAHOO, *Euonymus atropurpureus*
31. Seeds without red fleshy coverings 32
    32. Pod inflated and bladderlike, 1 to 2 inches long, with thin papery walls and usually 3 compartments, never splitting open . . . . . BLADDERNUT, *Staphylea trifolia*
    32. Pod slender, up to ¾ inch long, with leathery walls and 2 compartments, splitting open along two seams . . . . . JAPANESE TREE LILAC, *Syringa reticulata*
33. Leaf scars opposite or subopposite (i.e., associated in pairs at nodes, one on either side of twig, but not exactly opposite) 34
33. Leaf scars alternate 35
    34. Twigs tipped by terminal buds; fruit with 2 seeds . . . . . DOGWOODS, *Cornus* spp.
    34. Twigs tipped by short thorns or broken stubs; fruits usually 3 to 4 seeded . . . . . COMMON BUCKTHORN, *Rhamnus cathartica*
35. Fruits in large, compact, more or less flat-topped clusters; terminal bud ⅜ to ¾ inch long . . . . . MOUNTAIN-ASH, *Pyrus (Sorbus) aucuparia*
35. Fruits in small, open clusters; terminal bud usually less than ⅜ inch long 36
    36. Fruits with several small seeds that occupy center of fruit and are separated from flesh by thin, cartilaginous partitions; thorns absent, or if present, with leaf scars on them . . . . . APPLES, CRAB APPLES, PEARS, *Pyrus* spp.
    36. Fruits with 2 to 5 large, bony, light-colored seeds that occupy bulk of fruit; twigs bearing smooth thorns without leaf scars . . . . . HAWTHORNS, *Crataegus* spp.
37. Twigs or branchlets bearing thorns, spines, spur shoots, or exposed catkins 38
37. None of above-named structures present 53
    38. Twigs armed with thorns or spines 39
    38. Twigs not thorny or spiny 47
39. Twigs armed with stipular spines (spines in pairs at each node, one to either side of leaf scar) 40
39. Twigs armed with thorns (solitary at nodes) 41
    40. Buds apparently absent, actually buried beneath sur-

face of leaf scars . . . . BLACK LOCUST, *Robinia pseudoacacia*

40. Buds red, clearly visible on surface of twig above each leaf scar . . . . PRICKLY-ASH, *Xanthoxylum americanum*

41. Twigs very slender, densely coated with minute silver-gray scales that can be scratched off with fingernail; dried leaves from previous growing season often persisting on twigs in large numbers . . . . RUSSIAN-OLIVE, *Elaeagnus angustifolia*

41. Twigs not coated with silver-gray scales; dried leaves not persisting in winter 42

    42. Leaf scars subopposite (i.e., associated in pairs at nodes, one on either side of twig, but not exactly opposite); buds dark brown or black . . . . . COMMON BUCKTHORN, *Rhamnus cathartica*

    42. Leaf scars alternate; buds (if present) red, white, or light brown 43

43. Buds and/or leaf scars present along surface of thorns 44

43. Buds and leaf scars absent from thorns or present only at bases of thorns 45

    44. Buds densely coated with white hairs . . . . . WILD CRAB APPLE, *Pyrus (Malus) ioensis*

    44. Buds glabrous, either red or reddish (sometimes white along margins of scales) . . . . . AMERICAN PLUM, *Prunus americana*

45. Thorns ⅛ to ½ inch long . . . . . OSAGE ORANGE, *Maclura pomifera*

45. Thorns over ½ inch long 46

    46. Buds red, clearly visible on twigs above leaf scars; twig thorns unbranched (thorns sometimes branched on trunk of tree only) . . . . . HAWTHORNS, *Crataegus* spp.

    46. Buds brown, or embedded in twigs and not visible; thorns usually branched . . . . . HONEY LOCUST, *Gleditsia triacanthos*

47. Twigs bearing exposed catkins (spur shoots may be present) 48

47. Twigs bearing spur shoots but not catkins 51

    48. Buds globose to subglobose; catkins pale gray-brown; tall shrub of clearings, wood edges, and open woods; often forming thickets . . . . . HAZELNUT, *Corylus americana*

    48. Buds ovoid; catkins brown; a tree 49

49. Lateral buds with 6 or more visible scales; spur shoots absent . . . . . IRONWOOD, *Ostrya virginiana*

49. Lateral buds with 3 or 4 visible scales; spur shoots often present on branchlets 50

    50. Trunk bark white on saplings and mature trees, remaining fairly smooth or separating into thin papery strips; buds glabrous . . . . . PAPER BIRCH, *Betula papyrifera,* and EUROPEAN WHITE BIRCH, *B. pendula* (not easily distinguished during winter)

    50. Outer bark often white on saplings, though separating into papery scales that peel up and reveal orange inner bark, soon turning orange-brown and later dark gray; buds sometimes hairy . . . . . RIVER BIRCH, *Betula nigra*

51. Each leaf scar with 1 or 2 bundle scars 52

51. Each leaf scar with 3 bundle scars 53

    52. Bundle scar 1 . . . . . EUROPEAN LARCH, *Larix decidua*

    52. Bundle scars 2 . . . . . GINKGO, *Ginkgo biloba*

53. Leaf scars opposite or subopposite (i.e., associated in pairs but not exactly opposite) or in whorls of 3 54

53. Leaf scars alternate 67

    54. Leaf scars round, in whorls of 3 at many if not all of

the nodes . . . . . NORTHERN CATALPA, *Catalpa speciosa*

    54. Leaf scars opposite or subopposite 55

55. Buds plump with several overlapping scales, the largest ones ½ to 1 inch long; twigs stout with large shield-shaped, triangular, or half-round leaf scars 56

55. Characteristics of the buds and twigs not combined as described above 57

    56. Buds dark brown, sticky . . . . . HORSECHESTNUT, *Aesculus hippocastanum*

    56. Buds light brown, not sticky . . . . . OHIO BUCKEYE, *Aesculus glabra*

57. Bundle scar(s) forming a fine curved line in each leaf scar (Fig. 6.4) 58

57. Bundle scars not forming a line 60

    58. Bud at end of twig with 2 or 4 visible scales; bundle scars numerous, tiny, and very close together, forming a curved line (Fig. 6.4a) . . . . . ASHES, *Fraxinus* spp. (key to species on p. 132)

    58. Bud(s) at end of twig each with 6 to 10 visible scales; bundle scar 1 in each leaf scar, elongated into a continuous or broken line (Fig. 6.4b, c) 59

FIG. 6.4

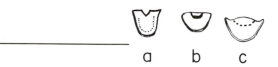

a   b   c

59. Twigs green or purple, often marked with 4 longitudinal lines; terminal bud present . . . . . WAHOO, *Euonymus atropurpureus*

59. Twigs gray or brown, not lined, usually tipped by 2 lateral buds instead of terminal bud . . . . JAPANESE TREE LILAC, *Syringa reticulata*

    60. Terminal bud present 61

    60. Terminal bud absent (twig may be tipped by a pair of lateral buds or a short thorn) 64

61. Terminal bud enclosed by 4 to 18 overlapping scales . . . . MAPLES, *Acer* spp. (key to species on p. 132)

61. Terminal bud with 2 scales 62

    62. Terminal bud ⅜ to 1 inch long . . . . NANNYBERRY, *Viburnum lentago*

    62. Terminal bud shorter 63

63. Leaf scars conspicuously raised above surface of twig on persisting petiole bases (Fig. 6.5a) . . . . . DOGWOODS, *Cornus* spp.

63. Leaf scars flush with surface of twig or only slightly raised (Fig. 6.5b); petioles completely deciduous in autumn . . . . . MAPLES, *Acer* spp. (key to species on p. 132)

FIG. 6.5

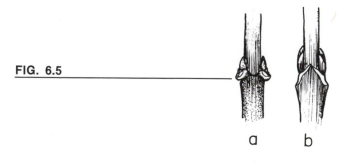

a   b

64. Twigs often tipped by short, thornlike projections; leaf scars subopposite . . . . COMMON BUCKTHORN, *Rhamnus cathartica*

64. Twigs not thorn-tipped; leaf scars mostly opposite 65

65. Small to large tree with slender twigs . . . . MAPLES, *Acer* spp. (key to species on p. 132)

65. Large native shrub with twigs moderate to stout 66

    66. Twigs gray or gray-brown with thick pith; stipule scars usually absent . . . . . ELDERBERRY, *Sambucus canadensis*

    66. Twigs green or purple; stipule scars present . . . . . BLADDERNUT, *Staphylea trifolia*

67. Several buds clustered together at tip of each twig (Fig. 6.6) 68

FIG. 6.6

67. Twigs tipped by 1 or 2 buds or tips of twigs lacking buds 70

    68. Buds covered with numerous tiny scales, usually arranged in vertical rows (Fig. 6.6); leaf scars half-round with many bundle scars; dried leaves from previous growing season sometimes persisting in large numbers . . . . . OAKS, *Quercus* spp. (key to species on p. 131)

    68. Without the above combination of charactristics 69

69. Leaf scars heart shaped, shield shaped, rounded, or lobed (illustrated in Chapter 3 and in Fig. 6.7) 85

69. Leaf scars half-round or broadly crescent-shaped 105

    70. Leaf scars very narrow: ring shaped, linear, crescent-shaped or U-shaped (illustrated in Chapter 3) 71

    70. Leaf scars some other shape 83

71. Terminal buds plump, ⅜ to ¾ inch long, partly to completely covered with soft hairs 72

71. Terminal buds absent or if present, then not as described above 74

    72. Each bud enclosed by a single visible scale; stipule scars forming a fine line from one side of leaf scar completely around twig to other side . . . . . SAUCER MAGNOLIA, *Magnolia* × *soulangeana*

    72. Each bud enclosed by two or more visible scales; stipule scars not encircling twigs 73

73. Leaf scars raised above twig on cushionlike bases colored like bud scales; bundle scars usually 5 . . . . . EUROPEAN MOUNTIAN-ASH, *Pyrus* (*Sorbus*) *aucuparia*

73. Leaf scars slightly raised, without obvious cushionlike bases; bundle scars 3 . . . . . CALLERY PEAR, *Pyrus calleryana*

    74. Each bud with a single visible scale* 75

    74. Each bud with 3 or more scales or with a dense covering of soft hairs that completely obscures the scales 76

75. Leaf scars ring shaped, completely encircling the buds . . . . . SYCAMORE, *Platanus occidentalis*

75. Leaf scars not ring shaped, not encircling the buds

    * If the buds appear to be absent, go to couplet 93

. . . . WILLOWS, *Salix* spp. (key to species on p. 131)

    76. Leaf scars C-shaped, nearly encircling the buds; twigs stout with thick, often brightly colored pith . . . . . SUMACS, *Rhus* spp. (see couplet 14 for key to species)

    76. Without the above combination of characteristics 77

77. Buds globose to subglobose (illustrated in Chapter 3) 78

77. Buds ovoid to elongate 79

    78. Lateral buds glabrous, with blunt or rounded tips and about a half-dozen scales . . . . . HAWTHORNS, *Crataegus* spp. (tree may have a few long thorns that are scattered and not immediately apparent)

    78. Lateral buds with about 4 scales, usually hairy, usually with pointed tips . . . . . CRAB APPLES, *Pyrus* spp.

79. Terminal bud elongate, its length at least 4 times greater than its basal diameter (measure with ruler) . . . . . DOWNY SERVICEBERRY, *Amelanchier arborea*

79. Terminal bud absent or if present, with its length no more than 3 times its basal diameter 80

    80. Lateral buds with 3 or 4 scales 81

    80. Lateral buds with about a half-dozen scales 107

81. Lowermost scale of each lateral bud centered directly over leaf scar (Fig. 6.9a) . . . . . POPLARS, *Populus* spp. (key to species on p. 131)

81. Lowermost scale of each lateral bud offset to one side of leaf scar (Fig. 6.9b) 82

    82. Ordinary elongated twigs tipped by false terminal buds (terminal buds present on spur shoots only if spur shoots are present) . . . . . BIRCHES, *Betula* spp. (see couplet 50 for key to species)

    82. Terminal bud usually present on both spur shoots and ordinary elongated twigs . . . . . CRAB APPLES, *Pyrus* spp.

83. Leaf scars heart shaped, shield shaped, round, or lobed (illustrated in Chapter 3 and in Fig. 6.7) 84

83. Leaf scars half-round or broadly crescent shaped or very tiny and inconspicuous 91

    84. Terminal bud present, usually much larger than the laterals 85

    84. Terminal bud absent (twig may be tipped by a false terminal bud the same size and shape as the laterals 89

85. Leaf scars with 3 bundle scars each (some of these may be split in two, so that there appear to be 4 to 6 bundle scars in 3 groups; see Fig. 6.9a) 86

85. Leaf scars with numerous bundle scars 88

    86. Pith of twigs chambered; buds usually superposed (in pairs at each leaf scar, one above the other) 87

    86. Pith continuous; buds only one at each leaf scar . . . . . POPLARS, *Populus* spp. (key to species on p. 131)

87. Leaf scar with a fringe of yellow-brown hairs along upper margin (Fig. 6.7a); terminal bud elongated, yellow-brown, ⅓ to ¾ inch long . . . . . BUTTERNUT, *Juglans cinerea*

87. Leaf scar not fringed (Fig. 6.7b); terminal bud subglobose, gray, 3/16 to ⅓ inch long . . . . . BLACK WALNUT, *Juglans nigra*

FIG. 6.7

    a   b

88. Stipule scars forming a line from one side of each leaf scar completely around twig to other side; terminal buds duckbill shaped . . . . TULIP TREE, *Liriodendron tulipifera*

88. Stipule scars absent; buds ovoid to elongate 110

89. Twigs very stout (¼ to ½ inch in diameter), with thick, often brightly colored pith 90

89. Twigs slender to moderate in diameter (less than ¼ inch in diameter) 93

90. Buds buried in small, craterlike depressions in twig, with only tips visible; leaf scars heart shaped with 3 to 5 bundle scars . . . . KENTUCKY COFFEE TREE, *Gymnocladus dioicus*

90. Buds dome shaped, plainly visible on surface of twig immediately above leaf scars; leaf scars shield shaped with 7 or more bundle scars . . . . TREE-OF-HEAVEN, *Ailanthus altissima*

91. Twigs partly to completely coated with minute silver-gray scales . . . . RUSSIAN-OLIVE, *Elaeagnus angustifolia*

91. Twigs not coated with scales, though sometimes hairy or marked with scattered dots (lenticels) 92

92. Terminal buds absent (twigs may tipped by false terminal buds, thornlike points, or broken stubs) 93

92. Terminal buds present on most if not all of the twigs 104

93. Buds buried in twig and thus apparently absent or with their bases buried so that only their tips are visible . . . . HONEY LOCUST, *Gleditsia triacanthos* var. *inermis*

93. Buds plainly visible on surface of twig 94

94. Buds subglobose, somewhat lopsided, with 2 (occasionally 3) red or reddish scales . . . . LINDENS (BASSWOODS), *Tilia* sp.

94. Buds lacking the above combination of characteristics 95*

95. Bundle scars embedded in a brown, corky material covering each of the leaf scars . . . . ELMS, *Ulmus* spp. (key to species on p. 132)

95. Leaf scars not covered with a brown corky material 96

96. Leaf scars round, roundish, or broadly half-round, conspicuous; bundle scars more than 3 in each leaf scar, either scattered or arranged in a circular pattern 97

96. Leaf scars half-round or broadly crescent shaped, very small, with 1 to 3 bundle scars (leaf scars may be so small that bundle scars are indistinct even with magnification) 98

97. Buds about as long as wide, closely pressed against side of twig; bark of branches (and trunks of small trees) pale orange-brown . . . . WHITE MULBERRY, *Morus alba*

97. Buds decidedly longer than wide, pointing away from twig at slight angle; bark of branches gray or brown . . . . RED MULBERRY, *Morus rubra*

98. Largest buds with 1 to 4 scales 99

98. Largest buds with more than 4 scales 101

99. Buds with one scale . . . . WILLOWS, *Salix* spp. (key to species on p. 131)

99. Buds with 3 or 4 scales 100

100. Buds somewhat triangle shaped, about ⅛ inch long, pressed closely to side of twig; pith intermittently chambered . . . . HACKBERRY, *Celtis occidentalis*

100. Buds ovoid, 3/16 to ¼ inch long; pith continuous; spur shoots often present . . . . BIRCHES, *Betula* spp. (see couplet 50 for key to species)

101. Lateral buds of two distinct kinds: tiny 2-scaled buds near the end of the twig and much larger, stalked, many-scaled buds closer to the base of the twig . . . . REDBUD, *Cercis canadensis*

101. Lateral buds not of 2 distinct kinds as described above 102

102. Buds with about 6 scales, sometimes collateral (in pairs above the leaf scars, one beside the other); twigs about as wide as the buds, or wider, often thorn tipped; dried leaves not normally persisting in winter . . . . WILD PLUM, *Prunus americana*

102. Buds with 6 to 12 scales; twigs very slender, often narrower than the buds; dried leaves from previous growing season often persisting on twigs in large numbers 103

103. Bud scales spirally arranged, often marked with fine vertical lines (seen with magnifying glass) (Fig. 6.8); trunk bark gray or brown, separating into vertical rows of small rectangular plates when trees are several inches in diameter . . . . IRONWOOD, *Ostrya virginiana*

FIG. 6.8

103. Bud scales arranged in 4 rows, not marked with fine lines; trunks having a distinct twisted or "muscle-bound" appearance, with smooth pale gray bark . . . . HORNBEAM, *Carpinus caroliniana*

104. Buds with many tiny scales usually arranged in vertical rows (Fig. 6.6); each leaf scar with many bundle scars; dried leaves from previous growing season sometimes persisting in large numbers . . . . OAKS, *Quercus* spp. (key to species on p. 131)

104. Without the above combination of characteristics 105

105. Buds with one scale; stipule scars forming a fine line from one side of leaf scar completely around twig to other side . . . . SAUCER MAGNOLIA, *Magnolia* × *soulangeana*

105. Buds with 2 or more overlapping scales 106

106. Buds globose to subglobose with rounded or blunt tips and thick, red, glabrous scales . . . . HAWTHORNS, *Crataegus* spp.

106. Buds ovoid to ovid-elongate, with pointed tips, either hairy or glabrous 107

107. Lowermost scale of each lateral bud centered directly over leaf scar (Fig. 6.9a) . . . . POPLARS, *Populus* spp. (key to species on p. 131)

107. Lowermost scale of each lateral bud offset to one side of leaf scar (Fig. 6.9b) 108

*The following species are among the most difficult to identify in winter. Accurate identification requires careful examination of buds and leaf scars, using a 10-power lens. Be sure to examine several buds or leaf scars at each step in the key.

FIG. 6.9

a   b

108. Buds with several glabrous scales; freshly bruised twigs with a strong unpleasant odor 109
   108. Buds with 2 to several scales that are bristle tipped and/or hairy; twigs lacking the odor described above . . . . . APPLES, CRAB APPLES, PEARS, MOUNTAIN-ASH, *Pyrus* spp.
109. Bud scales red or reddish . . . . BLACK CHERRY, *Prunus serotina*

109. Bud scales brown with gray margins . . . . . CHOKE-CHERRY, *Prunus virginiana*
   110. Terminal bud yellow, slender, with 2 scales that meet along the edges without overlapping . . . . BITTER-NUT HICKORY, *Carya cordiformis*
   110. Terminal bud brown or tan, plump, with several overlapping scales . . . . SHAGBARK HICKORY, *Carya ovata*

Key to Willows (*Salix*)

WILLOWS, which are difficult to identify when leaves and flowers are available, are especially troublesome to distinguish in winter. The following key distinguishes typical representatives of the most common species.

1. Tree with long, yellow, drooping branches that often reach or nearly reach the ground . . . . . GOLDEN WEEPING WILLOW, *S. ×sepulcralis*
1. Tree or large shrub; branches not long and drooping 2
   2. Buds ³⁄₁₆ to ³⁄₈ inch long, rather plump, opening to silky white catkins in late winter 3
   2. Buds ¹⁄₁₆ to ³⁄₁₆ inch long; twigs very slender 5
3. Native; buds often blackish . . . . . PUSSY WILLOW, *S. discolor*
3. Cultivated; buds usually brown or reddish 4
   4. Twigs and branchlets densely gray-hairy . . . . . GRAY WILLOW, *S. cinerea*
   4. Twigs and branchlets glabrous or partly hairy, often glossy . . . . . GOAT WILLOW, *S. caprea*
5. Small native tree with polelike stems and upright branches, forming thickets in floodplains and other moist, low-lying areas; twigs usually reddish-brown or orange-brown . . . . SANDBAR WILLOW, *S. interior*
5. Medium- to large-sized tree with spreading branches; twigs brown, greenish-brown, or yellowish (sometimes tinged with red on one side) 6
   6. Bud scale with freely overlapping edges on back (twig) side of bud (seen with magnifying glass); native tree 7
   6. Bud scale fused into a caplike structure with no visible edges; tree cultivated or wild . . . . WHITE WILLOW, *S. alba* and CRACK WILLOW, *S. fragilis* (not easily distinguished in winter)
7. Twigs brown or gray-brown, with brown buds . . . . . BLACK WILLOW, *S. nigra*
7. Twigs light yellow or yellowish-gray; buds brown or yellow, sometimes black on upper half . . . . PEACHLEAF WILLOW, *S. amygdaloides*

Key to Poplars (*Populus*)

1. Twigs coated with white, feltlike material that can be easily rubbed off . . . . WHITE POPLAR, *P. alba*
1. Twigs without such coating 2
   2. Twigs gray, gray-green, or yellow; glabrous 3
   2. Twigs brown (sometimes with grayish cast due to covering of fine gray hairs) 4
3. Terminal bud ³⁄₈ to ³⁄₄ inch long; tree with broad crown of spreading branches . . . . . COTTONWOOD, *P. deltoides*
3. Terminal bud ³⁄₁₆ to ¼ inch long; tree with narrow columnar crown of sharply ascending branches, frequently planted in rows for borders and windbreaks . . . . LOMBARDY POPLAR, *P. nigra* var. *italica*

4. Buds shiny dark brown, glabrous; lateral buds usually appressed to twigs . . . . . QUAKING ASPEN, *P. tremuloides*
4. Buds light brown, more or less covered with fine gray hairs; lateral buds diverging from twig at acute angle . . . . BIGTOOTH ASPEN, *P. grandidentata*

Key to Oaks (*Quercus*)

OAKS are difficult to identify in winter using characteristics of the twigs alone. The following key, which is based primarily on characteristics of the bark and acorns, will identify trees beyond the sapling stage.

1. Shell of acorn glabrous on inner surface; bark of branches either dark and prominently furrowed or light ashy gray and scaly (white oaks) 2
1. Shell of acorn hairy on inner surface; bark remaining smooth or only slightly roughened until branches are several inches in diameter, then becoming shallowly furrowed (red oaks) 5
   2. Acorn-cup with a conspicuous fringe of soft bristles around rim; buds and twigs more or less covered with fine grayish hairs; corky outgrowths often present on branchlets . . . . BUR OAK, *Q. macrocarpa*
   2. Acorn-cup lacking fringe of bristles; buds and twigs glabrous to slightly hairy; branchlets lacking corky outgrowths 3
3. Acorn-cup on stalk 1 to 4 inches long; tree native in moist, low-lying woods . . . . . SWAMP WHITE OAK, *Q. bicolor*
3. Acorn-cup unstalked or very short stalked; tree native in upland woods 4
   4. Acorn-cup with thick, warty scales; dried, lobed leaves often persisting in large numbers, especially on lower branches of tree . . . . . WHITE OAK, *Q. alba*
   4. Acorn-cup with thin scales; dried leaves not normally persisting in winter . . . . . CHINKAPIN OAK, *Q. muhlenbergii*
5. Scales at top of acorn-cup loose, forming fringe around rim of cup; buds ¼ to ½ inch long, densely hairy . . . . BLACK OAK, *Q. velutina*
5. Scales of acorn-cup tightly appressed to cup; buds mostly ¹⁄₁₆ to ¼ inch long, glabrous to partly hairy 6
   6. Acorn-cup bowl shaped or cone shaped, covering lower ⅓ to ½ of nut (Fig. 6.10a, c) 8
   6. Acorn-cup saucer shaped, covering only base of nut (Fig. 6.10b) 7

FIG. 6.10

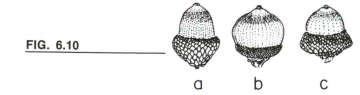

a   b   c

7. Acorn ⅝ to 1 inch long; buds mostly 3/16 to ¼ inch long . . . . . RED OAK, *Q. rubra*

7. Acorn ⅜ to ½ inch long; buds about ⅛ inch long . . . . . PIN OAK, *Q. palustris*

   8. Acorn 1½ to 2 times longer than wide, with cone-shaped cup (Fig. 6.10a) . . . . . HILL'S OAK, *Q. ellipsoidalis*

   8. Acorn only slightly longer than wide, with bowl-shaped cup (Fig. 6.10c) 9

9. Buds ⅛ to 3/16 inch long; leaves not lobed . . . . . SHINGLE OAK, *Q. imbricaria*

9. Buds 3/16 to ¼ inch long; leaves lobed . . . . . RED OAK, *Q. rubra*

Key to Elms (*Ulmus*)

1. Buds of two distinct types and sizes as follows: leaf buds less than ⅛ inch long near the tips of the twigs, and globose flower buds ⅛ to 3/16 inch long closer to the bases of the twigs . . . . . SIBERIAN ("CHINESE") ELM, *U. pumila*

1. Buds larger than described above 2

   2. Bud scales red-brown with dark margins, glabrous or nearly so; twigs brown or reddish-brown . . . . . AMERICAN ELM, *U. americana*

   2. Buds dark purple or purple-brown, usually covered with shiny copper-colored hairs, especially towards the tip; twigs gray . . . . . SLIPPERY ELM, *U. rubra*

Key to Maples (*Acer*)

1. Terminal bud with 10 to 18 visible scales . . . . . HARD (SUGAR, BLACK) MAPLE, *A. saccharum*

1. Terminal bud with 2 to 6 visible scales 2

   2. Largest buds about 1/16 inch long, terminal frequently absent; small, shrubby, cultivated tree . . . . . AMUR MAPLE, *A. ginnala*

   2. Largest buds ⅛ to ¼ inch long; a tree, cultivated or native 3

3. Buds white-hairy; twigs usually green or purple, often coated with white waxy material; fruits sometimes persisting on twigs in large numbers . . . . . BOXELDER, *A. negundo*

3. Buds glabrous or hairy along edges of scales only; twigs red or brown; fruits not persisting on twigs in large numbers 4

   4. Opposing leaf scars touching at edges (Fig. 6.11a); twigs brown . . . . . NORWAY MAPLE, *A. platanoides*

   4. Opposing leaf scars not normally touching, though sometimes connected by fine line (Fig. 6.11b); twigs red or red-brown . . . . . SILVER MAPLE, *A. saccharinum*

FIG. 6.11

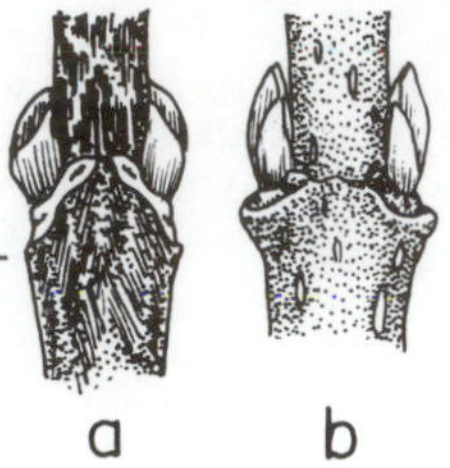

a   b

Key to Ashes (*Flaxinus*)

ASHES are highly variable in their characteristics and not easy to distinguish in winter. The following key will identify typical specimens.

1. Buds usually black (sometimes brown on small saplings); twigs very stout, with leaf scars rounded or elliptical in shape; wing of fruit extending to base of flattened and rather indistinct seed cavity . . . . . BLACK ASH, *F. nigra*

1. Buds light to dark brown; twigs moderate in diameter, with leaf scars usually half-round in shape; wing of fruit extending no further than upper half of seed cavity 2

   2. Lateral buds positioned in V-shaped notches in upper margins of leaf scars (Fig. 6.12a); wing of fruit not extending along edge of seed cavity (Fig. 6.13b); tree native in upland woods, sometimes cultivated . . . . . WHITE ASH, *F. americana*

   2. Lateral buds positioned immediately above leaf scars, which are straight or curved at top (Fig. 6.12b); wing of fruit extending along upper part of seed cavity (Fig. 6.13a); tree native in low-lying woods and widely cultivated . . . . . GREEN ASH, *F. pennsylvanica*

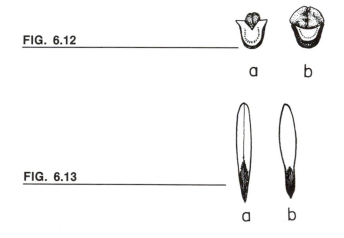

FIG. 6.12

a   b

FIG. 6.13

a   b

BIBLIOGRAPHY

Aikman, J. M., and A. Hayden. 1938. Iowa trees in winter. Iowa State Coll. Ext. Cir. 246.

Aikman, J. M., and A. W. Smelser. 1938. The structure and environment of forest communities in central Iowa. *Ecology* 19:141–50.

Aikman, J. M., and C. L. Gilly. 1948. A comparison of the forest floras along the Des Moines and Missouri rivers. *Proc. Iowa Acad. Sci.* 55:63–79.

Argus, G. W. 1986. The genus *Salix* (Salicaceae) in the southeastern United States. *Systematic Botany Monographs.* Vol. 9. The American Society of Plant Taxonomists.

Ball, C. R. 1899. The genus *Salix* in Iowa. *Proc. Iowa Acad. Sci.* 7:141–59.

_____. 1946. More plant study: Fewer plant names. *J. Arnold Arbor. Harv. Univ.* 27:373–85.

Bard, R. 1978. *Successful Wood Book.* Structures Publ., Farmington, Mich.

Becraft, R. J. 1924. Quercitron oak and its relation to soils. *Proc. Iowa Acad. Sci.* 31:129.

Bode, I. T., and G. B. MacDonald. 1928. A handbook of the native trees of Iowa. Iowa State Coll. Ext. Serv., Ames.

Borell, A. E. 1971. Russian-olive for wildlife and other conservation uses. USDA Leafl. 517.

Cahayla-Wynne, R., and D. C. Glenn-Lewin. 1978. The forest vegetation of the Driftless Area, northeast Iowa. *Am. Midl. Nat.* 100:307–19.

Campbell, R. B. 1961. Trees of Iowa. Iowa State Univ. Coop. Ext. Serv. Bull. P21 (rev.).

Carson, G. 1978. How the West was won. *Nat. Hist.* 87(9):84–98.

Carter, J. C. 1975. Diseases of midwest trees. Univ. Ill. Coll. Agric. Spec. Publ. 35.

Carter, J. L. 1960. *The Flora of Northwestern Iowa.* University Microfilms, Ann Arbor, Mich.

Clark, F. B. 1976. Planting black walnut for timber. USDA For. Serv. Leafl. 487.

Clark, O. R. 1926. An ecological comparison of two types of woodland. *Proc. Iowa Acad. Sci.* 33:131–34.

Clark, R. C. 1989. Chinkapin oak: Satisfaction for the homeowner, skulduggery for the botanist. *Morton Arbor. Quart.* 25:(1):10–16.

Coder, K. D. 1980. Management of floodplain forests. Iowa State Univ. Coop. Ext. Serv. For. Ext. Note 326.

Collier, H. O. J. 1963. Aspirin. *Sci. Am.* 209:97–108.

The Compact Edition of the Oxford English Dictionary. 1971. Oxford University Press.

Conard, H. S. 1952. The vegetation of Iowa. *Univ. Iowa Stud. Nat. Hist.* 19:1–166.

Cooperrider, M. 1957. Introgressive hybridization between *Quercus marilandica* and *Q. velutina* in Iowa. *Am. J. Bot.* 44:804–10.

Cooperrider, T. S. 1958. *The Flora of Clinton, Jackson, and Jones Counties, Iowa.* University Microfilms, Ann Arbor, Mich.

Cott, A. E., A. H. Epstein, V. M. Jennings, and S. O. Ryan. 1976. Ornamental and turf pest control. Category 3, Iowa Commercial Pesticide Applicator Manual. Iowa State Univ. Coop. Ext. Serv. CS-15.

Countryman, D. W., and D. P. Kelley. 1981. Management of existing hardwood stands can be profitable for private woodland owners. *Iowa State J. Res.* 56(2):119–30.

Davidson, R. A. 1957. *The Flora of Southeastern Iowa.* University Microfilms, Ann Arbor, Mich.

_____. 1961. Comparisons of the Iowa forest resource in 1832 and 1954. *Iowa State J. Sci.* 36:133–36.

Davis, E. F. 1928. The toxic principle of *Juglans nigra* as identified with synthetic juglone, and its toxic effects on tomato and alfalfa plants. *Am. J. Bot.* 15:620.

Del Tredici, P. 1991. Ginkgos and people: a thousand years of interaction. *Arnoldia* 51(2):2–15.

Desmarais, Y. 1952. Dynamics of leaf variation in the sugar maples. *Brittonia* 7:347–87.

Dick-Peddie, W. A. 1955. Presettlement forest types in Iowa. Ph.D. diss., Iowa State Univ.

Dirr, M. A. 1975. *Manual of Woody Landscape Plants: Their Identification, Ornamental Characteristics, Culture, Propagation, and Uses.* Stipes Publ., Champaign, Ill.

Dorn, R. D. 1975. A systematic study of *Salix* section *Cordatae* in North America. *Can. J. Bot.* 53:1491–1522.

_____. 1976. A synopsis of American *Salix. Can. J. Bot.* 54:2769–89.

Eilers, L. J. 1964. *The Flora and Phytogeography of the Iowan Lobe of the Wisconsin Glaciation.* University Microfilms, Ann Arbor, Mich.

Epstein, A. H., and H. S. McNabb. 1972a. Controlling oak wilt. Iowa State Univ. Coop. Ext. Serv. PM-482.

_____. 1972b. Shade tree diseases: Anthracnose. Iowa State Univ. Coop. Ext. Serv. PM-256 (rev.).

Erdmann, G. G. 1966. Promising conifers for western Iowa. USDA For. Serv. Res. Pap. NC-8.

Fay, M. J. 1951. The flora of Cedar County, Iowa. *Proc. Iowa Acad. Sci.* 58:107–31.

_____. 1953. *The Flora of Southwestern Iowa.* University Microfilms, Ann Arbor, Mich.

Fernald, M. L. 1950. *Gray's Manual of Botany.* 8th ed. D. Van Nostrand, New York.

Fitzpatrick, T. J., and M. F. L. Fitzpatrick. 1900a. Betulaceae of Iowa. *Proc. Iowa Acad. Sci.* 8:169–77.

_____. 1900b. The Fagaceae of Iowa. *Proc. Iowa Acad. Sci.* 8:177–95.

_____. 1900c. The Juglandaceae of Iowa. *Proc. Iowa Acad. Sci.* 8:160–69.

Franklin, A. H. 1959. *Ginkgo biloba:* Historical summary and bibliography. *Va. J. Sci.* 10:131–76.

Gleason, H. A. 1922. The vegetational history of the Middle West. *Ann. Assoc. Amer. Geog.* 12:39–85.

Gleason, H. A., and A. Cronquist. 1963. *Manual of Vascular Plants of Northeastern United States and Adjacent Canada.* D. Van Nostrand, New York.

Gorshkova, S. G. 1949. Elaeagnaceae. In Vol. XV, *Flora of the U.S.S.R.* Translated by N. Landau. Israel Program for Scientific Translations, Jerusalem, 1974.

Grant, M. L. 1950. Dickinson County flora. *Proc. Iowa Acad. Sci.* 57:91–129.

_____. 1953. Additions and notes on the flora of Dickinson Co., Iowa. *Proc. Iowa Acad. Sci.* 60:131–40.

Greuter, W., et al. 1988. *International Code of Botanical Nomenclature.* Koeltz Scientific Books, Königstein, Germany.

Guldner, L. F. 1960. The vascular plants of Scott and Muscatine counties. Davenport (Iowa) Public Museum Publ. Bot. 1.

Harlow, W. M. 1959. *Fruit Key and Twig Key to Trees and Shrubs.* Dover, New York.

Harlow, W. M., E. S. Harrar, and F. M. White. 1979. *Textbook of Dendrology.* 6th ed. McGraw-Hill, New York.

Harrington, H. D. 1934. The woody plants of Iowa in winter condition. *Univ. Iowa Stud. Nat. Hist.* 16:1–116.

_____. 1940. Keys to the woody plants of Iowa in vegetative condition. *Univ. Iowa Stud. Nat. Hist.* 17:371–484.

Harris, M. D. 1975. Effects of initial flooding on forest vegetation at two Oklahoma lakes. *J. Soil Water Conserv.* 30:294–95.

Harris, R. W., A. T. Leiser, and R. E. Fissel. 1975. Plant tolerance to flooding. Summary Report, 1971–1975. Dep. Environ. Hortic., University of California, Davis.

Hartley, T. G. 1962. *The Flora of the "Driftless Area."* University Microfilms, Ann Arbor, Mich.

Hayden, A. 1918. A botanical survey in the Iowa lakes region of Clay and Palo Alto counties. *Iowa State Coll. J. Sci.* 17:277–415.

Hess, W. J. 1977. Sumacs: Spectacle in autumn. Morton Arbor. Plant Inf. Bull. 15, Lisle, Ill.

Hightshoe, G. 1978. *Native Trees for Urban and Rural America.* Iowa State Univ. Res. Found., Ames.

Iowa Forest Industries Committee. 1968. Iowa Forest Facts. Dubuque, Iowa.

Jensen, R. J. 1977. A preliminary numerical analysis of the red oak complex in Michigan and Wisconsin. *Taxon* 26:399–407.

Jensen, R. J., and W. H. Eshbaugh. 1976. Numerical taxonomic studies of hybridization in *Quercus*. I and II. *Syst. Bot.* 1:1–19.

Johnson, H. 1973. *The International Book of Trees.* Mitchell Beaxley Publ., London.

Johnson, W. T., and H. H. Lyon. 1988. *Insects That Feed on Trees and Shrubs.* 2d ed. Cornell University Press, Ithaca.

Kielbaso, J. J., and M. R. Koelling. 1975. Pruning shade and ornamental trees. Mich. State Univ. Coop. Ext. Serv. Bull. E-804.

Kieran, J. 1966. *An Introduction to Nature.* Doubleday, Garden City, New York.

Kingsbury, J. M. 1965. *Deadly Harvest: A Guide to Common Poisonous Plants.* Holt, Rinehart and Winston, New York.

Kramer, P. M., and T. T. Kozlowski. 1960. *Physiology of Trees.* McGraw-Hill, New York.

Krüssmann, G. 1984. *Manual of Cultivated Broad-leaved Trees and Shrubs.* 3 Vols. Translated by M. E. Epp. Timber Press, Beaverton, Oregon.

Kucera, C. L. 1952. An ecological study of a hardwood forest area in central Iowa. *Ecol. Monogr.* 22:283–97.

Lammers, T. 1977. The vegetation of the Mississippi River floodplain in southeastern Iowa. Contributions from the Herbarium. 19. University of Wisconsin, La Crosse.

Landers, R. Q., and D. Graf. 1975. The oldest Iowa tree. II. Eastern red cedar on Cedar River bluffs. *Proc. Iowa Acad. Sci.* 82:123.

Larsen, J. A., and J. R. Dilworth. 1939. Notes on the forests of southern Iowa. *Proc. Iowa Acad. Sci.* 46:141–47.

Little, E. L. 1953. Checklist of native and naturalized trees of the United States (including Alaska). USDA For. Serv. Agr. Handb. 41.

McComb, A. L. 1955. The European larch: Its races, site requirements, and characteristics. *For. Sci.* 1:298–318.

McComb, A. L., and N. J. Hansen. 1954. A naturally occurring aspen-poplar hybrid. *J. For.* 52:528–29.

McCormick, J. 1966. *The Life of the Forest.* McGraw-Hill, New York.

Manning, W. E. 1973. The northern limit of the distribution of the mockernut hickory. *Mich. Bot.* 12:203–8.

Martin, A. C., H. S. Zim, and A. L. Nelson. 1951. *American Wildlife and Plants: A Guide to Wildlife Food Habits.* McGraw-Hill, New York. Reprint. Dover Publ., New York, 1961.

Monson, P. H. 1959. *Spermatophytes of the Des Moines Lobe in Iowa.* University Microfilms, Ann Arbor, Mich.

Morley, T. 1972. Deciduous trees of Minnesota: A winter key. *J. Minn. Acad. Sci.* 38:27–36.

Mueller, H. A. 1899. Trees and shrubs of Hamilton County. *Proc. Iowa Acad. Sci.* 7:204–9.

Municipal Tree Restoration Program. 1989. *Street Tree Fact Sheets.* Pennyslvania State University, University Park.

Olson, J. E., and P. H. Wray. 1980. Preventing construction damage to trees. Iowa State Univ. Coop. Ext. Serv. PM-909.

Olson, J. E., et al. 1984. Landscape plants for Iowa. Iowa State Univ. Coop. Ext. Serv. PM-212 (rev.).

Ostrom, A. J. 1976. Forest statistics for Iowa, 1974. USDA For. Serv. Res. Bull. NC-33.

Panshin, A. J., and C. de Zeeuw. 1970. *Textbook of Wood Technology.* Vol. 1. 3d ed. McGraw-Hill, New York.

Peattie, D. C. 1966. *A Natural History of Trees of Eastern and Central North America.* 2d ed. Bonanza Books, New York.

Peterson, R. P. 1980. *The Pine Tree Book.* Brandywine Press, New York.

Petrides, G. A. 1972. *A Field Guide to Trees and Shrubs.* 2d ed. Houghton Mifflin, Boston.

Preston, R. J. 1976. *North American Trees.* 3d ed. Iowa State University Press, Ames.

Rehder, A. 1940. *Manual of Cultivated Trees and Shrubs.* 2d ed. Macmillan, New York.

Rendle, B. J. 1969. *World timbers: Europe and Africa.* Vol. 1. Univ. Toronto Press, Toronto.

Rogers, W. E. 1935. *Tree Flowers of Forest, Park, and Street.* Reprint. Dover Publ., New York, 1975.

Rosendahl, C. O. 1955. *Trees and Shrubs of the Upper Midwest.* Univ. Minn. Press, Minneapolis.

Ryan, S. O. 1974. Bronze birch borers and their control. Iowa State Univ. Coop. Ext. Serv. IC-419.

_____. 1976. Shade tree galls and their control. Iowa State Univ. Coop. Ext. Serv. IC-417.

Santamour, F. S., Jr., and A. Jacot McArdle. 1988. Cultivars of *Salix babylonica* and other weeping willows. *J. Arboric.* 14(7):180–84.

Sargent, C. S. 1918. Notes on North American trees. II. *Carya. Bot. Gaz.* 66:229–58.

_____. 1922. *Manual of the Trees of North America.* 2d ed. Houghton Mifflin, New York. Reprint. Dover Publ., New York, 1961.

Settergren, C., and R. E. McDermott. 1964. Trees of Missouri. Missouri Agric. Exp. Stat. Bull. B767.

Shigo, A. L. Homeowner's guide for beautiful, safe, and healthy trees. USDA For. Serv. NE-INF-58-84.

Shimek, B. 1899. The distribution of forest trees in Iowa. *Proc. Iowa Acad. Sci.* 7:47–59.

_____. 1915. The plant geography of the Lake Okoboji region. Univ. Iowa Bull. Lab. Nat. Hist. 7.

_____. 1922. *Quercus lyrata* in Iowa. Bull. Torr. Bot. Club 49:293–94.

_____. 1948. The plant geography of Iowa. *Univ. Iowa Stud. Nat. Hist.* 18:1–178.

Silker, T. H. 1948. Planting of water-tolerant trees along margins of fluctuating-level reservoirs. *Iowa State Coll. J. Sci.* 22:431–48.

Sinclair, W. A., H. H. Lyon, and W. T. Johnson. 1987. *Diseases of Trees and Shrubs.* Cornell University Press, Ithaca, N.Y.

Smith, N. F. 1952. Michigan trees worth knowing. 3d ed. Michigan Dep. Conserv., Lansing.

Snyder, Leon C. 1980. *Trees and Shrubs for Northern Gardens.* Univ. Minn. Press, Minneapolis.

Spence, W. L. 1959. The Salicaceae of Iowa. Master's thesis. University of Iowa, Iowa City.

Steyermark, J. A. 1963. *Flora of Missouri.* Iowa State Univ. Press, Ames.

Tarr, M., and R. R. Rothacker. 1966. Landscape plants for Iowa. Iowa State Univ. Coop. Ext. Serv. PM-212 (rev.).

Thomson, B. F. 1977. *The Shaping of America's Heartland.* Houghton Mifflin, Boston.

Thomson, G. W. 1987. Iowa's forest area in 1832: A reevaluation. *Proc. Iowa Acad. Sci.* 94(4):116–20.

Thomson, G. W., and H. G. Hertel. 1981. The forest resources of Iowa in 1980. *Proc. Iowa Acad. Sci.* 88:(1):2–6.

Thorne, R. F. 1955. The flora of Johnson County, Iowa. *Proc. Iowa Acad. Sci* 62:155–97.

Trelease, W. 1931/1967. *Winter Botany.* 3d ed. Dover Publ., New York.

USDA Forest Service. 1965. Silvics of forest trees of the United States. Agric. Handb. 271. USGPO, Washington, D.C.

Van Bruggen, T. 1958. *The Flora of Southcentral Iowa.* University Microfilms, Ann Arbor, Mich.

Voss, E. G. 1985. *Michigan Flora.* Part II. Cranbrook Institute of Science Bull. 59, Ann Arbor.

Vyshenskii, V. A. 1935. Cited in Gorshkova, S. G. 1949. Elaeagnaceae. In Vol. XV, *Flora of the U.S.S.R.* Translated by N. Landau. Israel Program for Scientific Translations, Jerusalem, 1974.

Ware, G. 1977. Oaks for urban landscapes in northern Illinois. Morton Arbor. Plant Inf. Bull. 14, Lisle, Ill.

Ware, G., and V. K. Howe. 1974. The care and management of native oaks in northern Illinois. Morton Arbor. Plant Inf. Bull. 4, Lisle, Ill.

Watson, G. 1991. Attaining root-crown balance in landscape trees. *J. Arboric.* 17(8):211–16.

Weaver, J. E., and J. Kramer. 1932. Root system of *Quercus macrocarpa* in relation to the invasion of prairie. *Bot. Gaz.* 94:51–85.

Wilde, S. A. 1953. Trees of Wisconsin, their ecological and silvicultural silhouettes. Univ. Wis. Soils Dep., Madison.

Wray, P. H. 1976a. Planning and management of farmstead windbreaks. Iowa State Univ. Coop. Ext. Serv. PM-543 (rev.).

_____. 1976b. Tree planting in Iowa. Iowa State Univ. Coop. Ext. Serv. PM-496 (rev.).

_____. 1977. Iowa's forest reserve laws. Iowa State Univ. Coop. Ext. Serv. PM-605 (rev.).

Wray, P. H., and W. Farris. 1976. Woodland management in Iowa. Iowa State Univ. Coop. Ext. Serv. PM-718.

Wyman, D. 1965. *Trees for American Gardens.* Macmillan, New York.

Zimmerman, M. H., and C. L. Brown. 1971. *Trees: Structure and Function.* Springer-Verlag, New York.

INDEX